UKPDS: the first 30 years

EDITED BY

Rury R. Holman
Professor of Diabetic Medicine
Director, Diabetes Trials Unit
Oxford Centre for Diabetes, Endocrinology and Metabolism
Churchill Hospital
University of Oxford
Oxford, UK

Peter J. Watkins
Consultant Physician (retired)
King's College Hospital
London, UK

FOREWORD BY

David R. Matthews
Professor of Diabetic Medicine
Chairman, Oxford Centre for Diabetes, Endocrinology and
  Metabolism
National Institute for Health Research, Oxford Biomedical
  Research Centre
Churchill Hospital
University of Oxford
Oxford, UK

WILEY-BLACKWELL
A John Wiley & Sons, Ltd., Publication

This edition first published 2008, © 2008 by Blackwell Publishing Ltd

Blackwell Publishing was acquired by John Wiley & Sons in February 2007. Blackwell's publishing program has been merged with Wiley's global Scientific, Technical and Medical business to form Wiley-Blackwell.

Registered office: John Wiley & Sons Ltd, The Atrium, Southern Gate, Chichester, West Sussex, PO19 8SQ, UK

Editorial offices: 9600 Garsington Road, Oxford, OX4 2DQ, UK
The Atrium, Southern Gate, Chichester, West Sussex, PO19 8SQ, UK
111 River Street, Hoboken, NJ 07030-5774, USA

For details of our global editorial offices, for customer services and for information about how to apply for permission to reuse the copyright material in this book please see our website at www.wiley.com/wiley-blackwell

Library of Congress Cataloging-in-Publication Data
UKPDS : the first 30 years / edited by Rury R. Holman, Peter J. Watkins ; foreword by David R. Matthews.
    p. ; cm.
  ISBN 978-1-4051-9166-1
  1. UKPDS (Study) 2. Non-insulin-dependent diabetes--United Kingdom. I. Holman, Rury R. II. Watkins, Peter J.
  [DNLM: 1. UKPDS (Study) 2. Diabetes Mellitus, Type 2--drug therapy. 3. Randomized Controlled Trials as Topic--history. 4. Diabetes Mellitus, Type 2--complications. 5. History, 20th Century. 6. History, 21st Century. WK 810 U34 2008]
  RA645.D5U47 2008
  362.196′462--dc22

                                                                        2008039273

ISBN: 978-1-4051-9166-1

A catalogue record for this book is available from the British Library.

Set in 9.5/12 pt Palatino by Sparks, Oxford—www.sparkspublishing.com
Printed by GraphyCems, Navarra, Spain

1   2008

Contents

List of contributors

Amanda I. Adler
Consultant Physician
Institute of Metabolic Sciences
Addenbrooke's Hospital
Cambridge, UK

Rudy Bilous
Professor of Clinical Medicine
Newcastle University
Newcastle upon Tyne, UK

Anne Clark
Reader in Diabetic Medicine
Diabetes Research Laboratories
Oxford Centre for Diabetes, Endocrinology and
Metabolism
University of Oxford
Oxford, UK

Philip Clarke
Senior Research Fellow
School of Public Health
University of Sydney
New South Wales, Australia

Timothy M. E. Davis
Professor of Medicine
School of Medicine and Pharmacology
Fremantle Hospital
University of Western Australia
Perth, Australia

Minal Desai
Research Assistant
Diabetes Research Laboratories
Oxford Centre for Diabetes, Endocrinology and
Metabolism
University of Oxford
Oxford, UK

Charles Fox
Consultant Physician
Northampton General Hospital
Northampton, UK

Edwin A. M. Gale
Professor of Diabetic Medicine
Diabetes and Metabolism
Division of Medicine
University of Bristol
Medical School Unit
Southmead Hospital
Bristol, UK

Saul Genuth
Professor of Medicine
Department of Medicine
Case Western Reserve University
Cleveland, Ohio, USA

Anna L. Gloyn
University Research Lecturer
Diabetes Research Laboratories
Oxford Centre for Diabetes, Endocrinology and
Metabolism
University of Oxford
Oxford, UK

Alastair M. Gray
Professor of Health Economics
Health Economics Research Centre
Department of Public Health
University of Oxford
Oxford, UK

Philip Home
Professor of Diabetes Medicine and Consultant
Physician
Newcastle University and Newcastle Diabetes
Centre
Newcastle upon Tyne, UK

Eva M. Kohner
Professor of Medical Ophthalmology
Peninsula Medical School
Exeter, UK

Susan Manley
Clinical Scientist
Clinical Biochemistry
University Hospital Birmingham NHS
Foundation Trust from Selly Oak
Birmingham, UK

Mark I. McCarthy
Robert Turner Professor of Diabetic Medicine
Diabetes Research Laboratories
Oxford Centre for Diabetes, Endocrinology and
Metabolism;
Wellcome Trust Centre for Human Genetics
University of Oxford
Oxford, UK

Jennie Turner
Oxford, UK

Bryan Williams
Professor of Medicine
Department of Cardiovascular Sciences
University of Leicester School of Medicine
Leicester Royal Infirmary
Leicester, UK

Foreword

Everyone with even the slightest knowledge of diabetes medicine will have heard of the UKPDS. The story of its beginnings, financing, agonies, and triumph would make a fascinating epic. The hero, of course, would be Robert Turner who steadfastly refused to allow the 20-year gargantuan task of keeping the UKPDS afloat to pull him down. However, the UKPDS was also an extraordinary exemplar of all that is best in collaboration in medicine. The many staff who helped over the years deserve nothing but applause and those who worked deep into the night on many occasions should rightly feel proud of the ultimate achievement. In particular we should pay special homage to Rury Holman who, as Robert's aide-de-camp, guided the trial successfully past many potential metaphorical icebergs.

Of course the issues raised by the UKPDS have not all been answered yet. And maybe some of the questions will remain for decades to come. In particular, trials that have followed the UKPDS—including ProActive, ADOPT, ACCORD, ADVANCE, and the VADT—have all to some extent thrown a little light on the problems but in many respects have also demonstrated how difficult it is to run a successful trial in glycaemic control with cardiovascular outcomes. Ten years on from the first airing of the UKPDS results at Barcelona there has continued to be a scraping noise from icebergs as the newer trials have run into dark waters.

Why is the UKPDS different from any other trial? To begin with, it was by far the largest randomised trial in diabetes ever undertaken, with 5102 randomised patients, a longevity of 10 years median follow up, 20 years from inception to report, and 30 years duration in total when the post-study follow-up period is included. Furthermore, no other trial has produced a numbered series of publications to match that from the UKPDS, ranging from a study of GAD antibodies to theoretical modelling, and from genes to cost-effectiveness. This was possible only with the dedication of all those thousands of patients who volunteered to be part of the UKPDS and who attended the clinic every few months. The resulting information has puzzled, educated and illuminated us in equal measure.

This book celebrates the success of the UKPDS and its size and scope demonstrate the extent to which it still remains iconic. It is a great sadness to all of us that Robert Turner is not still with us to enjoy the 30-year anniversary and to be leading the post-study monitoring presentations. More than that, Robert's personal stature in Diabetes Research was such that many of the current academics working in diabetes passed through his laboratories. His skills were not just in trials methodology but were widely spread in physiology, genetics, hypoglycaemia and clinical medicine. He is still much missed by all of us who have such fond memories of him.

I warmly commend this book to you. You will see from the contents the extent to which the UKPDS continues to resonate throughout the diabetes world.

David R. Matthews
Oxford, 2008

Preface

The United Kingdom Prospective Diabetes Study (UKPDS) has radically altered our perceptions of the nature and treatment of type 2 diabetes. It was one of the longest clinical trials in medical history, embracing 20 years of study (1977–1997), and closing finally after its 30th birthday in 2007, following a further ten years of post-study monitoring. At its onset, some distinguished physicians had declared that it was an impossible undertaking, and at its close, one Egyptian physician declared that such a colossal task could only have been undertaken by an Englishman (page 144)—and that Englishman was of course the late Robert Turner (1938 to 1999). Tributes to Robert from his wife Jennie, Rury Holman, and many others are published in this book (Chapters 1 and 17).

The UKPDS involved 5102 patients with newly diagnosed type 2 diabetes, and was conducted by physicians, nurses, dieticians and many others in 23 clinical centres across the UK. That Robert Turner and Rury Holman could marshal the loyalty of so many for so long was an achievement in itself, and a major factor for the success of the study. The patients themselves understood the importance of their involvement, and often expressed 'the privilege and pleasure' of taking part (page 153), later deeply regretting the closure of the trial when one of them wrote: 'I am sorry I won't be hearing from you again' (page 153).

The beneficial effect of the UKPDS on diabetes teams across the UK has been remarkable. Indeed, this trial showed impressively what can be achieved when many people work together with a common purpose. Enthusiasms for clinical research were fired in many teams with no previous experience, and from Northampton, Charles Fox wrote that 'many of us have developed our own research interests and teams on the back of the UKPDS, and British diabetes would be a lot poorer without it' (page 142). Research teams became friends at the regular updates in Oxford, and the punting parties became famous or perhaps infamous (pages 145–8). A sense of bereavement affected many of the clinical teams and their patients at the closure of the study in 2007, when UKPDS became history.

This book celebrates the many facets of a clinical trial involving so many people over three decades. It not only presents the 11 reviews of the science evolving from the UKPDS, originally published in the August 2008 supplement to Diabetic Medicine, but also examines the historical origins of the study. It revisits the moments at the 1976 International Diabetes Federation Congress in Delhi, when its architect Robert Turner together with Rury Holman shared their ideas for a pilot study to re-examine the nature and treatment of type 2 diabetes. It reminds us of the constant struggle to maintain adequate funding against powerful opposition while the study skilfully steered its course and expanded its size and goals. It reminds our readers of the climax at the presentation of the results at the 1998 EASD Conference in Barcelona—hitherto held in absolute secrecy—and it recalls the excitement at the simultaneous publication of five papers in the Lancet and British Medical Journal on the day after the conference—12 September 1998.

This book also records and acknowledges with gratitude the multitude of people in many professions who created and made this study possible. We hope it will serve to refresh the memories of all those who participated, and might present new insights for others with ambitious plans for their own trials.

Peter J. Watkins

Acknowledgements

Preparation of this book represents a collaboration by many people who have made substantial contributions to its creation. Julie Carpenter and Jayne Starrett at the centre in the Diabetes Trials Unit at Oxford have handled mountains of paper and established necessary contacts with innumerable people involved in this undertaking, while Joanne Keenan ably helped in launching the project. The authors of the 11 scientific review articles presenting a comprehensive examination of the state of the art, all delivered their manuscripts in time, if not always on time. Professor Sally Marshall, editor of *Diabetic Medicine*, has given all her energy to the creation of this supplement published in August 2008 and in which these review articles first appeared, and we are immensely grateful for her collaboration. Our publisher, Wiley-Blackwell, and in particular Caroline Phillips, Jennifer Seward and Oliver Walter, have offered excellent support in the complex process of preparing this book, and we are most grateful to them. Support with an educational grant from Novo Nordisk is very much appreciated.

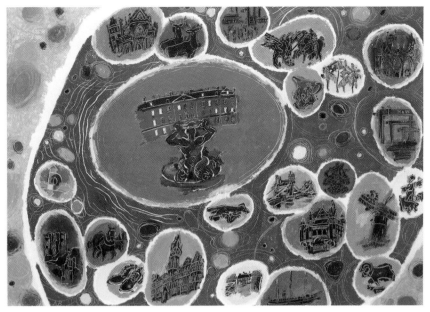

Painting by Alison Barratt commissioned to celebrate the 20 years (1977–1997) of the UK Prospective Diabetes Study, with the Radcliffe Infirmary, Oxford (centre) and the other 22 centres (clockwise from top left).

Cathedral—Exeter
Stags—Aberdeen
LS Lowry—Salford
St. George and Dragon—London St. George's
Jug—Stafford
Palm trees—Torquay
Cathedral—Peterborough
Harland & Wolff—Belfast City
Dick Whittington—London Whittington
Windmill—Norwich
Coat of arms—Stevenage

Bridge—London Hammersmith
General Hospital—Birmingham
Derby Rams—Derby
'Discovery'—Dundee
Gateposts—Belfast Royal Victoria
Running fox—Leicester
Town Hall—Manchester
Boots—Northampton
Suffolk Punch horses—Ipswich
Castle—Scarborough
Logo—St Helier Surrey

CHAPTER 1

Tributes to Robert Turner

Rury R. Holman[1] and Jennie Turner[2]
[1] Diabetes Trials Unit, Oxford Centre for Diabetes, Endocrinology and Metabolism, Churchill Hospital, University of Oxford, Oxford, UK
[2] Oxford, UK

Tribute by Professor Rury R. Holman

Robert Turner was born on 26 November 1938 and died peacefully on 1 August 1999 in Atlanta, Georgia, following a major stroke four days earlier (Fig. 1.1). While his untimely death came as a great shock, we celebrate the fact that he achieved so much more than most during his lifetime. His many colleagues and friends around the world were privileged to share in his work and aspirations. He is sorely missed.

Robert followed in the family tradition by electing to study medicine. He obtained an Exhibition in 1957 to Downing College, Cambridge, and subsequently completed his training at the Middlesex Hospital Medical School. His major interest in diabetes first developed while working for Dr John Nabarro as a Leverhulme Research Fellow. At this time he undertook a number of physiological studies and co-developed the charcoal separation phase insulin assay that was used subsequently to analyse UKPDS samples.

Figure 1.1 Professor Robert Turner, MA, MD, FRCP. Professor of Medicine, University of Oxford.

In 1970 Robert was awarded a named fellowship to study at the Massachusetts General Hospital, in Boston. He moved to Oxford in 1972, having been appointed as a clinical lecturer to Professor Paul Beeson in the Nuffield Department of Medicine. Robert was given two small laboratories in the Sir Hans Krebs Metabolic Research Laboratories. Here he started what was to become the Diabetes Research Laboratories, or DRL as it became known, with one nurse and one technician and myself as his first research fellow. This fledgling department was to grow inexorably over the years, gradually acquiring additional space and laboratories, and evolving into one of the largest and most successful clinical research units in Europe.

Above all, Robert was a visionary, an innovator and a fierce supporter of scientific method in clinical practice. Many projects which he undertook were only practicable because of his extraordinary ability to embrace and work creatively with different scientific disciplines to mutual benefit. Robert believed that the main metabolic problem in type 2 diabetes was insulin insufficiency, a view that proved controversial as many scientists thought a reduced sensitivity to insulin was the primary lesion. In the face of considerable uncertainty, Robert stuck to his guns and now, many years later, it is accepted that diminished insulin secretion, secondary to progressive beta cell failure, is indeed a central mechanism in the development of type 2 diabetes.

Robert was quick to acknowledge the help and inspiration of those with whom he worked. He regarded John Nabarro and Arnold Bloom as role models and was greatly influenced in his clinical trial work by Professor Sir Richard Doll and Professor Sir Richard Peto. Equally, Robert trained an entire generation of clinicians and scientists who came from many different countries to work with him in the DRL, many of whom have gone on to become the modern-day leaders in the field of type 2 diabetes. Robert was aided and abetted in his aspirations by a loyal band of dedicated co-workers including Irene Stratton, Dr Carole Cull and Dr Susan Manley. Professor David Matthews, Dr Anne Clark, Dr Jonathan Levy and I were privileged to have him as a mentor and confidante, and primarily as a friend.

Robert's research interests were diverse, and it is intriguing to note that several different scientific disciplines have claimed him as an expert in their own field, often unaware of his other talents. As well as physiological studies aimed at identifying the lesions that cause type 2 diabetes, he undertook studies of patients and their relatives to identify the heritability of different features of the disease. He then turned his attention to identifying both the genes that contribute to the initiation of type 2 diabetes, and those that may influence its subsequent complications. Robert worked extensively on the development and assessment of new pharmacological therapies and medical devices. Following the introduction of home blood glucose testing Robert co-developed the Autolet finger pricker, basing the mechanism on a toy cash register. He also undertook epidemiological studies and produced mathematical models for diabetes including the HOMA model for assessing beta cell function and insulin sensitivity, and a risk assessment simulation model based on UKPDS data.

Robert pioneered the early use of insulin therapy in type 2 diabetes and was an acknowledged expert on the diagnosis and treatment of insulinomas. He was quick to realize that long-term prospective studies were required in order to explore the causes and the most effective treatment of type 2 diabetes. His greatest achievement was the unveiling of the results of the 20-year United Kingdom Prospective Diabetes Study at the EASD meeting in Barcelona in 1998, following which he received many awards. It was characteristic of Robert that, even as the UKPDS was being presented, he was already planning an equally ambitious project to help implement and evaluate its findings.

Above all, Robert was a caring physician and leader. Patients, departmental staff, colleagues around the world and the many physicians and scientists he has helped to train can testify to his charisma, thoughtfulness and unstinting support. Numerous colleagues have expressed their profound sadness on hearing the news of Robert's demise, and each one has their own tale to tell of how he had assisted them in some venture, provided them with timely advice, or helped them personally.

Robert's interests, however, were not limited to medicine. He played golf, had a passionate interest in music, and took enormous pleasure from his garden. He enjoyed travelling and took an avid interest in the geography, history and culture of the places he visited. In 1970 Robert married Jennie, to whom he was devoted. At that time she was completing her PhD at the Brompton Hospital and worked subsequently on allergic lung diseases. The home they made together was to become a centre of hospitality for an international circle of students and colleagues.

The premature demise of such an important leader in the field of diabetes has been felt throughout the world and no more so than by the diabetes community in Oxford.

Tribute by Dr Jennie Turner

It was a great adventure to be married to Robert for 30 years. We had only been married for three months when we embarked on the *QE2* liner for a sabbatical at Harvard Medical School in Boston, USA.

We returned to Oxford in 1972, living first in Great Milton, a quintessentially English village just 12 miles from Oxford. While there we had our two sons who enjoyed the freedom of village life that would have been impossible in a city. We lived in a stone cottage with a large garden and it was here that Robert would relax, growing fruit and vegetables for the family. This would be a lifelong passion for him and one that was an essential 'bolt hole' from the pressures of the life he had chosen. A combination of teaching, devotion to his clinical work and of course the UKPDS would be the focus of his life, but always his family would come first if we needed him.

For me he was the perfect husband. He encouraged me to pursue my career as an immunologist in the field of allergic lung disease which I did, but I realized very early on that I enjoyed being with my sons and supporting Robert in his very exciting research. It was such fun to travel with Robert and I met so many doctors and researchers as a result from all over the world (Fig. 1.2).

We moved to our present house in 1981 and it is one of the few times that I gave Robert a lecture. I said that if he wanted to know his sons then he should try and be home for supper with them at 6.30 pm. As so many of the Fellows in the department will know, he did do this. In many ways he was very hungry by then as lunch would so often have been just a couple of chocolate bars. The telephone would ring at around 6.15 pm and this would mean that he was leaving work, but on many occasions it would go on ringing and when I would eventually pick it up Robert would tell me that he was bringing home this young doctor for dinner too. I soon realized that I was so lucky to be meeting these young doctors from all over the world, who have gone on to be leaders in the field of diabetes.

The UKPDS took up so much of Robert's time and energy that on the many trips to the opera and visiting friends, I would be the driver while Robert would work alongside me. However, the last few years of his life after the publication of the UKPDS were quite fantastic. He received the just recognition of this landmark study from colleagues all over the world. I know that Robert would be delighted that the UKPDS is to celebrate 30 years this year. I would like to take this opportunity to pay tribute to the many people who have ensured that this has happened. In particular I would like to thank Professor Rury Holman, who as you all know was a close colleague and the person who has ensured that the UKPDS continued after Robert's death.

Figure 1.2 Jennie and Robert Turner, Bermuda 1997.

2 Historical background

Rury R. Holman

Diabetes Trials Unit, Oxford Centre for Diabetes, Endocrinology and Metabolism, Churchill Hospital, University of Oxford, Oxford, UK

Before the UKPDS

The UK Prospective Diabetes Study (UKPDS) was conceived in the years of uncertainty following the premature termination in the late 1960s of the University Group Diabetes Program (UGDP) study which appeared to demonstrate excess cardiovascular mortality with tolbutamide ($P > 0.05$) and excess all-cause mortality with phenformin ($P > 0.05$). I moved to the Radcliffe Infirmary in Oxford in 1975 to work initially with Dr Derek Hockaday but by August of that year had joined Robert Turner as his first Research Fellow. Robert was convinced that relative insulin deficiency underpinned the hyperglycaemia seen in type 2 diabetes and together we published several papers demonstrating that fasting hyperglycaemia was a stable and repeatable characteristic for individual patients [1] which supported the Hepa-Beta feedback loop hypothesis we had proposed [2]. We went on to show that fasting hyperglycaemia could be corrected more effectively with a basal insulin supplement than with a long-acting sulfonylurea [1,3].

In 1976, while attending the International Diabetes Federation Congress in Delhi (Fig. 2.1), we proposed that 'Diabetes is an endocrine deficiency disease, a logical treatment of which is hormone replacement therapy'. We decided that a clinical trial would be needed to demonstrate the possible superior efficacy of insulin-mediated normo-glycaemia [1]; and outlined a study which would compare existing therapies as well as investigating the impact of improved glycaemic control on clinical outcomes. Robert then succumbed to 'Delhi belly' and was confined to barracks for 36 hours but emerged triumphantly bearing a paper which contained the outline protocol of what was to become the UKPDS (Fig. 2.2) and the funding required (Fig. 2.3).

By the time we returned to the UK we had agreed a protocol for a five-year pilot study which we proceeded to implement with a small grant from the Cloth Workers Foundation.

Figure 2.1 Rury Holman and Robert Turner at the International Diabetes Federation meeting in Delhi, India, 1976.

Prospective treatment of moderate diabetes.
6 centres, based from Oxford.
Initial period 7 years . Approx 400 - 500 pts per year.
                                      Enter for 5 years - Total 2,000 - 2,500 pts.
                                      ie. at 7 years 800 - 1000, have finished 5 years.

Study patients at 0 and 5 years.

Protocol
All new patients : not needing immediate treatment other than diet
          Rx Diet for 3/12 . If fasting plasma glucose > 5.5 mM
                    Then randomize a) further diet
                                   b) u.h. insulin
                                   c) sulphonylurea
          aiming in b) & c) for fasting glucose < 5.0 mM.

Figure 2.2 Robert Turner's projected plan for UKPDS, 1976.

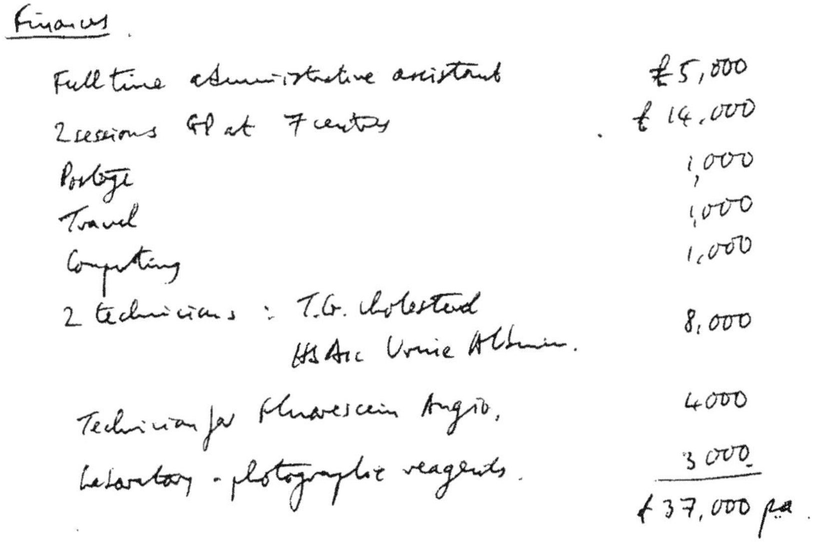

Finances

Full time administrative assistant	£5,000
2 sessions GP at 7 centres	£14,000
Postage	1,000
Travel	1,000
Computing	1,000
2 technicians : T.G. Cholesterol HbA1c Urine Albumin.	8,000
Technician for Fluorescein Angio,	4000
Laboratory - photographic reagents.	3000
	£37,000 pa .

Figure 2.3 Robert Turner's first calculation of funding for the UKPDS, 1976.

1977: UKPDS begins

Such was Robert's energy and drive that we had obtained ethical permission and were able to randomize the first patient in Oxford by December 1977. Having demonstrated the feasibility of the study and obtained data on likely event rates, we applied for and obtained funding from the UK Medical Research Council (MRC) and the British Diabetic Association (BDA) to expand the study first to five and then to fifteen centres with appropriate power calculations and sample size estimations.

It is often not appreciated that the UKPDS glucose study was essentially a monotherapy intervention as, following the unexpected results of the UGDP, there was great nervousness about the possibility that a sulfonylurea may increase cardiovascular events, with similar fears expressed by many opinion leaders regarding the use of insulin.

There was at the time a widespread belief that glucose control was not directly associated with diabetic complications, which it was thought might possibly be genetically related. The 'rescue' glucose level at which an additional intervention could be started was therefore set at 15 mmol/l (270 mg/dl), a threshold endorsed by the ethics committees. This arrangement certainly enhanced evaluation of the long-term 'natural history' of diabetes, but precluded the ability to achieve and maintain more near normal glucose values by the early use of combination therapy. This made it possible for the UKPDS to demonstrate the now well-recognized progressive nature of the condition, and to show that this was associated with declining beta cell function. It also meant that the degree of glycaemic separation between the conventional and intensive groups was modest with a median difference over the 10.0 years of follow-up of 0.9%.

The hypertension study

Early analyses of UKPDS data showed unequivocally that those patients who were hypertensive were at greater risk of diabetic complications, with a 45% increased risk for the primary 'any diabetes related endpoint' [4]. This finding led to the introduction in 1987 of the UKPDS blood pressure trial, in a factorial design with the glucose study. As with the glucose study, the blood pressure trial aimed to determine whether improved blood pressure control could reduce the risk of complications as well as comparing directly two therapies, a beta blocker (atenolol) and an ACE inhibitor (captopril). The blood pressure study, however, differed fundamentally from the glucose study in that it was designed from the outset as a treat-to-target study, with protocol specified stepwise addition of antihypertensive agents. This approach successfully achieved and maintained a 10/5 mmHg difference between the two groups over a median follow-up of 8.4 years.

Following the introduction of the blood pressure study the number of UKPDS centres was increased from 15 to 23 to ensure there would be no loss of power, given the likely reduction in events with improved blood pressure control. It also provided an opportunity to examine a revised treatment strategy in the last eight centres in which insulin was added to patients randomized to a sulphonylurea when a fasting plasma glucose less than 6 mmol/l could not be maintained, as opposed to the 15 mmol/l in the initial study [5].

A new hypoglycaemic agent

During the entire life of the UKPDS clinical trial only one new glucose-lowering agent was licensed which was the alpha glucosidase inhibitor, acarbose. The decision was made to include this in a double-blind fashion in the last three years of the trial from 1995 to 1997 inclusive. The trial closed out with a censor date of 30 September 1997, after which all patients were seen once more in the following three months to ascertain their clinical status at the end of the trial.

1998: the 20-year results

Early in 1998 an immense amount of work was undertaken to obtain the documentation needed to confirm endpoints, complete the cleaning and validation of the database, and perform the statistical analyses required for the preparation of eight manuscripts. These were submitted in advance of the study results to be presented at the European Association for the Study of Diabetes (EASD) 1998 meeting in Barcelona. Immediately before the EASD, staff from the UKPDS co-ordinating centre and clinical centres met with key members of the Data Safety and Monitoring Board and the Trial Steering Committees at a closed meeting in a hotel outside Barcelona to finalize the presentation. The results were presented in two 2-hour sessions on 10 and 11 September 1998, with five papers published simultaneously in *The Lancet* and the *British Medical Journal* [6–10]. These presentations were the high spot of the meeting, showing definitively for the first time that improved glucose control could reduce the risk of diabetic complications, although the 16% trend to reduction in myocardial infarction was only of borderline significance with a P value of 0.052.

Patients and their general practitioners were informed by letters summarizing the results and posted on the day of the presentation. A press release was made available at the EASD and to the local press for each of the UKPDS centres. International journalists were assembled at a meeting on the morning of 10 September in London to be briefed by a group of UKPDS investigators led by Peter Watkins. Their taped interviews were embargoed until the EASD presentation later that day but in the event these were never shown; and there was little mention of the UKPDS in the papers on the following day, as the Starr report outlining the case for Bill Clinton's impeachment and providing sordid details of the Clinton–Lewinsky relationship was released at the same time (Fig. 2.4). This was one event that Robert Turner had not anticipated although he did joke on the way to the conference that if Saddam Hussein invaded Kuwait again we might not get the publicity we anticipated. Subsequently however UKPDS results were widely promulgated, particularly in diabetes-related publications, and provided a major source of evidence that underpinned the revision of guidelines for diabetes management worldwide.

THE INDEPENDENT
Friday 11 September 1998

Treatment for diabetes inadequate

By JEREMY LAURANCE

ONE MILLION people in the UK who suffer from the commonest type of diabetes have received inadequate treatment over the last two decades, putting them at increased risk of death, blindness, kidney failure and amputations, researchers have found.

Intensive treatment to control blood pressure and glucose levels in sufferers can dramatically reduce their risk of complications, but it has not been routinely offered because there was no firm evidence until now that it made any difference. Instead, many patients have been left to control the disease by restricting their diet.

Results from a clinical study of diabetes that was started 20 years ago were presented yesterday at a conference in Barcelona and are published in a series of five papers in the *British Medical Journal* and *The Lancet* today.

controlled by diet. It accounts for 90 per cent of all cases of diabetes and is distinct from Type 1 which affects the young and requires daily insulin injections.

Type 2 diabetes is rising rapidly and is expected to affect 3 million people by 2010. It is commonest in the overweight.

Professor Robert Turner of Oxford University, who led the study of more than 5,000 patients, said: "This study shows for the first time that a substantial improvement in the health of people with Type 2 diabetes can be obtained."

Professor Turner said the drugs involved were cheap and the extra costs of intensive treatment would be largely offset by savings from reduced hospital admissions.

Poor detection of diabetes, which is marked by increased

Explosive Starr report outlines case for impeachment

Document provides sordid details of the Clinton-Lewinsky relationship

WASHINGTON (AllPolitics, Sept. 11) -- In an explosive report to Congress, Independent Counsel Ken Starr outlines a case for impeaching President Bill Clinton on 11 grounds, including perjury, obstruction of justice, witness-tampering and abuse of power, while providing graphic details of the sexual relationship between the president and former White House intern Monica Lewinsky.

Figure 2.4 Priorities in the press, September 1998 when the Clinton–Lewinsky story displaced coverage of UKPDS results. Articles taken from The Independent and CNN online. CNN article http://edition.cnn.com/ALLPOLITICS/stories/1998/09/11/starr.report/ Last accessed 2 September 2008.

Funding

Funding was the largest headache throughout the study. Following the successful pilot study from 1977 to 1982, the main study with five centres was funded for three years by the MRC, BDA and a consortium of pharmaceutical companies each contributing about one-third of the costs. In 1984 the decision was made to continue the study to a planned close-out in 1992 in order to give a six-year minimum follow-up, and funding agreed for the first five years to be renewed subject to review. In 1988 the Data Monitoring and Ethics Committee reported that there was only 67% power with a 1% alpha to detect a 15% advantage to the intensive glycaemic control policy compared to conventionally treated controls, and recommended that the study be extended to at least 1995.

In 1989 an application was submitted to the MRC and BDA for an extension which was approved, but only until 1994. In 1990 it became apparent that there was a major funding shortfall of £800,000 and this was made up by a BDA appeal launched by Jenny Hirst, together with her family and friends (see Chapter 3). A letter from the BDA on 18 September 1990 advised that their Council was unanimous in their view that the study should be completed as planned in 1994 and that no further extension would be considered. This caused Robert Turner, who never took no for an answer, to redouble his efforts, and by 1991 we had submitted more than Robert's weight in the total number of grant applications relating to the UKPDS. With the aid of the DMEC and a specially convened scientific review panel, the case for extending the study for a longer period was made successfully, and in December 1993 agreement was obtained to continue the study for four more years to 1997, with data to be reported in 1998 (Fig. 2.5).

30 December 1993

Dr Robert Turner
Diabetes Research Laboratories
Radcliffe Infirmary

Dear Robert

In all of my Christmas mail, the thing that gave me the most pleasure by far was the letter from you announcing that your diabetes study, which had been sentenced to abortion, is in fact to continue for 4 more years. This is very appropriate indeed from a medico-scientific viewpoint, as no other study has any serious hope during this century of sorting out the real clinical relevance of stricter glucose control. It is also appropriate from a personal viewpoint: the effort you and Rury Holman have put into the study is enormous, and this gives you a much better chance of generating reliable answers that will stand for decades in the international literature.

Best wishes for a happy quinquennium.

Richard

Richard Peto

Figure 2.5 Reprieve!

It should be acknowledged that the support of many pharmaceutical companies over this extended period, despite the lack of any positive feedback concerning the potential results, was a crucial element in the ability to maintain the study, and a prime example of academia, governmental, charity and industrial institutions working in harmony.

Acknowledgements

We would like to acknowledge the amazing contributions made by so many funders and individuals including physicians, nurses, dietitians, retinal photographers and laboratory technicians, but most of all the patients themselves. We thank all those who worked in the UKPDS Coordinating Centre (Fig. 2.6), including the two principal UKPDS statisticians, the late Dr Carole Cull and Mrs Irene Stratton. We would also like to thank those who served on the many UKPDS Committees over the years and in particular Professor David Matthews who has chaired the Endpoint Adjudication Committee from the outset.

We record with sadness that Dr Carole Cull died in June 2007. After a period of research in Cambridge, she retrained as a statistician, and joined the Oxford Diabetes team in 1987. During her 20 years in Oxford she contrib-

Figure 2.6 Oxford Coordinating Centre Group. Back row (l to r) Ian Kennedy, Heather McElroy, Caroline Wood, Robin Carter, Karen Fisher, Pauline Sutton, Richard Stevens. Middle row (l to r) Ziyah Mehta, Dianne Croft, Dick Jelfs, Valeria Frighi, Amanda Adler, Martin Payne. Front row (l to r) Philip Bassett, Carole Cull, David Matthews, Robert Turner, Rury Holman, Irene Stratton, Susan Manley.

Figure 2.7 Dr Carole Cull.

uted to more than 100 papers and gave numerous presentations worldwide. She was ordained as deacon in Christchurch Cathedral, Oxford, in 2006. Her contribution to our work was substantial and she will be greatly missed (Fig. 2.7).

Prizes and awards

Following the publication and widespread acceptance of the results, Robert Turner and the UKPDS group received many accolades, including Robert's presentation in 1999 of the BDA Banting Memorial Lecture, and the award to the UKPDS, also in 1999, of the ADA Charles H Best medal. Although Robert Turner's untimely death in August 1999 was a major tragedy, it is comforting to know that he was able to see the wide promulgation of the UKPDS results, receive congratulations from the scientific and lay community, and finalize the arrangements for the planned post-study monitoring.

Postscript

The final letter from Professor Robert Cohen, Chairman of the UKPDS Trial Steering Committee to Professor John Savill, Chairman of the Medical Research Council PMIB:

Professor J Savill   21th February 2004
Chairman, PMIB
Medical Research Council
20 Park Crescent
LondonW1B 1AL

Dear John

United Kingdom Prospective Diabetes Study(UKPDS)

The Trial Steering Committee for the UKPDS had its final meeting last week, and the
Committee felt that the end of this 25 year epic ought to be marked by a letter to the
PMIB Chairman, who might wish to draw it to the attention of the Board.

This trial ran in its full form for twenty years, in 23 centres in the UK, designed and
managed by the Oxford Diabetes Centre, under the leadership of the late Professor Robert
Turner and of Professor Rury Holman. A post-study monitoring (PSM) period, with
reduced surveillance, was continued for a further 5 years, led by Professor R Holman
after Robert Turner's untimely death.

Its scientific output demonstrated the value of good control both of glycaemia and blood
pressure in the prevention of microvascular complications of Type 2 diabetes. The PSM
has now added further information, namely of a legacy of benefit continuing into the
PSM despite the indices of control in the two groups (conventional v. intensive) coming
together in the PSM. The legacy of good glycaemic control persists for longer than that of
good blood pressure control. In 1997, at the end of the full study, there was little clear
effect on macrovascular disease, but the PSM has shown that the administration of
metformin appears to be associated with significant macrovascular benefit.

The UKPDS does for Type 2 diabetes what the American DCCT trial did for Type 1
diabetes. Though the UKPDS lasted for much longer than the DCCT, it did so at a cost
(approx £25M, funded from several agencies in addition to the MRC) which was a small
fraction of the DCCT cost. The Trial Steering Committee feels that the very successful
design of this trial – a hub and spokes model, with advice, encouragement and many
services provided from the hub, should be drawn to the attention of PMIB, as an
exemplar of how to run a large complex multicentre trial.

The trial is regarded world-wide as the definitive landmark investigation into the
treatment of Type 2 diabetes. The MRC can take considerable satisfaction in sticking
with it through some difficult periods and being a major funder for much of the time.

The Trial Steering Committee considered possible future directions for research in this
field. Whilst the UKPDS demonstrates the virtues of good control in the circumstances of
a trial, the question of helping patient compliance in a routine environment requires
serious study. There is scope both for the development of new drugs, and for research
into the prediction and prevention of Type 2 diabetes

The Trial Steering Committee wishes to express its appreciation of the leadership
provided by the Oxford team, and to Professor Holman in particular for guiding the
project to a successful conclusion.

Yours sincerely

R.D.Cohen
Chairman, UKPDS Trial Steering Committee

References

1 Holman RR, Turner RC. Diabetes: the quest for basal normoglycaemia. *Lancet* 1977;1:469-474.

2 Turner RC, Holman RR. Insulin rather than glucose homoeostasis in the pathophysiology of diabetes. *Lancet* 1976;1:1272-1274.

3 Holman RR, Turner RC. Basal normoglycemia attained with chlorpropamide in mild diabetes. *Metabolism* 1978;27:539-547.

4 Turner RC, Stratton IM, Frighi V, Holman R, Manley SE, Cull CA. Prevalence of hypertension in newly presenting type 2 diabetic patients and the association with risk factors for cardiovascular and diabetic complications. *Journal of Hypertension* 1993;11:309-317.

5 Wright A, Burden AC, Paisey RB, Cull CA, Holman RR; UK Prospective Diabetes Study Group. Sulfonylurea inadequacy: efficacy of addition of insulin over 6 years in patients with type 2 diabetes in the UK Prospective Diabetes Study: UKPDS 57. *Diabetes Care* 2002;25:330-336.

6 UK Prospective Diabetes Study (UKPDS) Group. Intensive blood-glucose control with sulphonylureas or insulin compared with conventional treatment and risk of complications in patients with type 2 diabetes: UKPDS 33. *Lancet* 1998;352:837-853.

7 UK Prospective Diabetes Study (UKPDS) Group. Effect of intensive blood-glucose control with metformin on complications in overweight patients with type 2 diabetes: UKPDS 34. *Lancet* 1998;352:854-865.

8 UK Prospective Diabetes Study Group. Tight blood pressure control and risk of macrovascular and microvascular complications in type 2 diabetes: UKPDS 38. *Br Med J* 1998;317:703-713.

9 UK Prospective Diabetes Study Group. Efficacy of atenolol and captopril in reducing risk of macrovascular and microvascular complications in type 2 diabetes: UKPDS 39. *Br Med J* 1998;317:713-720.

10 UK Prospective Diabetes Study Group. Cost effectiveness analysis of improved blood pressure control in hypertensive patients with type 2 diabetes: UKPDS 40. *Br Med J* 1998;317:720-726.

3 Rescuing the UKPDS

Charles Fox

Northampton General Hospital, Northampton, UK

Throughout the long history of the UKPDS, funding was always precarious; by 1987, the financial situation had become desperate. After the introduction of the Hypertension Study, the annual cost of the UKPDS was about £800,000. Funding came from a variety of sources including the British Diabetic Association (BDA), the pharmaceutical industry, the UK Medical Research Council and the US National Institutes of Health. Putting together all contributions towards the Study, there was an annual deficit of approximately £200,000. The BDA was not keen to deplete its own research funds, particularly as the main focus of its research funding was type 1 diabetes. It is hard to remember that in the late 1980s type 2 diabetes had a low profile.

Professor Harry Keen, Chairman of the BDA, was strongly supportive of the Study. He approached Jenny Hirst, the long-standing Chairman of the Branches Network, who had the vision to realize the value of the UKPDS and believed that it would catch the imagination of rank-and-file BDA members. Jenny set out to raise a million pounds to save the Study. Working through the branch structure, she appealed directly to members to save the UKPDS by contributing in person or by releasing any reserves they had stockpiled in their accounts.

Jenny was away from home on the first day of the appeal. By coincidence, she happened to be in Ipswich taking part in an education session run by John Day, who was himself a UKPDS investigator. Her daughter Beverly rang to say that donations were flooding in and causing chaos at home and she returned to find the dining room submerged in envelopes. The team set up to process the donations included Beverly, Dorothy Coope, Jenny's mother and Colin Clorley, Chairman of the Northampton BDA branch. Two BDA area coordinators, Sue Morris and Sue Wren, also took part and acted as auditors.

Jenny had opened a special account for the appeal and warned the bank to expect a flood of cheques. They were not particularly interested till Jenny arrived with thousands of cheques and the bank realized that they had to deal with serious sums of money. All donations had to be recorded in paper ledgers, since computers were not then available. Over two months Jenny raised the astonishing sum of £800,000, most of it in the form of individual donations of £5–£100 (Fig. 3.1). In addition many branches offered up their savings, and the Northern Irish branch was particularly generous in releasing £35,000.

By tapping into the membership of the British Diabetes Association, Jenny provided funds which allowed Robert Turner to keep the UKPDS afloat over a difficult period. The rest is history.

Figure 3.1 Jenny Hirst, family and friends raise £800,000.

CHAPTER 4

4 | 12 September 1998: simultaneous publication of pivotal results

Five papers reporting the primary results were published at the same time as the 1998 EASD presentation.

Intensive blood-glucose control with sulphonylureas or insulin compared with conventional treatment and risk of complications in patients with type 2 diabetes (UKPDS 33)

UK Prospective Diabetes Study (UKPDS) Group*

Summary

Background Improved blood-glucose control decreases the progression of diabetic microvascular disease, but the effect on macrovascular complications is unknown. There is concern that sulphonylureas may increase cardiovascular mortality in patients with type 2 diabetes and that high insulin concentrations may enhance atheroma formation. We compared the effects of intensive blood-glucose control with either sulphonylurea or insulin and conventional treatment on the risk of microvascular and macrovascular complications in patients with type 2 diabetes in a randomised controlled trial.

Methods 3867 newly diagnosed patients with type 2 diabetes, median age 54 years (IQR 48–60 years), who after 3 months' diet treatment had a mean of two fasting plasma glucose (FPG) concentrations of 6·1–15·0 mmol/L were randomly assigned intensive policy with a sulphonylurea (chlorpropamide, glibenclamide, or glipizide) or with insulin, or conventional policy with diet. The aim in the intensive group was FPG less than 6 mmol/L. In the conventional group, the aim was the best achievable FPG with diet alone; drugs were added only if there were hyperglycaemic symptoms or FPG greater than 15 mmol/L. Three aggregate endpoints were used to assess differences between conventional and intensive treatment: any diabetes-related endpoint (sudden death, death from hyperglycaemia or hypoglycaemia, fatal or non-fatal myocardial infarction, angina, heart failure, stroke, renal failure, amputation [of at least one digit], vitreous haemorrhage, retinopathy requiring photocoagulation, blindness in one eye, or cataract extraction); diabetes-related death (death from myocardial infarction, stroke, peripheral vascular disease, renal disease, hyperglycaemia or hypoglycaemia, and sudden death); and all-cause mortality. Single clinical endpoints and surrogate subclinical endpoints were also assessed. All analyses were by intention to treat and frequency of hypoglycaemia was also analysed by actual therapy.

Findings Over 10 years, haemoglobin A_{1c} (HbA_{1c}) was 7·0% (6·2–8·2) in the intensive group compared with 7·9% (6·9–8·8) in the conventional group—an 11% reduction. There was no difference in HbA_{1c} among agents in the intensive group. Compared with the conventional group, the risk in the intensive group was 12% lower (95% CI 1–21, p=0·029) for any diabetes-related endpoint; 10% lower (−11 to 27, p=0·34) for any diabetes-related death; and 6% lower (−10 to 20, p=0·44) for all-cause mortality. Most of the risk reduction in the any diabetes-related aggregate endpoint was due to a 25% risk reduction (7–40, p=0·0099) in microvascular endpoints, including the need for retinal photocoagulation. There was no difference for any of the three aggregate endpoints between the three intensive agents (chlorpropamide, glibenclamide, or insulin).

Patients in the intensive group had more hypoglycaemic episodes than those in the conventional group on both types of analysis (both p<0·0001). The rates of major hypoglycaemic episodes per year were 0·7% with conventional treatment, 1·0% with chlorpropamide, 1·4% with glibenclamide, and 1·8% with insulin. Weight gain was significantly higher in the intensive group (mean 2·9 kg) than in the conventional group (p<0·001), and patients assigned insulin had a greater gain in weight (4·0 kg) than those assigned chlorpropamide (2·6 kg) or glibenclamide (1·7 kg).

Interpretation Intensive blood-glucose control by either sulphonylureas or insulin substantially decreases the risk of microvascular complications, but not macrovascular disease, in patients with type 2 diabetes. None of the individual drugs had an adverse effect on cardiovascular outcomes. All intensive treatment increased the risk of hypoglycaemia.

Lancet 1998; **352:** 837–53

---

*Study organisation given at end of paper

Correspondence to: Prof Robert Turner, UKPDS Group, Diabetes Research Laboratories, Radcliffe Infirmary, Oxford OX2 6HE, UK

Effect of intensive blood-glucose control with metformin on complications in overweight patients with type 2 diabetes (UKPDS 34)

UK Prospective Diabetes Study (UKPDS) Group*

Summary

Background In patients with type 2 diabetes, intensive blood-glucose control with insulin or sulphonylurea therapy decreases progression of microvascular disease and may also reduce the risk of heart attacks. This study investigated whether intensive glucose control with metformin has any specific advantage or disadvantage.

Methods Of 4075 patients recruited to UKPDS in 15 centres, 1704 overweight (>120% ideal bodyweight) patients with newly diagnosed type 2 diabetes, mean age 53 years, had raised fasting plasma glucose (FPG; 6·1–15·0 mmol/L) without hyperglycaemic symptoms after 3 months' initial diet. 753 were included in a randomised controlled trial, median duration 10·7 years, of conventional policy, primarily with diet alone (n=411) versus intensive blood-glucose control policy with metformin, aiming for FPG below 6 mmol/L (n=342). A secondary analysis compared the 342 patients allocated metformin with 951 overweight patients allocated intensive blood-glucose control with chlorpropamide (n=265), glibenclamide (n=277), or insulin (n=409). The primary outcome measures were aggregates of any diabetes-related clinical endpoint, diabetes-related death, and all-cause mortality. In a supplementary randomised controlled trial, 537 non-overweight and overweight patients, mean age 59 years, who were already on maximum sulphonylurea therapy but had raised FPG (6·1–15.0 mmol/L) were allocated continuing sulphonylurea therapy alone (n=269) or addition of metformin (n=268).

Findings Median glycated haemoglobin (HbA$_{1c}$) was 7·4% in the metformin group compared with 8·0% in the conventional group. Patients allocated metformin, compared with the conventional group, had risk reductions of 32% (95% CI 13–47, p=0·002) for any diabetes-related endpoint, 42% for diabetes-related death (9–63, p=0·017), and 36% for all-cause mortality (9–55, p=0·011). Among patients allocated intensive blood-glucose control, metformin showed a greater effect than chlorpropamide, glibenclamide, or insulin for any diabetes-related endpoint (p=0·0034), all-cause mortality (p=0·021), and stroke (p=0·032). Early addition of metformin in sulphonylurea-treated patients was associated with an increased risk of diabetes-related death (96% increased risk [95% CI 2–275], p=0·039) compared with continued sulphonylurea alone. A combined analysis of the main and supplementary studies showed fewer metformin-allocated patients having diabetes-related endpoints (risk reduction 19% [2–33], p=0·033). Epidemiological assessment of the possible association of death from diabetes-related causes with the concurrent therapy of diabetes in 4416 patients did not show an increased risk in diabetes-related death in patients treated with a combination of sulphonylurea and metformin (risk reduction 5% [−33 to 32], p=0·78).

Interpretation Since intensive glucose control with metformin appears to decrease the risk of diabetes-related endpoints in overweight diabetic patients, and is associated with less weight gain and fewer hypoglycaemic attacks than are insulin and sulphonylureas, it may be the first-line pharmacological therapy of choice in these patients.

Lancet 1998; **352:** 854–65

*Study organisation given at end of paper

Correspondence to: Prof Robert Turner, UKPDS Group, Diabetes Research Laboratories, Radcliffe Infirmary, Oxford OX2 6HE, UK

Tight blood pressure control and risk of macrovascular and microvascular complications in type 2 diabetes: UKPDS 38

UK Prospective Diabetes Study Group

Abstract

Objective: To determine whether tight control of blood pressure prevents macrovascular and microvascular complications in patients with type 2 diabetes.

Design: Randomised controlled trial comparing tight control of blood pressure aiming at a blood pressure of < 150/85 mm Hg (with the use of an angiotensin converting enzyme inhibitor captopril or a β blocker atenolol as main treatment) with less tight control aiming at a blood pressure of < 180/105 mm Hg.

Setting: 20 hospital based clinics in England, Scotland, and Northern Ireland.

Subjects: 1148 hypertensive patients with type 2 diabetes (mean age 56, mean blood pressure at entry 160/94 mm Hg); 758 patients were allocated to tight control of blood pressure and 390 patients to less tight control with a median follow up of 8.4 years.

Main outcome measures: Predefined clinical end points, fatal and non-fatal, related to diabetes, deaths related to diabetes, and all cause mortality. Surrogate measures of microvascular disease included urinary albumin excretion and retinal photography.

Results: Mean blood pressure during follow up was significantly reduced in the group assigned tight blood pressure control (144/82 mm Hg) compared with the group assigned to less tight control (154/87 mm Hg) (P < 0.0001). Reductions in risk in the group assigned to tight control compared with that assigned to less tight control were 24% in diabetes related end points (95% confidence interval 8% to 38%) (P = 0.0046), 32% in deaths related to diabetes (6% to 51%) (P = 0.019), 44% in strokes (11% to 65%) (P = 0.013), and 37% in microvascular end points (11% to 56%) (P = 0.0092), predominantly owing to a reduced risk of retinal photocoagulation. There was a non-significant reduction in all cause mortality. After nine years of follow up the group assigned to tight blood pressure control also had a 34% reduction in risk in the proportion of patients with deterioration of retinopathy by two steps (99% confidence interval 11% to 50%) (P = 0.0004) and a 47% reduced risk (7% to 70%) (P = 0.004) of deterioration in visual acuity by three lines of the early treatment of diabetic retinopathy study (ETDRS) chart. After nine years of follow up 29% of patients in the group assigned to tight control required three or more treatments to lower blood pressure to achieve target blood pressures.

Conclusion: Tight blood pressure control in patients with hypertension and type 2 diabetes achieves a clinically important reduction in the risk of deaths related to diabetes, complications related to diabetes, progression of diabetic retinopathy, and deterioration in visual acuity.

Editorials by Orchard and Mogensen
Papers pp 713, 720

Members of the study group are given at the end of the paper.

This paper was prepared for publication by Robert Turner, Rury Holman, Irene Stratton, Carole Cull, Valeria Frighi, Susan Manley, David Matthews, Andrew Neil, Heather McElroy, Eva Kohner, Charles Fox, David Hadden, and David Wright.

Correspondence to: Professor R Turner, UK Prospective Diabetes Study Group, Diabetes Research Laboratories, Radcliffe Infirmary, Oxford OX2 6HE

BMJ 1998;317:703–13

Reprinted from the **BMJ** , 12 September 1998, Vol 317, p 713-720

Efficacy of atenolol and captopril in reducing risk of macrovascular and microvascular complications in type 2 diabetes: UKPDS 39

UK Prospective Diabetes Study Group

Abstract

Objective: To determine whether tight control of blood pressure with either a β blocker or an angiotensin converting enzyme inhibitor has a specific advantage or disadvantage in preventing the macrovascular and microvascular complications of type 2 diabetes.

Design: Randomised controlled trial comparing an angiotensin converting enzyme inhibitor (captopril) with a β blocker (atenolol) in patients with type 2 diabetes aiming at a blood pressure of < 150/ < 85 mm Hg.

Setting: 20 hospital based clinics in England, Scotland, and Northern Ireland.

Subjects: 1148 hypertensive patients with type 2 diabetes (mean age 56 years, mean blood pressure 160/94 mm Hg). Of the 758 patients allocated to tight control of blood pressure, 400 were allocated to captopril and 358 to atenolol. 390 patients were allocated to less tight control of blood pressure.

Main outcome measures: Predefined clinical end points, fatal and non-fatal, related to diabetes, death related to diabetes, and all cause mortality. Surrogate measures of microvascular and macrovascular disease included urinary albumin excretion and retinopathy assessed by retinal photography.

Results: Captopril and atenolol were equally effective in reducing blood pressure to a mean of 144/83 mm Hg and 143/81 mm Hg respectively, with a similar proportion of patients (27% and 31%) requiring three or more antihypertensive treatments.

More patients in the captopril group than the atenolol group took the allocated treatment: at their last clinic visit, 78% of those allocated captopril and 65% of those allocated atenolol were taking the drug (P < 0.0001). Captopril and atenolol were equally effective in reducing the risk of macrovascular end points. Similar proportions of patients in the two groups showed deterioration in retinopathy by two grades after nine years (31% in the captopril group and 37% in the atenolol group) and developed clinical grade albuminuria ≥ 300 mg/l (5% and 9%). The proportion of patients with hypoglycaemic attacks was not different between groups, but mean weight gain in the atenolol group was greater (3.4 kg v 1.6 kg).

Conclusion: Blood pressure lowering with captopril or atenolol was similarly effective in reducing the incidence of diabetic complications. This study provided no evidence that either drug has any specific beneficial or deleterious effect, suggesting that blood pressure reduction in itself may be more important than the treatment used.

Editorials by Orchard and Mogensen

Papers pp 703, 720

Members of the study group are given at the end of the accompanying paper on p 703.

This paper was prepared for publication by Rury Holman, Robert Turner, Irene Stratton, Carole Cull, Valeria Frighi, Susan Manley, David Matthews, Andrew Neil, Eva Kohner, David Wright, David Hadden, and Charles Fox.

Correspondence to: Professor R Holman, UK Prospective Diabetes Study Group, Diabetes Research Laboratories, Radcliffe Infirmary, Oxford OX2 6HE

BMJ 1998;317:713-20

Cost effectiveness analysis of improved blood pressure control in hypertensive patients with type 2 diabetes: UKPDS 40

UK Prospective Diabetes Study Group

Editorials by Orchard and Mogensen *Papers* pp 703, 713

Members of the study group are given at the end of the accompanying paper on p 703. This paper was prepared for publication by Maria Raikou, Alastair Gray, Andrew Briggs, Richard Stevens, Carole Cull, Alistair McGuire, Paul Fenn, Irene Stratton, Rury Holman, and Robert Turner.

Correspondence to: Dr Alastair Gray, Health Economics Research Centre, Institute of Health Sciences, Oxford University, Oxford OX3 7LF alastair.gray@ ihs.ox.ac.uk

Reprint requests to: UK Prospective Diabetes Study Group, Diabetes Research Laboratories, Radcliffe Infirmary, Oxford OX2 6HE

BMJ 1998;317:720–6

Abstract

Objectives: To estimate the economic efficiency of tight blood pressure control, with angiotensin converting enzyme inhibitors or β blockers, compared with less tight control in hypertensive patients with type 2 diabetes.

Design: Cost effectiveness analysis incorporating within trial analysis and estimation of impact on life expectancy through use of the within trial hazards of reaching a defined clinical end point. Use of resources driven by trial protocol and use of resources in standard clinical practice were both considered.

Setting: 20 hospital based clinics in England, Scotland, and Northern Ireland.

Subjects: 1148 hypertensive patients with type 2 diabetes from UK prospective diabetes study randomised to tight control of blood pressure (n = 758) or less tight control (n = 390).

Main outcome measure: Cost effectiveness ratios based on (*a*) use of healthcare resources associated with tight control and less tight control and treatment of complications and (*b*) within trial time free from diabetes related end points, and life years gained.

Results: Based on use of resources driven by trial protocol, the incremental cost effectiveness of tight control compared with less tight control was cost saving. Based on use of resources in standard clinical practice, incremental cost per extra year free from end points amounted to £1049 (costs and effects discounted at 6% per year) and £434 (costs discounted at 6% per year and effects not discounted). The incremental cost per life year gained was £720 (costs and effects discounted at 6% per year) and £291 (costs discounted at 6% per year and effects not discounted).

Conclusions: Tight control of blood pressure in hypertensive patients with type 2 diabetes substantially reduced the cost of complications, increased the interval without complications and survival, and had a cost effectiveness ratio that compares favourably with many accepted healthcare programmes.

5 The UKPDS and its global impact

Saul Genuth

Department of Medicine, Case Western Reserve University, Cleveland, Ohio, USA

Introduction

Virtually all journal articles dealing with the complications and/or treatment of diabetes cite the publications detailing the main results from the UK Prospective Diabetes Study (UKPDS) [1, 2] and Diabetes Control and Complications Trial (DCCT) [3] in the first paragraph and often in the first sentence. This fact alone attests to the huge impact the UKPDS has had on the world of diabetes. Although the DCCT results were presented in 1993 and the UKPDS results in 1998, the UKPDS was started first in 1977 with a pilot study that recruited 600 patients in five centres [4], whereas recruitment for the comparable DCCT feasibility phase did not begin until 1983 [3]. The results of these two seminal studies were mutually reinforcing, demonstrating that intensive treatment which targeted the range of normoglycaemia reduced the risks of microvascular and neuropathic complications. Neither randomized trial was able to prove conclusively that complications of cardiovascular disease (CVD) were reduced by intensive treatment [1, 5], although subsequent observational follow-up of the DCCT cohort has finally also shown the accrual of this benefit [6]. The UKPDS main results were succinctly summarized by one commentator and are shown in Table 5.1.

Table 5.1 Main UK Prospective Diabetes Study (UKPDS) results

Improved control of blood glucose or blood pressure reduced the risk of:
Major diabetic eye disease by one-quarter
Serious deterioration of vision by nearly one-half
Early kidney damage by one-third
Strokes by one-third
Death from diabetes-related causes by one-third
Reproduced with permission from Leslie RD. Diabetes Metab Res Rev 15: 65–71, 1999 [16].

Originally published: Genuth S. The UKPDS and its global impact. *Diabetic Medicine* 2008; 25 (Suppl. 2): 57–62

Context

Although insulin became available for therapy in 1921, it was not until the 1930–1940 era that it became apparent that the development of long-term complications might be influenced by the type and degree of glycaemic control employed [7]. A controversy ensued, but a body of animal model and human data was built up to support the hypothesis that hyperglycaemia was a cause of, or at least a contributor to, the pathogenesis of these complications [8]. The hypothesis was conclusively tested and supported by the results of the DCCT and the Stockholm Diabetes Intervention Study for Type 1 diabetes in 1993 [9, 10]. But did the DCCT results apply to type 2 diabetes?

The only prior randomized clinical trial in type 2 diabetes, the University Group Diabetes Program (UGDP), had failed to show any benefit from lowering blood glucose, even with insulin. However, this trial lacked power, a reliable long-term measure of glycaemic levels, accurate sophisticated assessment of complications and probably included participants who may have only had impaired glucose tolerance [11]. The many deficiencies in the UGDP study were one of the main stimuli to the UKPDS investigators to organize a much larger and better designed trial which took advantage of the improvements in treatment and monitoring since the UGDP period.

A position statement on the DCCT by the American Diabetes Association (ADA) [12] said: '...there is no reason to believe that the effects of better control of blood glucose levels would not apply to people with NIDDM. The eye, kidney, and nerve complications appear quite similar in IDDM and NIDDM and it is likely that the same or similar underlying mechanisms of disease apply.' However, a DCCT investigator noted in 1995 that 'the debate regarding the effect of intensive therapy on the long-term complications of NIDDM cannot be resolved satisfactorily at the current time.' [13]. The report of the Kumamoto study in 1995 [14] demonstrating a reduction in retinopathy, nephropathy and neuropathy in Japanese patients with type 2 diabetes did not settle the issue for many investigators, given the small number of participants (110), their low body mass index (20), decreased urinary C-peptide excretion and need for insulin treatment before being studied.

Response of the scientific diabetes community

There was a universal sigh of relief in Barcelona when the UKPDS results were presented in painstaking detail. Not only were the risks of microvascular complications reduced 25% by intensive treatment that lowered glycated haemoglobin (HbA$_{1c}$) by 0.9%, but the absolute rate of severe hypoglycaemic episodes with insulin administration was at least an order of magnitude lower than DCCT intensive treatment had caused in type 1 diabetes. Moreover, the spectre of sulfonylurea-induced CVD death raised by the UGDP was dispelled. The positive impact of these UKPDS results was attested to by numerous commentators [15-20] whose words outweighed those of a minority of critics of the study [21-23]. It is important to note that the results of the simultaneous blood pressure trial were equally important clinically: for example, this was the first demonstration that deterioration in visual acuity could be mitigated by intensive treatment of hypertension that lowered blood pressure by 10/5 mmHg compared with conventional treatment [24].

However, many investigators were disappointed that the 16% reduction in the cumulative incidence of myocardial infarction did not meet the conventional statistical test of significance, i.e. $P < 0.05$. This author preferred to interpret this crucial finding more literally by probability statistics: the P-value of 0.052 meant that if the UKPDS had been exactly replicated 19 times (instead of 20 times), the 16% reduction in myocardial infarction might have been observed one time only by chance alone. This contribution of the UKPDS to the CVD issue is strengthened by the fact that in meta-analyses of the positive epidemiological relationship between HbA_{1c} and CVD [25] or of randomized clinical trials testing the beneficial effect of intensive glycaemic treatment [26] in type 2 diabetes, the UKPDS is the dominant contributor to the data because of its large number of participating research volunteers and long duration. Moreover, the final story of CVD and intensive treatment remains to be told when the data from a further 10-year observational follow-up of the cohort become available. The statistical 'near miss' of a beneficial effect of intensive treatment on CVD has encouraged other investigators to design other randomized clinical trials to test this critical question (ACCORD, VADT, ADVANCE) and helped attract funding for them by government agencies and drug companies.

The impact of the UKPDS on the scientific community can also be seen in the tens of thousands of continuing medical education programmes on type 2 diabetes and its management that have been conducted since 1998. The UKPDS results quickly became a staple of such programmes. Moreover, they have been cited in educational material directed at nurses, dieticians and other healthcare professionals, as well as of equal importance, to patients.

While a direct linkage to the UKPDS results cannot be averred, it is likely that the effort of pharmaceutical companies to develop new drugs and new classes of drugs has been enhanced [20]. This stimulating effect comes not only from the demonstration of benefit to complications. It has also been made necessary by the crucial UKPDS observation that, after an initial period of blood glucose control in the study cohort by sulfonylurea drugs, metformin and even insulin, HbA_{1c} appears to rise inexorably despite continuation of therapy [1] because pancreatic β-cell function declines [27]. This experience also led to the recommendation that combination therapy with different classes of glucose-lowering drugs should be started earlier in the course of type 2 diabetes [28] and used more often [29].

The use of metformin as the first-choice drug, certainly for the 80% of type 2 diabetic patients who are obese, was strengthened by the UKPDS observation [2] that metformin treatment led to a significant 39% reduction in myocardial infarction (MI) and a 36% reduction in total mortality, despite maintaining an

HbA_{1c} of only 7.4% compared with 8.0% in the comparison group. Metformin is now 'officially endorsed' as the number-one drug for starting treatment when nutrition therapy fails, by consensus of the ADA and the European Association for the Study of Diabetes, referencing the UKPDS paper as support for this conclusion [30].

In the small country of Luxembourg, based on questionnaires sent to all general practitioners, internists and endocrinologists, a fourfold increase in metformin use and a doubling of prescriptions for combined use of insulin plus oral glucose-lowering drugs has been observed between 1991 and 2002. The authors suggest the change may reflect 'the helpful impact of studies like the UKPDS' [31].

Objective evidence of impact on diabetes care

The only certain way to have obtained Grade A evidence of the effect of the UKPDS on diabetes care would have been a randomized trial: namely, to have compared the subsequent course, management and HbA_{1c} in two cohorts of physicians and their patients, randomly assigned to either being offered intensive indoctrination with the UKPDS results or being offered little or no knowledge of the study results. Obviously such a design to test the effect of the UKPDS worldwide would have been unfeasible and unethical. Thus, one can only seek information as to diabetes outcomes since 1998, without being able to conclusively impute a cause-and-effect relationship between the UKPDS and those outcomes, from *post hoc propter hoc* reasoning.

The most obvious outcome to inspect is HbA_{1c} where it has been systematically collected and recorded. In the USA, the National Health and Nutrition Examination Survey (NHANES) is carried out at regular intervals on nationally representative, population-based samples of adults. Figure 5.1 shows the results for three waves (400–500 individuals each) of sampling: 1999–2000, 2001–2002 and 2003–2004 [32]. The mean HbA_{1c} decreased from 7.8 to 7.5 to 7.2% during that period, while the percentage with HbA_{1c} <7.0% (the existing ADA target during that period) increased from 37 to 50 to 57%. A much larger, although not a population-based, sample of HbA_{1c} results was obtained from Quest Laboratories [33], which estimated that it performs 1/4 to 1/3 of all laboratory tests in the USA. From a review of 23 million results obtained from 4.8 million patients, a progressive fall in HbA_{1c} from 2001 to 2006 of 0.4% in type 1 diabetes and 0.6% in type 2 diabetes was noted [33]. Each separate cohort of patients who were tested yearly showed a fall in HbA_{1c} during the first year of follow-up, but then began to increase again in successive years, although generally remaining below their first value.

Data from the UK itself also show recent improvement. The percentage of patients with HbA_{1c} <7.4% increased from 59% in 2004–2005 to 68% in 2006–2007 [34]. Those numbers compare favourably with a median HbA_{1c} of 8.1% in the intensively treated group and 8.7% in the conventionally treated group during the last 5-year period of the UKPDS [1].

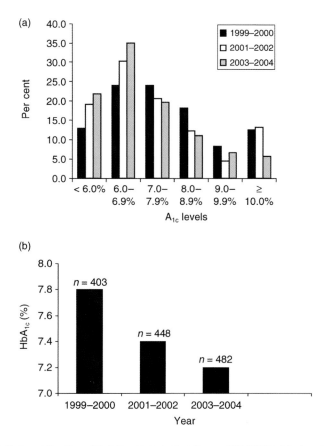

Figure 5.1 National Health and Nutrition Examination Survey (NHANES) data from the USA. (a) Distribution of HbA_{1c} among the three separate NHANES cohorts. Note the increase in HbA_{1c} within the American Diabetes Association guideline target of < 7.0%. Copyright © 2008 American Diabetes Association from [32]. (b) Mean glycated haemoglobin (HbA_{1c}) in successive population-based samples of diabetic patients (the majority being type 2) obtained by NHANES. Drawn using data from [32].

The Swedish National Diabetes Registry has noted in cross-sectional data a decrease in HbA_{1c} from 7.8% in 1996 to 7.2% in 2003 [35]. The percentage of patients with HbA_{1c} <7.3% increased from 41 to 68% during that time. In Israel, the percentage of patients with HbA_{1c} <7.0% increased from 30% in 1995 to 43% in 2003 [36] and increased further to 59% in 2005 [37].

There are other non-systematic scattered data from various countries and from different years that suggest a general trend toward improvement in the world of diabetes as a whole. A survey of over 24 000 patients in 230 centres in 12 countries in Asia in 1998 yielded a mean HbA_{1c} of 8.6%, similar to the UKPDS conventional group just prior to that time [38]. By contrast, in the Czech Republic, the mean HbA_{1c} in 2002 was 8.0% [39]. In a recent survey in

Spain, 51% of patients had $HbA_{1c} < 7.0\%$ [40]. In Japan [41], the yearly mean HbA_{1c} of type 2 diabetic patients was stable at 7.0–7.1% during the period of 2000–2002.

A report from Germany and Austria provides a longitudinal analysis in 27000 adolescents and young adults with type 1 diabetes managed in 207 treatment centres [42]. The median HbA_{1c} (taking values only after the honeymoon remission period) decreased from 8.5 to 7.6% from the periods of 1995–1997 to 2001–2005. While it is arguable whether the UKPDS could have directly influenced the course of type 1 diabetes in young people, the consistency of the microvascular results of the UKPDS with those of the DCCT surely buttressed the conclusion that improved blood glucose control was very beneficial to anyone with diabetes.

It would also be of interest to know whether there are temporal trends in treatment of type 2 diabetes since 1998; however, much less data are readily available. In Sweden, the average HbA_{1c} at which insulin is either substituted for or added to oral glucose-lowering agents decreased from 8.8% in 1996 to approximately 8.0% in 2003 [43]. In the USA, data from a market survey [44] on insulin use suggest slow intensification of treatment. In the past 5 years, the percentages of type 2 patients on intensive vs. conventional treatment has changed from 24 vs. 76% to 34 vs. 66%. In the past 2 years, the percentage of type 2 insulin users who are taking insulin exclusively has increased from 42 to 46% and the mean number of injections has risen from 2.1 to 2.3 per day. Another result of the UKPDS is a growing emphasis on the earlier use of insulin in treatment of type 2 diabetes, before HbA_{1c} has risen to 9.0% [45].

Interpretation of data not obtained from single cohorts of patients followed longitudinally is, of course, confounded by other possible explanations for the trends. The early death of patients with higher HbA_{1c} could lead to a fall in national levels (survivor bias). The addition of patients with newly diagnosed diabetes picked up by more aggressive screening would enrich later data with lower HbA_{1c} levels. The growing number of underinsured or uninsured patients with diabetes in the USA, whose glycaemic control is known to be poorer [46], would select out such individuals from those having more recent tests because they cannot afford to pay for them. Nonetheless, it appears reasonable to conclude that there has been a slow global decrease in HbA_{1c} of treated diabetic patients and that the global impact of the UKPDS contributed to that trend.

The results of the UKPDS and its analysis of cost-effectiveness have probably influenced public health agency efforts to limit the damage to patients and increasingly to society itself, as the global type 2 diabetes epidemic gains momentum [47]. In 2004 pounds sterling, each quality-adjusted life year (QALY) gained by intensive blood glucose control cost approximately £6028; the cost for intensive blood pressure control, which was—and is—easier to implement, was only £369; these values are well below an 'acceptability ceiling' of £20000 per QALY [48]. Metformin treatment of obese patients was actually cost saving (~ £1000 less than conventional treatment) and it increased QALYs by 0.55 [48, 49]. This economic analysis has further supported the predominant position of metformin in the management of type 2 diabetes [30]. Of great importance from a societal perspective and to public healthcare planners, the total yearly cost of UKPDS treatment that would reduce complications represented less than 1% of the annual proposed expenditure of the UK National Health Service for 2001–2005 [50]. This intrusion on other healthcare needs may, of course, be different in other countries and be judged differently depending on what those other national healthcare needs are.

Conclusion

The UKPDS was an enormous undertaking by a very committed group of primary investigators, ably led by Robert Turner. Remarkably, it was actually implemented in the field by 305 clinical practitioners who referred their newly diagnosed diabetic patients for recruitment in 23 clinical centres [1, 4].

Was the UKPDS a perfect study? Of course not; no study is. There were considerable therapeutic drug crossovers among the treatment arms and 80% of the original diet policy (conventional) group ultimately required some drug therapy mandated by unacceptable glycaemic control. However, this confounding would have been an impediment to observing a difference in complications outcomes, not an aid. The imbedding of several other studies within the UKPDS added to its complexity and made interpretation somewhat more difficult [21]. One of the sub-studies, the randomized addition or not of metformin to sulfonylurea failure patients [2], left considerable confusion in its wake.

Nonetheless, the large size, scope of outcome and covariate measurements, long median follow-up period, multiple treatment arms, sophisticated analysis and numerous ancillary studies gave it greater weight than any previous study of the treatment of type 2 diabetes. The post hoc epidemiological analyses of the data [51-54] have further enriched the value of the UKPDS and its impact on the world of diabetes. It has stood as a model for numerous studies that have succeeded it. Further observational follow-up of this uniquely valuable cohort of patients will very likely yield more insights into diabetes, its complications and the benefits of treatment.

Summary

This article reviews the worldwide impact of the United Kingdom Prospective Diabetes Study (UKPDS) on diabetes health care since publication of the main study results in 1998.

The major papers published by the UKPDS were reviewed, e-mails and faxes were sent to diabetes associations in various regions of the world seeking information on trends in HbA$_{1c}$ over the past decade and similar information was obtained from a major USA laboratory.

The UKPDS extended to type 2 diabetes and brought to completion the case for linking the microvascular vascular complications of diabetes to control of blood glucose initially demonstrated by the Diabetes Control and Complications Trial (DCCT). This helped set the standard of care for diabetes to seek an HbA$_{1c}$ goal of at least < 7.0% with intensive glycaemic treatment and formed a fundamental part of continuing medical education. This also helped stimulate new hypoglycaemic drug development and the preferential use of metformin as first line therapy was supported by UKPDS results. In many areas of the world, including the United Kingdom and the USA, a national trend to lower HbA$_{1c}$ levels has been seen.

Economic analyses have shown UKPDS intensive treatment to be cost-effective at £6028 per quality life year gained, imposing a reasonable burden on the British National health care budget.

The UKPDS was a landmark study in the treatment of type 2 diabetes from the time of diagnosis that has influenced standards of care and treatment guidelines throughout the world.

Acknowledgements

I appreciate the assistance of all of the following in obtaining data from their countries: George Alberti (United Kingdom); Bjorn Eliasson (Sweden); Richard Furlanetto (USA); Ofra Kalter-Leibovici (Israel); Masashi Kobayashi (Japan); Laura Ladd (United Kingdom); Jan Skrha (Czech Republic); and Laura Pavlik for expert secretarial work.

References

1 UKPDS Group. Intensive blood-glucose control with sulphonylureas or insulin compared with conventional treatment and risk of complications in patients with type 2 diabetes (UKPDS 33). *Lancet* 1998;352:837-853.

2 UKPDS Group. Effect of intensive blood-glucose control with metformin on complications in overweight patients with type 2 diabetes (UKPDS 34). *Lancet* 1998;352:854-865.

3 The DCCT Research Group. The effect of intensive treatment of diabetes on the development and progression of long-term complications in insulin-dependent diabetes mellitus. *N Eng J Med* 1992;329:977-986.

4 UK Prospective Diabetes Study Group. UK Prospective Diabetes Study (UKPDS). *Diabetologia* 1991;34:877-890.

5 DCCT Research Group. Effect of intensive diabetes management on macrovascular events and risk factors in the Diabetes Control and Complications Trial. *Am J Cardiol* 1995;75:894-903.

6 DCCT/EDIC Study Research Group. Intensive diabetes treatment and cardiovascular disease in patients with type 1 diabetes. *N Eng J Med* 2005;353:2643-2653.

7 Johnsson S. Retinopathy and nephropathy in diabetes mellitus: comparison of the effects of two forms of treatment. *Diabetes* 1960; 9:1-8.

8 Genuth SM. The case of blood glucose control. *Adv Inter Med* 1995;40:573-623.
 9 Reichard P, Berglund B, Britz A, Cars I, Nilsson BY, Rosenqvist U. Intensified conventional insulin treatment retards the microvascular complications of insulin-dependent diabetes mellitus (IDDM): the Stockholm Diabetes Intervention Study (SDIS) after 5 years. *J Intern Med* 1991;230:101-108.
10 Reichard P, Nilsson BY, Rosenqvist U. The effect of long-term intensified insulin treatment on the development of microvascular complications of diabetes mellitus. *N Eng J Med* 1993;329:304-309.
11 Genuth S. Exogenous insulin administration and cardiovascular risk in non-insulin-dependent and insulin-dependent diabetes mellitus. *Ann Intern Med* 1996;124:104-109.
12 American Diabetes Association. Implications of the Diabetes Control and Complications Trial. *Diabetes* 1993;42:1555-1558.
13 Nathan DM. Do results from the Diabetes Control and Complications Trial apply in NIDDM? *Diabetes Care* 1995;18:251-257.
14 Ohkubo Y, Kishikawa H, Araki E, Miyata T, Isami S, Motoyoshi S *et al*. Intensive insulin therapy prevents the progression of diabetic microvascular complications in Japanese patients with non-insulin-dependent diabetes mellitus: a randomized prospective 6-year study. *Diabetes Res Clin Pract* 1995;28:103-117.
15 American Diabetes Association. Implications of the UK Prospective Diabetes Study. *Diabetes Care* 1998;21:2180-2184.
16 Leslie RD. UK Prospective Diabetes Study (UKPDS): What now or so what? *Diabetes Metab Res Rev* 1999;15:65-71.
17 Baldeweg SE, Yudkin JS. Implications of the UK Prospective Diabetes Study. *Prim Care* 1999;26:809-827.
18 Laakso M. Benefits of strict glucose and blood pressure control in type 2 diabetes. Lessons from the UK Prospective Diabetes Study. *Circulation* 1999;99:461-462.
19 Mehnert H. Diabetologische Realitäten und Wünsche. UKPDS nach einem Jahr. *Dtsch med Wschr* 1999;124:1021.
20 Pontiroli AE, Folli F. Is it worth treating diabetes? Lessons from the UKPDS. *Acta Diabetol* 1998;335:170-171.
21 Nathan DM. Some answers, more controversy, from UKPDS. *Lancet* 1998;352:832-833.
22 Budenholzer B. Glycaemia and vascular effects of type 2 diabetes. *Br Med J* 2001;322:1245.
23 McCormack J, Greenhalgh T. Seeing what you want to see in randomized controlled trials: versions and perversions of UKPDS data. *Br Med J* 2000;320:1720-1723.
24 UK Prospective Diabetes Study Group. Tight blood pressure control and risk of macrovascular and microvascular complications in type 2 diabetes: UKPDS 38. *Br Med J* 1998;317:703-713.
25 Selvin E, Marinopoulos S, Berkenblit G, Rami T, Brancati FL, Powe NR *et al*. Meta-analysis: glycosylated hemoglobin and cardiovascular disease in diabetes mellitus. *Ann Intern Med* 2004;141:421-431.
26 Stettler C, Allemann S, Jüni P, Cull CA, Holman RR, Egger M *et al*. Glycemic control and macrovascular disease in types 1 and 2 diabetes mellitus: meta-analysis of randomized trials. *Am Heart J* 2006;152:27-38.
27 UK Prospective Diabetes Study Group. UK Prospective Diabetes Study 16. *Diabetes* 1995;44:1249-1258.
28 UK Prospective Diabetes Study (UKPDS) Group. Glycemic control with diet, sulfonylurea, metformin, or insulin patients with type 2 diabetes mellitus. *J Am Med Assoc* 1999;281:2005-2012.

29 Inzucchi SE. Oral antihyperglycemic therapy for type 2 diabetes. *J Am Med Assoc* 2002;287:360-372.

30 Nathan DM, Buse JB, Davidson MB, Heine RJ, Holman RR,Sherwin R *et al*. Management of hyperglycemia in type 2 diabetes: a consensus algorithm for the initiation and adjustment of therapy. *Diabetes Care* 2006;29:1963-1972.

31 Perquin M, Michel GH, de Beaufort C, Keipes M, Wirion R, Haas N. Changes in diabetes prevalence and treatment in the last ten years in Luxembourg. A lesson from the UK Prospective Diabetes Study? *Diabetes Metab* 2005;31:499-502.

32 Hoerger TJ, Segel JE, Gregg EW, Saaddine JB. Is glycemic control improving in US adults? *Diabetes Care* 2008;31:81-86.

33 Huang X, Reichberg S, Green M, Koski E, Kaufman H, Kaufman F *et al*. Factors affecting the seasonal pattern in hemoglobin A_{1c} values: analyses of data from a large reference laboratory database. Presented at the American Diabetes Association Annual Meeting, Washington DC, USA, June 9–13, 2006.

34 Department of Health. *Quality and Outcomes Framework*. NHS Information Centre for Health and Social Care, September 2007. UK: Department of Health. http://www. dh.gov.uk/en/Healthcare/Primarycare/Primarycarecontracting/QOF/index.htm Last accessed 2 September 2008.

35 Eliasson B, Cederholm J, Nilsson P, Gudbjörnsdóttir, for the Steering Committee of the Swedish National Diabetes Register. The gap between guidelines and reality: Type 2 diabetes in a National Diabetes Register 1996–2003. *Diabet Med* 2005;22:1420-1426.

36 Goldfracht M, Levin D, Peled O, Poraz I, Stern E, Weiss D *et al*. Diabetes in the community—ten years of chronic disease management program. Community Division, Clalit Health Services, Tel Aviv Israel, 2006.

37 Elis A, Rosenmann L, Chodick G, Heymann AD, Kokia E, Shalev V. The association between glycemic, lipids and blood pressure control among Israeli diabetic patients. *Q J Med* 2008;101:275-280.

38 Chuang LM, Tsai ST, Huang BY, Tai TY. The status of diabetes control in Asia—a cross-sectional survey of 24 317 patients with diabetes mellitus in 1998. *Diabet Med* 2002;19:978-985.

39 Skrha J for the Committee of the Czech Diabetes Society. Diabetes mellitus 2002 in the Czech Republic—Epidemiological Study. *Diabetol Metab Endokrinol* 2005;8:5–12.

40 Orozco-Beltrán D, Gil-Guillen VF, Quirce F, Navarro-Perez J, Pineda M, Gomez-de-la-Cámara A *et al*. Collaborative diabetes study investigators. Control of diabetes and cardiovascular risk factors in patients with type 2 diabetes in primary care. The gap between guidelines and reality in Spain. *Int J Clin Pract* 2007;61:909-915.

41 Kobayashi M, Yamazaki K, Hirao K, Oishi M, Kanatsuka A, Yamauchi M *et al*. The status of diabetes control and anti-diabetic drug therapy in Japan—a cross-sectional survey of 17 000 patients with diabetes mellitus (JDDM 1). *Diabetes Res Clin Pract* 2006;73:198-204.

42 Gerstl EM, Rabl W, Rosenbauer J, Gröbe H, Hofer SE, Krause U *et al*. Metabolic control as reflected by HbA_{1c} in children, adolescents and young adults with type 1 diabetes mellitus: combined longitudinal analysis including 27 035 patients from 207 centers in Germany and Austria during the last decade. *Eur J Pediatr* 2008;167:447-453.

43 Eliasson B, Eeg-Olofsson K, Cederholm J, Nilsson PM, Gudbjörnsdóttir S, for the Steering Committee of the Swedish National Diabetes Register. Antihyperglycaemic treatment of type 2 diabetes: results from a national diabetes register. *Diabetes Metab* 2007;33:269-276.

44 GfK Market Measures, 2007. http://www.gfk.com/gfkmm/ Last accessed 2 September 2008.

45 LeRoith D. Our evolving understanding of getting to goal using insulin in type 2 diabetes. *Endocrinol Metab Clin. North Am* 2007;36(Suppl. 2):9-19.

46 Philis-Tsimikas A, Walker C, Rivard L, Talavera G, Reimann JO, Salmon M *et al*. Improvement in diabetes care of underinsured patients enrolled in Project Dulce. A community-based, culturally appropriate, nurse care management and peer education diabetes care model. *Diabetes Care* 2004;27:110-115.

47 King H, Aubert RE, Herman WH. Global burden of diabetes, 1995–2025; prevalence, numerical estimates, and projections. *Diabetes Care* 1998;21:1414-1431.

48 Clarke PM, Gray AM, Briggs A, Stevens RJ, Matthews DR, Holman RR, on behalf of the UK Prospective Diabetes Study (UKPDS). Cost–utility analyses of intensive blood glucose and tight blood pressure control in type 2 diabetes (UKPDS 72). *Diabetologia* 2005;48:868-877.

49 Clark P, Gray A, Adler A, Stevens R, Raikou M, Cull C *et al*. on behalf of the UKPDS Group. Cost-effectiveness analysis of intensive blood-glucose control with metformin in overweight patients with Type II diabetes (UKPDS No. 51). *Diabetologia* 2001;44:298-304.

50 Gray A, Clarke P, Farmer A, Holman R. Implementing intensive control of blood glucose concentration and blood pressure in type 2 diabetes in England: cost analysis (UKPDS 63). *Br Med J* 2002;325:860.

51 Stratton IM, Adler AI, Neil HA, Matthews DR, Manley SE, Cull CA *et al*. on behalf of the UK Prospective Diabetes Study Group. Association of glycaemia with macrovascular and microvascular complications of type 2 diabetes (UKPDS 35): prospective observational study. *Br Med J* 2000;321:405-412.

52 Adler AI, Stratton IM, Neil HA, Yudkin JS, Matthews DR, Cull CA *et al*. on behalf of the UK Prospective Diabetes Study Group. Association of systolic blood pressure with macrovascular and microvascular complications of type 2 diabetes (UKPDS 36): prospective observational study. *Br Med J* 2000;321:412-419.

53 Stratton IM, Cull CA, Adler AI, Matthews DR, Neil HA, Holman RR. Additive effects of glycaemia and blood pressure exposure on risk of complications in type 2 diabetes: a prospective observational study (UKPDS 75). *Diabetologia* 2006;49:1761-1769.

54 Stevens RJ, Kothari V, Adler AI, Stratton IM, on behalf of the UK Prospective Diabetes Study Group. The UKPDS risk engine: a model for the risk of coronary heart disease in type 2 diabetes (UKPDS 56). *Clin Science* 2001;101:671-679.

6 Genetics: how the UKPDS contributed to determining the genetic landscape of type 2 diabetes

Anna L. Gloyn[1] and Mark I. McCarthy[2]

[1] Diabetes Research Laboratories, Oxford Centre for Diabetes, Endocrinology and Metabolism, University of Oxford, Oxford, UK
[2] Diabetes Research Laboratories, Oxford Centre for Diabetes, Endocrinology and Metabolism; Wellcome Trust Centre for Human Genetics, University of Oxford, Oxford, UK

Introduction

Type 2 diabetes (T2DM) is the archetypal multifactorial trait, an individual's risk is defined by the complex interplay of both genetic and environmental factors. The enormous increase in the worldwide prevalence of T2DM is well documented and largely driven by the dramatic changes in individual environmental exposure, most notably in diet, exercise and other lifestyle changes that predispose to obesity. However, it is also evident from twin, family and admixture studies that T2DM and related intermediate traits show substantial heritability, which supports the role played by genetic variation in modifying an individual's response to these factors.

Over the past 18 months, as a result of an explosion of data from genome-wide association scans (GWAS), performed by several international groups, there has been a dramatic increase in our understanding of the genetic factors underlying the susceptibility to T2DM [1–6]. This eruption of data has seen our list of so called 'T2DM genes' increase from three robustly associating genes (*PPARG, KCNJ11, TCF7L2*) [7–10] to 17 in less than 2 years [1–6, 11–13]. New genes include *CDKAL1, CDKN2A/B, IGF2BP2, HHEX/IDE, FTO, SLC30A8, WFS1, HNF1B, JAZF1, CDC123-CAMK1D, TSPAN8-LGR5, THADA, ADAMTS9* and *NOTCH2* (Table 6.1). It would be hard to argue that, among this list of culprits, there are many of the traditional 'candidates' which were the focus of study by many in the field, including the UK Prospective Diabetes Study (UKPDS) group, over the past 20 years and, consequently, there are many new and unexpected insights into biology [14–16]. Despite these new revelations, there are a number of concepts which have come to fruition, exemplified by the recently identified genes, and it is fair to say that some of these were the basis for a number of the early studies performed on the UKPDS data set. This review will concentrate on these paradigms and illustrate how the UKPDS study employed them.

Originally published: Gloyn AL, McCarthy MI. Genetics: how the UKPDS contributed to determining the genetic landscape of type 2 diabetes. *Diabetic Medicine* 2008; 25 (Suppl. 2): 35–40

The genes encoding key proteins involved in pancreatic β-cell function are excellent candidates for type 2 diabetes

For many years the primary defect in T2DM has been hotly debated, with two distinct camps rooting for either pancreatic β-cell dysfunction or insulin resistance as the primary defect [17, 18]. The elucidation of the genes responsible for an individual's genetic susceptibility to T2DM is one approach that can be utilized to tease out the underlying primary defect. During the 1990s through to the early 2000s many groups performed genetic association studies, taking their favourite T2DM candidate gene, typically from the insulin secretion or insulin signalling pathways, and trying to determine whether genetic variants (typically only a single or at most a handful of single nucleotide polymorphisms, so called SNPs) within this gene were more common in patients with diabetes than in population or non-diabetic control subjects [19]. During these early years, the true architecture of genetic susceptibility was not even partially understood and consequently these studies were inadequately designed, with insufficient statistical power. This left the research community bewildered by a literature littered with false positives, which could not be replicated, and false negatives which resulted in strong biological candidates being discarded before they had been properly investigated [20]. Despite these poorly designed underpowered studies and the limited genetic resources available (the majority of studies were performed pre-human genome and HapMap projects), there were some perceptive concepts driven by an understanding of human physiology behind a number of these studies.

The genetic association studies performed by the UKPDS research team epitomized this as they were largely focused on genes involved in pancreatic β-cell function and in subjects selected for study on the basis of a clinical phenotype enriched for an insulin secretory defect (e.g. slim patients with a body mass index $< 27 \text{kg/m}^2$) and 'loaded' for a genetic aetiology (by selecting individuals with a family history of diabetes) [21–27]. In fact, one of the three robustly associating T2DM candidate genes (*KCNJ11*) identified in the pre-GWAS era was initially identified in the UKPDS dataset [23] and subsequently confirmed 2 years later in a large case–control study supported by a meta-analysis [8]. *KCNJ11* encodes one of the two essential subunits (Kir6.2) of the β-cell potassium ATP-sensitive (K_{ATP}) channel. Kir6.2, a member of the inwardly rectifying potassium channel family, forms the pore of the K_{ATP} channel, whilst the sulfonylurea receptor 1 (SUR1) provides the target for Mg-ADP and ATP and for the oral glucose-lowering agents, sulfonylureas. This key component of the stimulus–secretion machinery of the β-cell was an attractive candidate for a number of reasons, which are discussed in greater detail below.

The results from the past 18 months strongly support a defect in pancreatic β-cell function and/or mass as the primary progenitor of this disease, with ~70% of genes playing a role in islet function and influencing insulin secretion [6, 13, 28–31] (Table 6.1). The gene with the biggest effect size reported to date, *TCF7L2*, encodes a protein clearly influencing islet function [28, 32]. If our understanding of human pancreatic β-cell development, maintenance and physiology had been better, would we have selected the 'real T2DM susceptibility genes' as candidates and detected these associations earlier? It remains doubtful as we would still have been inadequately armed to tackle these questions, with limited sample sizes, inadequate genetic tools and an inability to consider variants without an obviously biological role (many current T2DM signals are intronic and their functional effect unclear). From the recently reported GWAS results, it would appear that the debate is no longer simply one of β-cell dysfunction vs. insulin action but one of β-cell dysfunction or reduced functional β-cell mass.

The genes involved in monogenic diabetes are likely to play a role in susceptibility to type 2 diabetes

Approximately 1-2% of non-autoimmune diabetes is because of monogenic disorders, largely affecting genes involved in β-cell development and function [33]. One such monogenic form of diabetes is as a result of a maternally inherited mitochondrial mutation (mt3243A>G), which causes a variable clinical phenotype, including diabetes and deafness. An early paper from the UKPDS team demonstrated that the prevalence of this mt3243A>G mutation was approximately 0.1–0.2% in Caucasians, a prevalence which has held up in subsequent larger studies in this population [34].

It is now commonly accepted that the genes involved in these rare aetiologies are excellent candidates for a role in susceptibility to T2DM [35, 36]. The premise is that a rare mutation in the gene leads to a severe clinical phenotype presenting at a young age, whilst a common genetic variant present in the normal population can play a role in an individual's susceptibility to T2DM. The UKPDS research group showed an early interest (as did others) in pursuing this research line and were among the first to screen the *HNF1A* (MODY3) gene for common variants and then test for association in T2DM [27]. Although these early studies did not have the statistical power to demonstrate the modest associations of common genetic variants in the *HNF1A* gene with T2DM, they did identify mutations in three patients who had been wrongly diagnosed as having T2DM rather than HNF1A-MODY. The identification of mutations in these individuals has implications for their clinical management and also highlights the diagnostic challenge in young adults presenting with diabetes [37, 38]. UKPDS 31 also identified common coding SNPs which have subsequently been investigated in large-scale association studies and have shown some evidence for a role in susceptibility to T2DM [12, 39, 40].

When the UKPDS research group were investigating the role of common genetic variation in the K_{ATP} channel genes (*KCNJ11* and *ABCC8)* and T2DM susceptibility, it had already been established that rare inactivating mutations (in both genes) were a common cause of congenital hyperinsulinaemia of infancy (CHI) [41, 42]. More recently, it has been demonstrated that activating mutations in both genes are a major cause of the opposite phenotype of neonatal diabetes [43–46]. This once again exemplifies the overlap between monogenic and multifactorial forms of β-cell dysfunction (Table 6.1).

Table 6.1 Type 2 diabetes susceptibility genes reaching genome-wide significance

Gene	Example variant	Mode of identification	Known/putative gene function	Evidence for an involvement in a monogenic form of diabetes	Evidence that variant influences β-cell function in man	References
PPARG	P12A (rs1801282)	Candidate	Transcription factor involved in adipocyte differentiation	Yes—mutations cause familial lypodystrophy	No	[7, 53]
KCNJ11	E23K (rs5215)	Candidate	Stimulus-secretion coupling in pancreatic β-cells	Yes—mutations cause neonatal diabetes and congenital hyperinsulinaemia of infancy	Yes—evidence for functional effect on β-cell K_{ATP} channel in vitro and evidence in vivo of post-OGTT serum insulin response	[8, 9, 30, 42, 43]
TCF7L2	rs7901695	Positional candidate	Wnt signalling	No	Yes	[10, 28, 50]
CDKAL1	rs10946398	Genome wide	Cell cycle control—inhibitor of cyclin-dependent kinase 5 (CDK5) activation	No	Yes—in vivo evidence that risk variant affects measures of insulin secretion	[2, 4-6, 29, 54]
CDKN2A/B	rs10811661	Genome wide	Cell cycle control—KO mouse displays reduced islet proliferation	No	Yes—in vivo evidence that risk variant affects measures of insulin secretion	[2, 4, 5, 54-56]
FTO	rs8050136	Genome wide	Nucleic acid demethylase	No	No	[3]
IGFBP2	rs4402960	Genome wide	Binding protein for insulin-like growth factor	No	No	[2, 4, 5, 54, 56]

Gene	SNP	Platform	Function	Monogenic/syndrome evidence	in vivo secretion evidence	References
HHEX/IDE	rs1111875	Genome wide	Transcription factor—KO mouse displays disrupted pancreas development	No	Yes—in vivo evidence that risk variant affects measures of insulin secretion	[1, 2, 4, 5, 29, 54, 56-59]
SLC30A8	rs13266634	Genome wide	Islet zinc transporter	No	Yes—evidence in vivo that risk variant affects measures of insulin secretion	[1, 2, 4-6, 54, 58]
WFS1	rs10010131	Candidate	Calcium channel involved in unfolded protein response	Yes—mutations cause wolfram syndrome	No	[11, 60]
HNF1B	rs4430796 *	Candidate	Transcription factor involved in pancreas development	Yes—mutations cause HNF1B-MODY	No	[12, 61]
JAZF1	rs864745	Genome wide	Transcription factor which regulates NR2C2—NR2C2 KO mice show growth retardation, perinatal and early post-natal hypoglycaemia	No	No	[13, 62]
CDC123-CAMK1D	rs12779790	Genome wide	Calcium-dependent protein kinase	No	No	[13]
TSPAN8-LGR5	rs7961581	Genome wide	Cell surface glycoprotein expressed in pancreatic carcinomas	No	No	[13]
THADA	rs7578597	Genome wide	Unknown function	No	No	[13]
ADAMTS9	rs4607103	Genome wide	Inhibitor of angiogenesis	No	No	[13]
NOTCH2	rs10923931	Genome wide	Control of cell differentiation—expressed in embryonic ductal cells of branching pancreatic buds during pancreatic organiogenesis	No	No	[13, 63]

*Single nucleotide polymorphism (SNP) not captured on genome-wide association (GWA) platforms. KO, knockout; OGTT, oral glucose tolerance test.

Type 2 diabetes susceptibility variants could influence response to treatment (pharmacogenetics)

Over the past 15 years we have seen spectacular success with the identification of the different genetic aetiologies of monogenic disorders of the pancreatic β-cell, which have not only led to a greater understanding of the molecular mechanisms of the β-cell but have also paved the way for the individualization of therapy for patients based on their aetiology, leading to improved quality of life for patients with these conditions [37, 38].

With the identification of replicated and established genetic variants influencing T2DM susceptibility, we are now in a position to consider if they can be used to predict T2DM risk and in the individualization of treatment for T2DM. Studies to date have shown a fourfold variation in T2DM risk between carriers of all known risk alleles and non-carriers [5]. However, as the known susceptibility variants have only modest effect sizes, their combined predictive power is currently too small to be clinically useful [47, 48].

It is interesting to note that the first two robustly associating T2DM genes (*KCNJ11* and *PPARG)* are both current drug targets for the T2DM treatment, raising the question of pharmacogenetics. In fact, the UKPDS investigators also instigated studies exploring the effect of the *KCNJ11* E23 K variant on response to sulfonylureas (UKPDS 53) [23]. This study, although among the first of its kind in diabetes, was underpowered to detect any statistical differences between genotypes. Different pharmacological responses to sulfonylureas in patients with the E23 K variant of *KCNJ11* and to thiazolidinediones in patients with different genetic variants in the *PPARG* gene (encoding the nuclear receptor peroxisome proliferator-activated receptor-γ) have subsequently been reported by other groups in different data sets [49–51]. However, of these 'pharmacogenetic' studies, it is only those on *TCF7L2* which really have been tested in appropriately large sample sizes. Variation in *TCF7L2* has been shown to reduce insulin secretion, influence progression from impaired glucose tolerance to diabetes and the response to sulfonylureas [50, 52]. This is an area of research very much in its infancy and it is only over the past 18 months that investigators have had an appropriate list of replicated susceptibility variants to explore the role of in determining therapeutic response. The challenge now is to use these variants in appropriately designed and statistically powered studies to investigate their influence. Over the coming months this will be an area of active research, with a genuine hope of improved diagnostics, prognostics and clinical management for patients with T2DM.

The current genetic landscape for type 2 diabetes

Despite the enormous advances that have been made over the past 18 months, there is still a great deal to be achieved if we are to fully understand the genetic landscape in T2DM. The genetic variants discovered to date only account for a small proportion of the familial aggregation of T2DM. The sibling relative risk (λs) attributable to all known variants combined is <1.10, far below the epidemiologically-derived estimate of ~3 overall. So what are the remaining T2DM susceptibility genes and what types of genetic variation underlie the undiscovered signals? These questions are the current focus of research in the field and will require international collaborative efforts, similar to those already seen, to unearth the answers. The interplay between statistical geneticists, clinicians, islet and molecular biologists will continue to be essential to make biological sense of our expanding appreciation of the genetic landscape of T2DM.

Summary

The identification and functional characterisation of genetic variants that either cause or predispose to diabetes is a major focus of biomedical research. The molecular basis is now known for the majority of monogenic forms of diabetes arising from pancreatic β-cell dysfunction; however finding the genetic variants underlying susceptibility to type 2 diabetes (T2DM) has been a greater technical, statistical and biological challenge. The advent of biology–agnostic approaches made possible by the improved arsenal of research platforms and genetic tools available has increased the number of known T2DM genes dramatically and provided important insights into the pathophysiology of T2DM. Over the past 18 months, the list of T2DM susceptibility genes has grown from three to close to 20, illustrating the substantial progress which has been made. These recent milestones have not only illustrated the limited knowledge we have of the pancreatic β-cell, but have also reinforced our belief in the involvement of common genetic variants in the genes involved in monogenic forms of diabetes in the susceptibility to T2DM and have clearly shown a primary role for pancreatic β-cell dysfunction in T2DM. Both of these concepts were explored in the early work of the UK Prospective Diabetes Study (UKPDS) genetics research groups.

Acknowledgements

The authors thank their many colleagues and collaborators who have contributed to the UKPDS work cited and the significant advances made in the field over the past 20 years. ALG thanks Diabetes UK and the Medical Research Council (MRC) for support. MIM thanks Diabetes UK, National Institute of Health, the MRC and the Wellcome Trust for support.

References

1 Sladek R, Rocheleau G, Rung J, Dina C, Shen L, Serre D *et al.* A genome-wide association study identifies novel risk loci for type 2 diabetes. *Nature* 2007;445:881-885.

2 Zeggini E, Weedon MN, Lindgren CM, Frayling TM, Elliott KS, Lango H *et al.* Replication of genome-wide association signals in UK samples reveals risk loci for type 2 diabetes. *Science* 2007;316:1336-1341.

3 Frayling TM, Timpson NJ, Weedon MN, Zeggini E, Freathy RM, Lindgren CM *et al.* A common variant in the FTO gene is associated with body mass index and predisposes to childhood and adult obesity. *Science* 2007;316:889-894.

4 Saxena R, Voight BF, Lyssenko V, Burtt NP, de Bakker PI, Chen H *et al.* Genome-wide association analysis identifies loci for type 2 diabetes and triglyceride levels. *Science* 2007;316:1331-1336.

5 Scott LJ, Mohlke KL, Bonnycastle LL, Willer CJ, Li Y, Duren WL *et al.* A genome-wide association study of type 2 diabetes in Finns detects multiple susceptibility variants. *Science* 2007;316:1341-1345.

6 Steinthorsdottir V, Thorleifsson G, Reynisdottir I, Benediktsson R, Jonsdottir T, Walters GB *et al.* A variant in CDKAL1 influences insulin response and risk of type 2 diabetes. *Nat Genet* 2007;39:770-775.

7 Altshuler D, Hirschhorn JN, Klannemark M, Lindgren CM, Vohl M-C, Nemesh J *et al.* The common PPARg Pro12Ala polymorphism is associated with decreased risk of type 2 diabetes. *Nat Genet* 2000;26:76-80.

8 Gloyn AL, Weedon MN, Owen K, Turner MJ, Knight BA, Hitman GA *et al.* Large-scale association studies of variants in genes encoding the pancreatic β-cell K-ATP channel subunits Kir6.2 (*KCNJ11*) and SUR1 (*ABCC8*) confirm that the *KCNJ11* E23K variant is associated with type 2 diabetes. *Diabetes* 2003;52:568-572.

9 Nielsen EM, Hansen L, Carstensen B, Echwald SM, Drivsholm T, Glumer C *et al.* The E23K variant of Kir6.2 associates with impaired post-OGTT serum insulin response and increased risk of type 2 diabetes. *Diabetes* 2003;52:573-577.

10 Grant SF, Thorleifsson G, Reynisdottir I, Benediktsson R, Manolescu A, Sainz J *et al.* Variant of transcription factor 7-like 2 (TCF7L2) gene confers risk of type 2 diabetes. *Nat Genet* 2006;38:320-323.

11 Sandhu MS, Weedon MN, Fawcett KA, Wasson J, Debenham SL, Daly A *et al.* Common variants in WFS1 confer risk of type 2 diabetes. *Nat Genet* 2007;39:951-953.

12 Winckler W, Weedon MN, Graham RR, McCarroll SA, Purcell S, Almgren P *et al.* Evaluation of common variants in the six known maturity-onset diabetes of the young (MODY) genes for association with type 2 diabetes. *Diabetes* 2007;56:685-693.

13 Zeggini E, Scott LJ, Saxena R, Voight BF, Marchini JL, Hu T *et al.* Meta-analysis of genome-wide association data and large-scale replication identifies additional susceptibility loci for type 2 diabetes. *Nat Genet* 2008;40:638–645.

14 Frayling TM. Genome-wide association studies provide new insights into type 2 diabetes aetiology. *Nat Rev Genet* 2007;8:657-662.

15 Gerken T, Girard CA, Tung YC, Webby CJ, Saudek V, Hewitson KS *et al.* The obesity-associated FTO gene encodes a 2-oxoglutarate-dependent nucleic acid demethylase. *Science* 2007; 318:1469-1472.

16 Liu Z, Habener JF. Glucagon-like peptide-1 activation of TCF7L2-dependent Wnt signaling enhances pancreatic β-cell proliferation. *J Biol Chem* 2008;283:8723–8735.

17 O'Rahilly S, Nugent Z, Rudenski A, Hosker J, Burnett M, Darling P *et al.* Beta-cell dysfunction, rather than insulin insensitivity, is the primary defect in familial type 2 diabetes. *Lancet* 1986;ii:360-364.

18 Yki-Jarvinen H. Evidence for a primary role of insulin resistance in the pathogenesis of type 2 diabetes. *Ann Med* 1990;22:197-200.

19 Gloyn A, McCarthy M. The genetics of type 2 diabetes. *Best Pract Res Clin Endocrinol Metab* 2001;15:293-308.

20 Hattersley AT, McCarthy MI. What makes a good genetic association study? *Lancet* 2005;366:1315-1323.

21 Varadi A, Lebel L, Hashim Y, Metha Z, Ashcroft SJH, Turner R. Sequence variants of the sarco(endo)plasmic reticulum Ca^{2+}-transport ATPase 3 gene (SERCA3) in Caucasian type II diabetic patients (UK Prospective Diabetes Study 48). *Diabetologia* 1999;42:1240–1243.

22 Gloyn AL, Desai M, Clark A, Levy JC, Holman RR, Frayling TM *et al.* Human calcium/cal-modulin-dependent protein kinase II gamma gene (*CAMK2G*): cloning, genomic structure and detection of variants in subjects with type II diabetes. *Diabetologia* 2002;45:580-583.

23 Gloyn AL, Hashim Y, Ashcroft SJH, Ashfield R, Wiltshire S, Turner RC. Association studies of variants in promoter and coding regions of β-cell ATP-sensitive K-channel genes SUR1 and Kir6.2 with type 2 diabetes mellitus (UKPDS 53). *Diabet Med* 2001;18:206-212.

24 Zhang Y, Warren-Perry M, Sakura H, Adelman J, Stoffel M, Bell GI *et al.* No evidence for mutations in a putative β-cell ATP-sensitive K$^+$ channel subunit in MODY, NIDDM, or GDM. *Diabetes* 1995;44:597-600.

25 Inoue H, Ferrer J, Warren-Perry M, Zhang Y, Millns H, Turner RC *et al.* Sequence variants in the pancreatic Islet β-cell inwardly rectifying K$^+$ channel Kir6.2 (Bir) gene. Identification and lack of role in Caucasian patients with NIDDM. *Diabetes* 1997;46:502-507.

26 Inoue H, Ferrer J, Welling CM, Elbein SC, Hoffman M, Mayorga R *et al.* Sequence variants in the sulfonylurea receptor (SUR) gene are associated with NIDDM in Caucasians. *Diabetes* 1996;45:825-831.

27 Cox RD, Southam L, Hashim Y, Horton V, Mehta Z, Taghavi J *et al.* UKPDS 31: Hepatocyte nuclear factor-1αlpha (the MODY3 gene) mutations in late-onset type II diabetic patients in the UK. UK Prospective Diabetes Study. *Diabetologia* 1999;42:120-121.

28 Shu L, Sauter NS, Schulthess FT, Matveyenko AV, Oberholzer J, Maedler K. Transcription factor 7-like 2 regulates β-cell survival and function in human pancreatic islets. *Diabetes* 2008;57:645-653.

29 Pascoe L, Tura A, Patel SK, Ibrahim IM, Ferrannini E, Zeggini E *et al.* Common variants of the novel type 2 diabetes genes CDKAL1 and HHEX/IDE are associated with decreased pancreatic β-cell function. *Diabetes* 2007;56:3101-3104.

30 Schwanstecher C, Meyer U, Schwanstecher M. K(IR)6.2 polymorphism predisposes to type 2 diabetes by inducing overactivity of pancreatic β-cell ATP-sensitive K($^+$) channels. *Diabetes* 2002;51:875-879.

31 Lyssenko V, Lupi R, Marchetti P, Del Guerra S, Orho-Melander M, Almgren P *et al.* Mechanisms by which common variants in the TCF7L2 gene increase risk of type 2 diabetes. *J Clin Invest* 2007;117:2155-2163.

32 Weedon MN. The importance of *TCF7L2. Diabet Med* 2007;24:1062-1066.

33 Murphy R, Ellard S, Hattersley AT. Clinical implications of a molecular genetic classification of monogenic β-cell diabetes. *Nat Clin Pract Endocrinol Metab* 2008;4:200-213.

34 Saker PJ, Hattersley AT, Barrow B, Hammersley MS, Horton V, Gillmer MD *et al.* UKPDS 21: low prevalence of the mitochondrial transfer RNA gene {tRNA[Leu(UUR)]} mutation at position 3243 bp in UK Caucasian type 2 diabetic patients. *Diabet Med* 1997;14:42-45.

35 McCarthy MI. Progress in defining the molecular basis of type 2 diabetes mellitus through susceptibility-gene identification. *Hum Mol Genet* 2004;13:R33-41.

36 Weedon MN, Frayling TM. Insights on pathogenesis of type 2 diabetes from MODY genetics. *Curr Diab Rep* 2007;7:131-138.

37 Gloyn AL, Ellard S. Defining the genetic aetiology of monogenic diabetes can improve treatment. *Expert Opin Pharmacother* 2006;7:1759-1767.

38 Hattersley AT, Pearson ER. Minireview: pharmacogenetics and beyond: the interaction of therapeutic response, β-cell physiology, and genetics in diabetes. *Endocrinology* 2006;147:2657-2663.

39 Weedon MN, Owen KR, Shields B, Hitman G, Walker M, McCarthy MI *et al.* A large-scale association analysis of common variation of the HNF1α gene with type 2 diabetes in the UK Caucasian population. *Diabetes* 2005;54:2487-2491.

40 Winckler W, Burtt NP, Holmkvist J, Cervin C, de Bakker PI, Sun M *et al.* Association of common variation in the HNF1α gene region with risk of type 2 diabetes. *Diabetes* 2005;54:2336-2342.

41 Thomas PM, Cote GJ, Wohilk N, Haddad B, Mathew PM, Rabel W *et al.* Mutations in the sulphonylurea receptor and familial persistent hyperinsulinemic hypoglycemia of infancy. *Science* 1995;268:426-429.

42 Thomas PM, Yuyang Y, Lightner E. Mutation of the pancreatic islet inward rectifier, Kir6.2 also leads to familial persistent hyperinsulinemic hypoglycemia of infancy. *Hum Mol Genet* 1996;5:1809-1812.

43 Gloyn AL, Pearson ER, Antcliff JF, Proks P, Bruining GJ, Slingerland AS *et al.* Activating mutations in the gene encoding the ATP-sensitive potassium-channel subunit Kir6.2 and permanent neonatal diabetes. *N Engl J Med* 2004;350:1838-1849.

44 Gloyn AL, Reimann F, Girard C, Edghill EL, Proks P, Pearson ER *et al.* Relapsing diabetes can result from moderately activating mutations in *KCNJ11*. *Hum Mol Genet* 2005;14:925-934.

45 Babenko AP, Polak M, Cave H, Busiah K, Czernichow P, Scharfmann R *et al.* Activating mutations in the *ABCC8* gene in neonatal diabetes mellitus. *N Engl J Med* 2006;355:456-466.

46 Proks P, Arnold AL, Bruining J, Girard C, Flanagan SE, Larkin B *et al.* A heterozygous activating mutation in the sulphonylurea receptor SUR1 (*ABCC8*) causes neonatal diabetes. *Hum Mol Genet* 2006;15:1793-1800.

47 Weedon MN, McCarthy MI, Hitman G, Walker M, Groves CJ, Zeggini E *et al.* Combining information from common type 2 diabetes risk polymorphisms improves disease prediction. *PLoS Med* 2006;3:e374.

48 Lyssenko V, Almgren P, Anevski D, Orho-Melander M, Sjogren M, Saloranta C *et al.* Genetic prediction of future type 2 diabetes. *PLoS Med* 2005;2:e345.

49 Sesti G, Laratta E, Cardellini M, Andreozzi F, Del Guerra S, Irace C *et al.* The E23K variant of KCNJ11 encoding the pancreatic β-cell adenosine 5'-triphosphate-sensitive potassium channel subunit Kir6.2 is associated with an increased risk of secondary failure to sulfonylurea in patients with type 2 diabetes. *J Clin Endocrinol Metab* 2006;91:2334-2339.

50 Florez JC, Jablonski KA, Bayley N, Pollin TI, de Bakker PI, Shuldiner AR *et al.* TCF7L2 polymorphisms and progression to diabetes in the Diabetes Prevention Program. *N Engl J Med* 2006;355:241-250.

51 Wolford JK, Yeatts KA, Dhanjal SK, Black MH, Xiang AH, Buchanan TA *et al.* Sequence variation in *PPARG* may underlie differential response to troglitazone. *Diabetes* 2005;54:3319-3325.

52 Pearson ER, Donnelly LA, Kimber C, Whitley A, Doney AS, McCarthy MI *et al.* Variation in *TCF7L2* influences therapeutic response to sulfonylureas: a GoDARTs study. *Diabetes* 2007;56:2178-2182.

53 Barroso I, Gurnell M, Crowley VE, Agostini M, Schwabe JW, Soos MA *et al*. Dominant negative mutations in human PPARγ associated with severe insulin resistance, diabetes mellitus and hypertension. *Nature* 1999;402:880-883.

54 Kirchhoff K, Machicao F, Haupt A, Schafer SA, Tschritter O, Staiger H *et al*. Polymorphisms in the *TCF7L2, CDKAL1* and *SLC30A8* genes are associated with impaired proinsulin conversion. *Diabetologia* 2008;51:597-601.

55 Krishnamurthy J, Ramsey MR, Ligon KL, Torrice C, Koh A, Bonner-Weir S *et al*. p16INK4a induces an age-dependent decline in islet regenerative potential. *Nature* 2006;443:453-457.

56 Grarup N, Rose CS, Andersson EA, Andersen G, Nielsen AL, Albrechtsen A *et al*. Studies of association of variants near the *HHEX, CDKN2A/B*, and *IGF2BP2* genes with type 2 diabetes and impaired insulin release in 10 705 Danish subjects: validation and extension of genome-wide association studies. *Diabetes* 2007;56:3105-3111.

57 Bort R, Martinez-Barbera JP, Beddington RS, Zaret KS. Hex homeobox gene-dependent tissue positioning is required for organogenesis of the ventral pancreas. *Development* 2004;131:797-806.

58 Staiger H, Machicao F, Stefan N, Tschritter O, Thamer C, Kantartzis K *et al*. Polymorphisms within novel risk loci for type 2 diabetes determine β-cell function. *PLoS ONE* 2007;2:e832.

59 Staiger H, Stancakova A, Zilinskaite J, Vanttinen M, Hansen T, Marini MA *et al*. A candidate type 2 diabetes polymorphism near the *HHEX* locus affects acute glucose-stimulated insulin release in European populations: results from the EUGENE2 study. *Diabetes* 2008;57:514-517.

60 Inoue H, Tanizawa Y, Wasson J, Behn P, Kalidas K, Mizrachi EB *et al*. A gene encoding a transmembrane protein is mutated in patients with diabetes mellitus and optic atrophy (Wofram syndrome). *Nat Genet* 1998;20:143-148.

61 Horikawa Y, Iwasaki N, Hara M, Furuta H, Hinokio Y, Cockburn B *et al*. Mutation in hepatocyte nuclear factor-1b gene (*TCF2*) associated with MODY. *Nat Genet* 1997;17:384-385.

62 Collins LL, Lee YF, Heinlein CA, Liu NC, Chen YT, Shyr CR *et al*. Growth retardation and abnormal maternal behaviour in mice lacking testicular orphan nuclear receptor 4. *Proc Natl Acad Sci USA* 2004;101:15058-15063.

63 Lammert E, Brown J, Melton DA. Notch gene expression during pancreatic organogenesis. *Mech Dev* 2000;94:199-203.

7 Autoimmune diabetes in adults: lessons from the UKPDS

Minal Desai and Anne Clark

Diabetes Research Laboratories, Oxford Centre for Diabetes, Endocrinology and Metabolism, University of Oxford, Oxford, UK

Introduction

Autoimmune diabetes (hyperglycaemia associated with serological markers of pancreatic β-cell autoimmunity) occurring in adults has a relatively slow onset compared with childhood-onset type 1 diabetes and is usually diagnosed and treated as type 2 diabetes; most of these adult-onset (typically over the age of 30 years) patients retain adequate residual β-cell function to prevent ketoacidosis and avoid the need for insulin replacement therapy for a number of years [1]. This subgroup of patients is usually only distinguished from those with classical type 2 diabetes by testing for autoantibodies against β-cell proteins and is most commonly called latent autoimmune diabetes in adults (LADA) [2-4]. Other nomenclature includes slowly progressive insulin-dependent diabetes, latent type 1 diabetes, type 1 diabetes masquerading as type 2 diabetes and type 1.5 diabetes [5]. Although the presence of autoimmune diabetes developing in adults has been recognized for more than 30 years [6], LADA remains a clinical controversy [7, 8]. Immunological, genetic and physiological studies on large and small cohorts in different parts of the world have provided often conflicting evidence to support or disprove LADA as a separate disease entity [8-11]. A recent proposal for diagnostic criteria for LADA as age >30 years at clinical presentation and not requiring insulin for >6 months post-diagnosis might aid definition of this disease [12].

LADA patients represent a variable proportion (2–22%) of diagnosed type 2 diabetic subjects, depending on the ascertainment criteria and population examined (reviewed by van Deutekom *et al.* [8] and Pozzilli and Di Mario [13]). The prevalence is ~10% of diagnosed type 2 diabetes in Caucasian populations [14, 15], but lower in an Asian population [16]. If the prevalence of type 2 diabetes in the UK population is ~4%, and up to 10% of these are LADA patients, the prevalence of LADA is at least half of that of classical childhood-onset

Originally published: Desai M, Clark A. Autoimmune diabetes in adults: lessons from the UKPDS. *Diabetic Medicine* 2008; 25 (Suppl. 2): 30–34

type 1 diabetes [17]. The UKPDS included ~12% of patients with autoimmune diabetes and is one of the largest studies to ascertain clinical, immunological and genetic features of this form of diabetes.

LADA in the UKPDS

Immunological markers

The UKPDS cohort included over 500 patients who were thought to have newly diagnosed type 2 diabetes (aged >25 years at diagnosis), clinically managed within the protocol of this type 2 diabetes study, but who were subsequently shown to possess autoantibodies to islet cell proteins and thus have autoimmune diabetes [18-20]. Initially, the UKPDS LADA cohort was defined by positivity for autoantibodies to islet cell antigen (ICA) and/or GADA using extracted glutamic acid decarboxylase (GAD) protein [18, 21]. Later, positivity for autoantibodies to the protein tyrosine phosphatase isoform, IA-2A was assessed with a radiobinding assay against recombinant peptide and similar types of assay were used to determine GADA positivity post-diagnosis and epitope reactivities [19, 20, 22, 23]. Of the approximately 4500 UKPDS patients examined, 11.6% were positive for either ICA, GADA or IA-2A, with GADA being the most common autoantibody found in 84% of antibody positive patients, followed by IA-2A (16.5%) [19, 20]. Recently, the zinc transporter protein ZnT8 [24] has been identified as a major autoantigen in childhood onset type 1 diabetes; its increasing prevalence with age suggests that it could be a useful marker for LADA. Potentially, identification of more autoantigens with high predictive ability and frequency could increase the detection of autoimmune diabetes; however, in most cases, autoantibodies coexist, suggesting that there are probably few adult-onset patients tested for one of these humoural markers that remain undiagnosed.

GAD antibodies persist in LADA for several years post-diagnosis [23, 25], which is less commonly observed in classical type 1 diabetic patients [26]. The significance of antibody persistence in the clinical progression of autoimmune diabetes is not understood. The degree of pancreatic β-cell destruction and rate of decline can be assessed directly by measurement of fasting or glucose-stimulated C-peptide concentrations [27, 28], or indirectly by requirement for intensification of therapeutic regimens to regulate hyperglycaemia, particularly the eventual requirement for exogenous insulin treatment [19, 23]. However, in the UKPDS, neither GADA levels nor their GAD65 epitope specificity were deemed useful as clinical markers of disease progression in the post-diagnosis period of LADA [23].

Autoantibody screening can identify individuals at risk for classical type 1 diabetes, for example, first-degree relatives of type 1 diabetic patients [29], but prospective studies for LADA are more difficult to undertake [30]. In type 1 diabetes, multiple antibody positivity in the pre-diabetic period is associated with a shorter latency of onset compared with subjects with only one antibody [31]; this has been interpreted as an association of multiple antibody positivity with increased severity of the β-cell autoimmune response. In the UKPDS, positivity for both GADA and IA-2A at diagnosis was associated with an increased proportion of patients requiring insulin therapy by 3 or 6 years (ratio 1.5 : 1.0—two antibodies : one antibody) [19, 20, 23].

The 'positivity' of autoantibodies is a contentious issue. Antibody level positivity is defined by a laboratory-based cut-off established by measurement of samples from non-diabetic and diabetic subjects; however, this arbitrary cut-off lies in a continuous distribution of serum reactivities [7]. Although there are international workshops for the standardization of autoantibody assays [32], many studies adopt different criteria for positivity [15]. Thus, comparisons between studies should be made with caution [8].

Genetic markers

Genetic association studies in the UKPDS LADA cohort have demonstrated similarities with observations reported in the literature for classical type 1 diabetes [33]; HLA haplotypes *DRB1*0301_DQB1*0201* and *DRB1*0401_DQB1*0302* were shown to be susceptibility determinants for LADA (*DRB1*0401_DQB1*0302* : frequencies, 16.9% in LADA patients, 7.3% in control subjects, UKPDS [34]; 34% in type 1 diabetes, 12.5% in control subjects [33]) whereas *DRB1*1501-6_DQB1*0602* conferred protection (frequencies, 3.3% in LADA patients, 14% in control subjects, UKPDS [34]; 0.4% in type 1 diabetes, 12.0% in control subjects [33]). As seen in type 1 diabetes, there was a variable level of susceptibility to LADA conferred by different alleles within the DR4 serological specificity [33-35]. Analysis of the insulin gene locus *(IDDM2)* in UKPDS LADA patients demonstrated further similarities in association patterns to that reported in classical type 1 diabetes and other LADA cohorts [36, 37]; Class I variable number of tandem repeats (VNTR) alleles were predisposing (69% in LADA patients, 49% in control subjects UKPDS [34]; 73% in LADA patients, 55% in type 1 diabetes, 45% in control subjects [37]) and Class III alleles protective (31% in LADA, 51% in control subjects UKPDS [38]; 31% in LADA, 27% in type 1 diabetes, 45% in control subjects [37]). However, there may be subtle differences between type 1 diabetes and LADA in fine-structure association patterns in the *IDDM2* region [38].

Aetiology: is LADA an age-related extension of type 1 diabetes?

As with both type 1 and type 2 diabetes, the exact aetiopathology of LADA is not well understood. The pancreatic insulitis and cellular immune responses to GAD65 observed in type 1 diabetes [39] have been demonstrated in LADA [40, 41]. The factors that govern the later age of onset and milder phenotype (less severe symptoms at diagnosis onset and slower disease progression) of LADA compared with classical type 1 diabetes are unclear. Whether LADA represents a unique disease entity is a much-debated area [8-11]. Current hypotheses suggest that LADA could be an intermediate form of diabetes in a phenotypic continuum, with childhood-onset type 1 diabetes at one end of the spectrum and type 2 diabetes at the other [7, 8]. The proposition that increased body mass could trigger an autoimmune response in type 2 diabetic patients culminating in LADA [8, 42] is unlikely as LADA patients are not always overweight or in possession of other features of the metabolic syndrome often observed in type 2 diabetes [19, 23, 43]. The overall similarities in immunological and genetic features of LADA and classical type 1 diabetes indicate a common disease aetiopathology, suggesting that autoimmune diabetes developing in adults is an age-related extension of type 1 diabetes [44, 45]. In this hypothesis, the slower onset and progression of disease in LADA compared with type 1 diabetes could result from a combination of decreased genetic susceptibility for autoimmune diabetes conferred from HLA and INS susceptibility alleles, increased levels of protection also from HLA protective alleles and fewer environmental pressures. Studies in the UKPDS LADA cohort show higher frequency of protective HLA alleles associated with increasing age at diagnosis [38, 46], providing support for this hypothesis. Similarly, in type 1 diabetes in a study over a wide age range (1–49 years), high-risk HLA genotypes were associated with a younger age of diagnosis, lower C-peptide levels and early insulin requirement [28]. The recent demonstration that the type 2 diabetes-associated single nucleotide polymorphisms (SNPs) of *TCF7L2* are also associated with LADA [37] suggest a possible underlying insulin secretory defect [47]. Taken together, these findings support the proposal that an autoimmune disease continuum exists of decreasing autoimmune genetic susceptibility and severity of islet dysfunction with increasing age, starting with childhood-onset type 1 diabetes and extending into LADA [27, 45, 46]. Furthermore, as in type 1 and type 2 diabetes, there is clear heterogeneity in LADA, reflecting the complex interactions of genetic and environmental factors in determining clinical phenotype.

Clinical management

There is concern amongst clinicians that, because of the difference in disease aetiology, LADA patients do not receive the correct treatment—but what is the correct therapy [45, 48, 49]? The aetiology of autoimmune diabetes predicts eventual reduction of pancreatic β-cell mass to very low levels consistent with a progressive decline in C-peptide concentrations. However, many LADA patients remain insulin-independent and retain some C-peptide secretion for many years post-diagnosis [28, 50]. The concept of 'β-cell rest' using insulin replacement therapy from diagnosis has been proposed [51]. In the UKPDS, over a 10-year period there were no major differences in clinical variables or glycaemic control in the LADA subjects compared with antibody-negative type 2 diabetic subjects within either randomization arm (oral glucose-lowering agents or insulin therapy), but antibody-positive patients were more likely to progress to eventual insulin requirement [19, 23]; this suggests that LADA can be initially treated with sulphonylurea therapy [19].

Conclusion

LADA remains a clinical enigma and probably not a separate disease entity, but an adult form of autoimmune diabetes. A list of diagnostic features for screening [52] and defined clinical management regimens [27, 49] are unlikely to improve outcomes for adult-onset autoimmune patients who benefit from regular and careful clinical care with flexible treatment plans.

Summary

Latent autoimmune diabetes in adults (LADA) is characterized by a relatively mild diabetes onset, autoantibody positivity and eventual requirement for insulin therapy. Twelve per cent of newly diagnosed, UK Prospective Diabetes Study (UKPDS) patients were positive for autoantibodies to GAD65 (GADA) and/or insulinoma-associated antigen-2A (IA-2A) and managed as if they had type 2 diabetes according to the UKPDS protocol. Here, we compare data from UKPDS LADA patients with that from other cohorts. In common with other groups, UKPDS LADA patients required insulin therapy earlier post-diagnosis than non-LADA patients. Reduction of islet function was similar in UKPDS LADA groups randomised to oral glucose-lowering agents or insulin replacement therapy, contesting the current hypothesis of reduced decline of insulin secretion in LADA by immediate insulin therapy. Disease progression was not predicted by post-diagnosis GADA levels or epitope specificities as has been suggested. Slowly progressing insulitis and pancreatic β-cell loss at post-mortem are consistent with sustained retention of residual C-peptide secretion in LADA. Genetic association patterns at the human leucocyte antigen (*HLA*) and insulin gene (*INS*) regions are similar in UKPDS LADA patients and individuals with adult and childhood-onset type 1 diabetes. The combined evidence suggests that LADA is an adult-onset form of type 1 diabetes, rather than a separate condition or an intermediate state in a continuum of phenotype from type 1 to type 2 diabetes.

Acknowledgements

Some of the UKPDS studies referred to here were originally funded by Diabetes UK (MD). We are grateful to the Wellcome Trust for past financial support. We also thank the late Carole Cull for her committed and expert statistical analyses for these studies of LADA in the UKPDS and all other authors who have contributed to publications of the LADA cohort.

References

1 Zimmet PZ. The pathogenesis and prevention of diabetes in adults. Genes, autoimmunity, and demography. *Diabetes Care* 1995;18:1050-1064.

2 Zimmet PZ, Tuomi T, Mackay IR, *et al.* Latent autoimmune diabetes mellitus in adults (LADA): the role of antibodies to glutamic acid decarboxylase in diagnosis and prediction of insulin dependency. *Diabet Med* 1994;11:299-303.

3 Groop LC, Bottazzo GF, Doniach D. Islet cell antibodies identify latent type I diabetes in patients aged 35–75 years at diagnosis. *Diabetes* 1986;35:237-241.

4 Tuomi T, Groop LC, Zimmet PZ, Rowley MJ, Knowles W, Mackay IR. Antibodies to glutamic acid decarboxylase reveal latent autoimmune diabetes mellitus in adults with a non-insulin-dependent onset of disease. *Diabetes* 1993;42:359-362.

5 Juneja R, Palmer JP. Type 1 1/2 diabetes: myth or reality? *Autoimmunity* 1999;29:65-83.

6 Irvine WJ, McCallum CJ, Gray RS, Duncan LJ. Pancreatic islet-cell antibodies in diabetes mellitus correlated with the duration and type of diabetes, coexistent autoimmune disease, and HLA type. *Diabetes* 1977;26:138-147.

7 Gale EA. Latent autoimmune diabetes in adults: a guide for the perplexed. *Diabetologia* 2005;48:2195-2199.

8 van Deutekom AW, Heine RJ, Simsek S. The islet autoantibody titres: their clinical relevance in latent autoimmune diabetes in adults (LADA) and the classification of diabetes mellitus. *Diabet Med* 2008;25:117-125.

9 Palmer JP, Hirsch IB. What's in a name: latent autoimmune diabetes of adults, type 1.5, adult-onset, and type 1 diabetes. *Diabetes Care* 2003;26:536-538.

10 Groop L, Tuomi T, Rowley M, Zimmet P, Mackay IR. Latent autoimmune diabetes in adults (LADA)—more than a name. *Diabetologia* 2006;49:1996-1998.

11 Fourlanos S, Dotta F, Greenbaum CJ, Palmer JP, Rolandsson O, Coleman PG *et al.* Latent autoimmune diabetes in adults (LADA) should be less latent. *Diabetologia* 2005;48:2206-2212.

12 Palmer JP, Hampe CS, Chiu H, Goel A, Brooks-Worrell BM. Is Latent Autoimmune Diabetes in Adults distinct from Type 1 diabetes or just Type 1 diabetes at an older age? *Diabetes* 2005;54:S62-S67.

13 Pozzilli P, Di Mario U. Autoimmune diabetes not requiring insulin at diagnosis (latent autoimmune diabetes of the adult): definition, characterization, and potential prevention. *Diabetes Care* 2001;24:1460-1467.

14 Landin-Olsson M, Nilsson KO, Lernmark A, Sundkvist G. Islet cell antibodies and fasting C-peptide predict insulin requirement at diagnosis of diabetes mellitus. *Diabetologia* 1990;33:561-568.

15 Tuomi T, Carlsson A, Li H, Isomaa B, Miettinen A, Nilsson A,Nissén M *et al.* Clinical and genetic characteristics of type 2 diabetes with and without GAD antibodies. *Diabetes* 1999;48:150-157.

16 Kawasaki E, Eguchi K. Current aspects on the clinical immunology and genetics of autoimmune diabetes in Japan. *Diabetes Res Clin Pract* 2007;77(Suppl 1):S104-109.

17 Narendran P, Estella E, Fourlanos S. Immunology of type 1 diabetes. *Quart J Med* 2005;98:547-556.

18 Turner R, Stratton I, Horton V, Manley S, Zimmet P, Mackay IR *et al.* UKPDS 25: autoantibodies to islet-cell cytoplasm and glutamic acid decarboxylase for prediction of insulin requirement in type 2 diabetes. UK Prospective Diabetes Study Group. *Lancet* 1997;350:1288-1293.

19 Davis TM, Wright AD, Mehta ZM, Cull CA, Stratton IM, Bottazzo GF *et al.* Islet autoantibodies in clinically diagnosed type 2 diabetes: prevalence and relationship with metabolic control (UKPDS 70). *Diabetologia* 2005;48:695-702.

20 Bottazzo GF, Bosi E, Cull CA *et al*. IA-2 antibody prevalence and risk assessment of early insulin requirement in subjects presenting with type 2 diabetes (UKPDS 71). *Diabetologia* 2005;48:703-708.

21 Rowley MJ, Mackay IR, Chen QY, Knowles WJ, Zimmet PZ. Antibodies to glutamic acid decarboxylase discriminate major types of diabetes mellitus. *Diabetes* 1992;41:548-551.

22 Bonifacio E, Lampasona V, Genovese S, Ferrari M, Bosi E. Identification of protein tyrosine phosphatase-like IA2 (islet cell antigen 512) as the insulin-dependent diabetes-related 37/40K autoantigen and a target of islet-cell antibodies. *J Immunol* 1995; 155:5419-5426.

23 Desai M, Cull CA, Horton VA, Christie MR, Bonifacio E, Lampasona V *et al*. GAD autoantibodies and epitope reactivities persist after diagnosis in latent autoimmune diabetes in adults but do not predict disease progression: UKPDS 77. *Diabetologia* 2007;50:2052-2060.

24 Wenzlau JM, Juhl K, Yu L, Moua O, Sarkar SA, Gottlieb P *et al*. The cation efflux transporter ZnT8 (Slc30A8) is a major autoantigen in human type 1 diabetes. *Proc Natl Acad Sci USA* 2007;104:17040-17045.

25 Borg H, Gottsater A, Fernlund P, Sundkvist G. A 12-year prospective study of the relationship between islet antibodies and beta-cell function at and after the diagnosis in patients with adult-onset diabetes. *Diabetes* 2002; 51:1754-1762.

26 Hampe CS, Kockum I, Landin-Olsson M, Törn C, Ortqvist E, Persson B *et al*. GAD65 antibody epitope patterns of type 1.5 diabetic patients are consistent with slow-onset autoimmune diabetes. *Diabetes Care* 2002;25:1481-1482.

27 Stenstrom G, Gottsater A, Bakhtadze E, Berger B, Sundkvist G. Latent autoimmune diabetes in adults: definition, prevalence, beta-cell function, and treatment. *Diabetes* 2005;54(Suppl 2):S68-72.

28 Petrone A, Galgani A, Spoletini M, Alemanno I, Di Cola S, Bassotti G *et al*. Residual insulin secretion at diagnosis of type 1 diabetes is independently associated with both, age of onset and HLA genotype. *Diabetes Metab Res Rev* 2005;21:271-275.

29 Bingley PJ, Bonifacio E, Williams AJ, Genovese S, Bottazzo GF, Gale EA. Prediction of IDDM in the general population: strategies based on combinations of autoantibody markers. *Diabetes* 1997;46:1701-1710.

30 Hampe CS, Hall TR, Agren A, Rolandsson O. Longitudinal changes in epitope recognition of autoantibodies against glutamate decarboxylase 65 (GAD65Ab) in prediabetic adults developing diabetes. *Clin Exp Immunol* 2007;148:72-78.

31 Bingley PJ, Christie MR, Bonifacio E, Bonfanti R, Shattock M, Fonte MT *et al*. Combined analysis of autoantibodies improves prediction of IDDM in islet cell antibody-positive relatives. *Diabetes* 1994;43:1304-1310.

32 Bingley PJ, Bonifacio E, Mueller PW. Diabetes Antibody Standardization Program: first assay proficiency evaluation. *Diabetes* 2003;52:1128-1136.

33 Erlich H, Valdes AM, Noble J, Carlson JA, Varney M, Concannon P *et al*. HLA DR-DQ haplotypes and genotypes and type 1 diabetes risk: analysis of the type 1 diabetes genetics consortium families. *Diabetes* 2008;57:1084-1092.

34 Desai M, Zeggini E, Horton VA, Owen KR, Hattersley AT, Levy JC *et al*. An association analysis of the HLA gene region in latent autoimmune diabetes in adults. *Diabetologia* 2007;50:68-73.

35 Rewers A, Babu S, Wang TB, Bugawan TL, Barriga K, Eisenbarth GS *et al*. Ethnic differences in the associations between the HLA-DRB1*04 subtypes and type 1 diabetes. *Ann N Y Acad Sci* 2003;1005:301-309.

36 Bennett ST, Todd JA . Human type 1 diabetes and the insulin gene: principles of mapping polygenes. *Annu Rev Genet* 1996;30:343-370.

37 Cervin C, Lyssenko V, Bakhtadze E, Lindholm E, Nilsson P, Tuomi T et al. Genetic similarities between LADA, type 1 and type 2 Diabetes. *Diabetes* 2008;57:1433–1437.

38 Desai M, Zeggini E, Horton VA, Owen KR, Hattersley AT, Levy JC et al. The variable number of tandem repeats upstream of the insulin gene is a susceptibility locus for Latent Autoimmune Diabetes in Adults. *Diabetes* 2006;55:1890-1894.

39 Foulis AK, McGill M, Farquharson MA. Insulitis in type 1 (insulin-dependent) diabetes mellitus in man—macrophages, lymphocytes, and interferon-gamma containing cells. *J Pathol* 1991;165:97-103.

40 Shimada A, Imazu Y, Morinaga S, Funae O, Kasuga A, Atsumi Y et al. T-cell insulitis found in anti-GAD65+ diabetes with residual beta-cell function. A case report. *Diabetes Care* 1999;22:615-617.

41 In't Veld P, Lievens D, De Grijse J, Ling Z, Van der Auwera B, Pipeleers-Marichal M et al. Screening for insulitis in adult autoantibody-positive organ donors. *Diabetes* 2007;56:2400-2404.

42 Wilkin TJ. The accelerator hypothesis: weight gain as the missing link between Type I and Type II diabetes. *Diabetologia* 2001;44:914-922.

43 Gale EA. To boldly go—or to go too boldly? The accelerator hypothesis revisited. *Diabetologia* 2007;50:1571-1575.

44 Hosszufalusi N, Vatay A, Rajczy K, Prohászka Z, Pozsonyi E, Horváth L et al. Similar genetic features and different islet cell autoantibody pattern of latent autoimmune diabetes in adults (LADA) compared with adult-onset type 1 diabetes with rapid progression. *Diabetes Care* 2003;26:452-457.

45 Leslie RD, Williams R, Pozzilli P. Clinical review: Type 1 diabetes and latent autoimmune diabetes in adults: one end of the rainbow. *J Clin Endocrinol Metab* 2006;91:1654-1659.

46 Horton V, Stratton I, Bottazzo GF, Shattock M, Mackay I, Zimmet P et al. Genetic heterogeneity of autoimmune diabetes: age of presentation in adults is influenced by HLA DRB1 and DQB1 genotypes (UKPDS 43). UK Prospective Diabetes Study (UKPDS) Group. *Diabetologia* 1999;42:608-616.

47 Lyssenko V, Lupi R, Marchetti P, Del Guerra S, Orho-Melander M, Almgren P et al. Mechanisms by which common variants in the TCF7L2 gene increase risk of type 2 diabetes. *J Clin Invest* 2007;117:2155-2163.

48 Falorni A, Brozzetti A. Diabetes-related antibodies in adult diabetic patients. *Best Pract Res Clin Endocrinol Metab* 2005;19:119-133.

49 Brophy S, Brunt H, Davies H, Mannan S, Williams R. Interventions for latent autoimmune diabetes (LADA) in adults. *Cochrane Database Syst Rev* 2007; CD006165.

50 Borg H, Gottsater A, Landin-Olsson M, Fernlund P, Sundkvist G. High levels of antigen-specific islet antibodies predict future beta-cell failure in patients with onset of diabetes in adult age. *J Clin Endocrinol Metab* 2001;86:3032-3038.

51 Palmer JP. Beta-cell rest and recovery—does it bring patients with latent autoimmune diabetes in adults to euglycemia? *Ann N Y Acad Sci* 2002;958:89-98.

52 Fourlanos S, Perry C, Stein MS, Stankovich J, Harrison LC, Colman PG. A clinical screening tool identifies autoimmune diabetes in adults. *Diabetes Care* 2006;29:970-975.

8 Glucose control in the UKPDS: what did we learn?

Edwin A.M. Gale

Diabetes and Metabolism, Division of Medicine, University of Bristol, Medical School Unit, Southmead Hospital, Bristol, UK

Introduction

'You see things; and you say "Why?"
But I dream things that never were; and I say "Why not?"'

George Bernard Shaw

The UK Prospective Diabetes Study (UKPDS) changed everything: so much so that it takes a real effort to think ourselves back into the pre-UKPDS mindset. When the study was planned, we did not know whether blood glucose control influenced progression of the vascular complications of diabetes. We had no idea that blood pressure might be an important influence upon microvascular risk. We did not have routine home blood glucose monitoring or glycated haemoglobin (HbA$_{1c}$). We worried that tablet therapy might actually do more harm than good. Insulin was a last resort, used only when unavoidable, a custom enshrined by the terms insulin-dependent and insulin-independent diabetes. Insulin was considered ineffective in the obese, merely contributing to further weight gain. The 1980 World Health Organization (WHO) diagnostic classification of diabetes [1,2] was based on epidemiological studies showing that cardiovascular risk begins to climb above a blood glucose value of 6.0 mmol/l, whereas the risk of microvascular complications takes off after 7.8 mmol/l. Would the same glucose thresholds translate into useful therapeutic targets? A prospective clinical trial would be needed to arbitrate the issue, but previous experience already suggested that this would not be a task for the faint-hearted.

This brings us to the odd history of the University Group Diabetes Program (UGDP) study. This flagship trial, launched in 1961, was intended to show if the vascular complications of diabetes were influenced by its treatment. It concluded, amid a storm of protest, that flexible insulin therapy was no better

Originally published: Gale EAM. Glucose control in the UKPDS: what did we learn? *Diabetic Medicine* 2008; 25 (Suppl. 2): 9–12

than an oral placebo (i.e. diet alone) in preventing cardiovascular deaths and that treatment with a sulfonylurea (tolbutamide) or a biguanide (phenformin) might actually increase mortality. Consternation at the results was followed by ferocious infighting, prompting the investigators to protest that 'the main difficulty with the UGDP is not its design, execution or analysis, but rather that it reached an unpopular conclusion' [3,4]. UGDP would not be the last big diabetes trial to provoke unresolved controversy.

As UGDP had ended in confusion, a study such as the UKPDS was badly needed to set things straight. Anyone should have been able to see this, but there are times when it takes a real visionary to appreciate the obvious. The fact is that support and understanding were in short supply at the time, however, and that the UKPDS was launched in an atmosphere of doubt and controversy, with relatively little concept of the enormity of the undertaking. In retrospect it is hard to imagine how the UKPDS could have been launched at all—let alone piloted through stormy waters to a successful conclusion—without the iron nerves of the late Robert Turner. Admiral Horatio Nelson clapped a telescope to his blind eye when shown the signal to retire. Robert, in much the same spirit, experienced selective deafness when he encountered the word 'no'.

Controlling plasma glucose

The central aim of the study was to establish the effect of glucose control upon the late complications of diabetes and, if possible, the level of control needed to produce such an effect. A further aim was to establish whether glucose control could be better or more safely achieved with tablets or insulin. Before it could measure the consequences of improved glucose control, the UKPDS had first to achieve it. The target fasting plasma glucose of 6.0 mmol/l selected for those on intensive therapy was derived from the epidemiological threshold for cardiovascular risk, using the newly defined category of impaired glucose tolerance, and appeared almost impossibly rigorous at the time. The emphasis upon fasting glucose arose from the concept of basal normoglycaemia [5]. At a time when all the leading experts were busy hunting the phantom of insulin resistance, Rury Holman and Robert Turner saw diabetes as a disease of insulin deficiency. While others assumed that hyperglycaemia was the passive consequence of insulin deficiency, Turner and Holman saw that fasting plasma glucose is relatively constant in the early stages of glucose intolerance, and inferred a control system. They argued that fasting hyperglycaemia is mandated by the need to promote insulin secretion from a failing pancreatic β-cell mass, a view that has stood the test of time [6].

The concept had direct therapeutic implications. Insulin sensitivity can be increased by diet and weight loss, but this (as they initially believed and went on to demonstrate) was insufficient to achieve treatment goals in most patients. Contemporary thinking reserved metformin for the overweight, and the drug was undervalued; at the time there was (sadly enough) no reason for them to try it in everybody. Their preferred strategy was to increase basal insulin levels, either with a long-acting sulfonylurea such as chlorpropamide or with beef ultralente, topped up with soluble insulin before meals as the need arose. This would become the famous basal–bolus approach, although the term does not seem to have entered general circulation until the 1990s. Logical though it might seem, however, ultralente insulin was never particularly popular outside Oxford and some of us feel mild regret that the investigators did not settle for overnight neutral protamine Hagedorn (NPH) insulin instead.

The UKPDS broke almost all the rules of trial design. We are taught to believe that a study protocol should be predetermined and set in stone, but this study went to the other extreme, elevating the ad hoc into an art form, weathering the rapidly changing fashions in diabetes management and sprouting new heads like a hydra. There were times when the study seemed destined to meander on without ever reaching a conclusion and some of us could not suppress a groan when blood pressure control was squeezed in as an apparent afterthought or (as we considered, with some justification) as a means of tapping into a source of additional funding. But Robert was right and we were wrong and flexibility of means coupled with fixity of purpose carried the day.

This was a study that actually drew strength from its own limitations. Its approach to classification, for example, was to triage all those with an immediate need for insulin (based on symptoms, ketonuria or a fasting plasma glucose in excess of 15.0 mmol/l) and to recruit all the rest. This meant that the iconic study of type 2 diabetes would incorporate a sizeable minority of patients who would now be assigned to type 1 diabetes or latent autoimmune diabetes in adults (LADA). In consequence, the UKPDS, quite unwittingly, conducted the biggest and best prospective randomized controlled trial of early insulin vs. other therapies in people with LADA [7,8]. The UKPDS also showed that it is safe and effective to randomize patients diagnosed over the age of 25 years and with no immediate need for insulin to the same treatment pathway, regardless of presumed classification. The lesson is perfectly clear, but the world of diabetes is not yet ready to hear it, preferring as it does to persist in the quaint belief that it is both possible and useful to discriminate effectively between the major types of diabetes and to base therapeutic decisions upon this assumption [9].

The therapies

Diet

All patients in the UKPDS started with 3 months on diet alone, with the target of a fasting plasma glucose of 6.0 mmol/l. This allowed them to be classed as diet satisfactory or unsatisfactory before randomization to diet alone, tablets or insulin. Only 16% achieved the 6.0 mmol/l target within 3 months. The presence or absence of obesity did not (as previously expected) determine the response to diet, but the fall in glucose did correlate with weight loss as well as energy restriction. The overall correlation conceals a wide range of individual variation, but an average loss of 16% ideal body weight was required to achieve the target value of 6.0 mmol/l if the initial fasting plasma glucose was between 6.0 and 8.0 mmol/l, whereas 41% must be shed if the initial fasting value was between 12.0 and 14.0 mmol/l. The study showed that only a minority could achieve glucose control by diet alone and that this degree of success was associated with a level of dietary privation that was hard to achieve and rarely sustainable [10].

Those who were considered diet unsatisfactory were then randomized to continue on diet alone or to other therapies. Addition of chlorpropamide, glibenclamide or insulin achieved a similar level of control (HbA$_{1c}$ 6.8, 6.9 and 7.0% respectively), whereas diet alone fared worse at HbA$_{1c}$ 7.6% ($P < 0.001$); only 23% of those allocated to diet alone had a fasting plasma glucose below 7.8 mmol/l 3 years after diagnosis [11]. A small sub-study of the UKPDS found that reported dietary intake is unaffected by the allocation to other treatments [12], but the extent to which dietary compliance determines the success or failure of additional therapies has yet to be established.

Early effects of therapy

The UKPDS was built around the diagnostic scaffold of the 1980 WHO classification, both in terms of glucose targets and of the division into insulin-dependent and -independent forms of diabetes. The WHO subdivided non-insulin-dependent diabetes into obese and non-obese forms and the UKPDS followed suit, allocating metformin only to the obese. Experience with the sulfonylureas showed that chlorpropamide, a drug which has since fallen into disfavour, actually performed well in comparison with glibenclamide, with rather fewer minor hypoglycaemic episodes, but a similar rate (2%) of serious episodes requiring third-party intervention each year for the first 3 years; the rate had fallen to 0.7% by 6 years [13]. Metformin was rather less effective in controlling fasting plasma glucose at 6 months, but produced a more sustained effect at 3 years and was also weight neutral in the obese, whereas the sulfonylureas, like insulin, induced weight gain of 3–5 kg over the same period [11].

A progressive disorder

No presentation about type 2 diabetes is complete without a slide showing the tick-shaped response to therapy in the UKPDS, in which the initial dip towards better control (associated with an average weight loss of 5 kg) is followed by an inexorable rise in HbA$_{1c}$ and fasting glucose levels. This progression stood in marked contrast to the relatively stable baseline achieved in patients with type 1 diabetes in the Diabetes Control and Complications Trial (DCCT). The UKPDS documented that deteriorating control reflects progressive loss of insulin secretory capacity and showed that treatment with insulin or sulfonylureas was equally effective over a 6-year period, with equivalent levels of fasting plasma glucose, similar weight gain, but rather more severe hypoglycaemia on insulin (2.3 vs. 0.7% per annum). Metformin was equally effective in lowering fasting glucose levels, but without the weight gain or hypoglycaemia. It does seem remarkable that three such diverse therapies should achieve almost exactly the same degree of glucose control, particularly as oral medications, unlike insulin, have a therapeutic ceiling: but this is what the data show.

Emerging from the labyrinth

Twenty-one years after it started, the UKPDS emerged into the light of day with answers to many of the original questions. Some of the answers seemed very clear, others very complicated. There were indeed so many items of information, so many arms to the study, so many variables, so many endpoints and so many approaches to analysis (intention to treat or epidemiological) that commentators appeared on every street corner to tell you what it all meant. In time, as always happens, received opinion would focus upon some conclusions while ignoring others, would sidestep the complexities and would simplify the message into something subtly different from what was actually shown.

To take one example: the message that reached the diabetes community around the world in 1998 was that more people with type 2 diabetes should be treated with insulin. This was undoubtedly a useful message, but it was not what the study showed. The UKPDS tested the introduction of insulin at diagnosis, which clinicians would scarcely dream of doing, and indeed showed that early insulin therapy had no advantage over oral agents. What the study did not set out to show, and could not have demonstrated, was that people inadequately controlled on tablets should be transferred to insulin. This was, however, to be its main impact upon clinical care and who but a pedant could complain about that?

The UKPDS had some grim messages when it came to control and complications. For example: 50% of patients already had evidence of tissue complications of diabetes before they were diagnosed and exposed to therapy. Or consider that, within 9 years of study entry, 20% of patients had experienced a macrovascular complication (myocardial infarction, stroke or angina) and one-third of these had died in consequence [14]. The study did indeed achieve its objective by demonstrating that glucose control could influence progression to macrovascular disease, but this demonstration was trumped by the observation that a range of non-glycaemic risk factors are both more important and more amenable to therapy. Thus, and by another paradox, the UKPDS both confirmed and demoted the role of glucose control in macrovascular complications. The findings in microvascular disease were much as anticipated when it came to glucose control, but brought the unexpected finding that hypertension was almost as much of a factor in the development of retinopathy as in that of nephropathy. Here again, the wayward course of the UKPDS resulted in a major unanticipated benefit that went far beyond the glucocentric assumptions upon which the study was founded.

Some ends, some beginnings

The main outcomes of the UKPDS have been extensively summarized else-where and I will not attempt to do so here. Our understanding of diabetes has grown in parallel with the study and because of the study. Here are some of the things we learned in the process:

We learned that glucose control is easy at the onset of type 2 diabetes and becomes progressively more difficult. Ironically, our understanding of the difficulties involved has grown hand in hand with the popular belief that type 2 diabetes can and should be managed by the non-specialist in primary care. We have learned that different therapies are roughly equipotent. This is bad news for those who pontificate about the rational basis of therapy for type 2 diabetes, but good news for the pragmatists.

We learned (although many have since forgotten) that sulfonylureas are safe and effective and reduce cardiovascular risk to the same extent as insulin. Current arguments against their use are largely theoretical, but the case for the sulfonylureas is based upon solid evidence. Metformin was, however, the big bonus of the study, both in terms of efficacy and cardiovascular risk. It achieved the same glycaemic benefit as sulfonylureas or insulin, but with greater risk reduction. The mysterious 'factor X' that this implies has been the cause of much conjecture. Sales of metformin took off mightily in the aftermath of the UKPDS, and we have the study to thank for the fact that the glitazones (one of which may actually increase cardiovascular risk, while the other may lower it slightly) did not achieve greater market penetration in Europe.

We learned that insulin is a useful and acceptable form of treatment for type 2 diabetes. No longer wielded as a threat, it is now a routine part of our treatment plan and we talk to patients about when, rather than if, they will need insulin. As to how the insulin should be formulated and how often administered, trial evidence suggests that basal insulin has no intrinsic advantage over prandial or biphasic insulin. Once again, expectation must defer to the evidence [15].

The UKPDS set out to establish the importance of glucose control in type 2 diabetes and, in doing so, also showed us the limits of glucose lowering as an intervention. It showed us that we intervene too late, for 50% of our patients already carry the marks of vascular disease by the time they come to our attention. And it showed us that pancreatic β-cells go on dying after diagnosis despite our best efforts at glucose control. Diabetes therapy is played out against the backdrop of an incoming tide and one therapy must be piled upon another in the attempt to hold it back [16]. The two comparison groups in the UKPDS showed a parallel yet superimposable deterioration in glucose control and the effect of intensive therapy was to separate the curves by 2–3 years. Not much, you might think, but what a difference to the lives of those affected. Buying time is all that medicine can ever do and the UKPDS has shown that we can do it.

In conclusion, the UKPDS changed the way we think about and manage type 2 diabetes, to the extent that it would be very hard to imagine where we would be without it. The two central lessons are that glucose must be tackled aggressively (although there may be a limit to this) and that vascular risk reduction is the main objective of therapy. This is the basis of everything we do. I will close with two further reflections. The first is that the UKPDS would have been much less useful to us if it had been conducted according to the rules. If the original hypotheses had been followed through to a logical conclusion, we would have learned that improved glucose control reduces microvascular risk to a useful extent, which we knew already, and that it has a borderline effect in reducing cardiovascular risk; scarcely a revolution in our understanding. The second reflection concerns the difference that one person with vision can make to the course of clinical science. The UKPDS showed us what can be achieved by many people working together to a common purpose. It is a lasting testimonial to the wisdom and organizational genius of Rury Holman and the dedication of the core team that ran the study so effectively. But, in the end, it all depended upon Robert Turner, the man who said 'why not?'.

Summary

The UK Prospective Diabetes Study (UKPDS) set out to establish whether improved glucose control could alleviate the macrovascular and microvascular complications of diabetes and to compare the relative merits of diet, oral glucose-lowering agents or insulin in achieving this objective. The study broke many of the rules of trial design, not least by constant addition of further interventions and analyses, but this flexibility would, paradoxically, prove to be one of its greatest strengths. The UKPDS taught us that glucose control must be tackled aggressively in type 2 diabetes. It taught us that treatment must be escalated in parallel with the evolution of pancreatic β-cell failure. It also taught us that glucose control is not enough: the central objective of therapy is to reduce vascular risk by any means available. This commentary looks back along the winding road that led to these conclusions.

References

1 National Diabetes Data Group. Classification and diagnosis of diabetes mellitus and other categories of glucose intolerance. *Diabetes* 1979;28:1039–1057.

2 WHO Expert Committee on Diabetes Mellitus. Second Report. Geneva: World Health Organization, 1980.

3 Kilo C, Miller JP, Williamson JR. The crux of the UGDP. Spurious results and biologically inappropriate data analysis. *Diabetologia* 1980;18:179–185.

4 Schwartz TB, Meinert CL. The UGDP controversy. Thirty-four years of contentious ambiguity laid to rest. *Perspectives Biol Med* 2004;47:564–574.

5 Holman RR, Turner RC. Diabetes: the quest for basal normoglycaemia. *Lancet* 1977; i: 469–474.

6 Stumvoll M. Control of glycaemia: from molecules to men. *Diabetologia* 2004;47:770–781.

7 Davis TME, Wright AD, Mehta ZM, Cull CA, Stratton JM, Bottazzo GF *et al*. Islet autoantibodies in clinically diagnosed type 2 diabetes: prevalence and relationship with metabolic control (UKPDS 70). *Diabetologia* 2005;48:695–702.

8 Gale EAM. Latent autoimmune diabetes in adults: a guide for the perplexed. *Diabetologia* 2005;48:2195–2199.

9 Gale EAM. Declassifying diabetes. *Diabetologia* 2006;49:1989–1995.

10 UKPDS Group. UK Prospective Diabetes Study 7: Response of fasting plasma glucose to diet therapy in newly presenting type II diabetic patients. *Metabolism* 1990;39:905–912.

11 UKPDS Study Group. UKPDS 13. Relative efficacy of randomly allocated diet, sulphonylurea, insuin or metformin in patients with newly diagnosed non-insulin dependent diabetes followed for 3 years. *Br Med J* 1995;310:83–88.

12 Eeley EA, Stratton IM, Hadden DR, Turner RC, Holman RR on behalf of the UKPDS Study Group. UKPDS 18. Estimated dietary intake in type 2 diabetic patients randomly allocated to diet, sulphonylurea or insulin therapy. *Diabet Med* 1996;13:656–662.

13 UKPDS Study Group. UKPDS 16. Overview of 6 years' therapy of type II diabetes: a progressive disease. *Diabetes* 1995; 44:1249–1258.

14 Turner RC. The UK Prospective Diabetes Study. A review. *Diabetes Care* 1998;21:C35–38.

15 Holman RR, Thorne KI, Farmer AJ, Davies MJ, Keenan JF, Paul S *et al*. for the 4-T Study Group. Addition of biphasic, prandial or basal insulin to oral therapy in type 2 diabetes. *N Eng J Med* 2007;357:1716–1730.

16 Turner RC, Cull CA, Frighi V, Holman RR for the UKPDS Group. Glycemic control with diet, sulfonylurea, metformin or insulin in patients with type 2 diabetes mellitus. Progressive requirement for multiple therapies (UKPDS 49). *J Am Med Assoc* 1999; 281:2005–2012.

9

The Hypertension in Diabetes Study (HDS): a catalyst for change

Bryan Williams

Department of Cardiovascular Sciences, University of Leicester School of Medicine,
Leicester Royal Infirmary, Leicester, UK

Introduction

'Whether the adverse effects of hypertension can be reversed by antihypertensive treatment … remains to be determined …'
  Hypertension in Diabetes Study group of UKPDS, *J. Hypertension*, 1993 [4]

Hypertension is now accepted as a major risk factor for macrovascular and microvascular complications in people with diabetes and a major contributor to the associated premature morbidity and mortality. However, it is important to put into context how recent the recognition of the importance of blood pressure (BP) as a risk factor in diabetes has been. The recording of BP in the medical records of patients with diabetes was not diligent or routine until the last decade. Although patients often had admirably detailed records of their blood glucose, BP records were sparse and even when BP was recorded, if it was high it was rarely treated, except in patients with evidence of nephropathy. There were a number of reasons for this, the most important of which was a lack of clinical trial evidence demonstrating the safety and efficacy of blood pressure lowering in people with diabetes. Indeed, until recently, the whole area of BP treatment in diabetes was fraught with many myths and misconceptions. These included concerns that BP lowering might be poorly tolerated because of autonomic dysfunction and potentially hazardous if perfusion to vital organs was compromised as a result of impaired blood flow autoregulation in people with diabetes. Even if doctors decided to treat, they were then confronted with a blizzard of cautions with regard to specific treatments: 'don't use diuretics as they may worsen glycaemic control' (which was perceived to be the only thing that mattered—and still is by some!), 'don't use β-blockers as they might impair recognition of hypoglycaemia', 'don't use ACE-inhibitors in type 2 diabetes

Originally published: Williams B. The Hypertension in Diabetes Study (HDS): a catalyst for change. *Diabetic Medicine* 2008; 25 (Suppl. 2): 13–19

as these patients are more likely to have renovascular disease', and 'don't use calcium channel blockers as they are just dangerous!'. All of these myths flourished in an evidence-free zone, compounded by the fact that the presence of diabetes was often an exclusion criterion for the early BP-lowering trials. All of these myths and misconceptions have now been dismissed in the only way they can be: by clinical trials evidence; a journey that began in earnest for people with type 2 diabetes with the UK Prospective Diabetes Study (UKPDS).

Although the UKPDS was originally established as a study of intensified glycaemic control in type 2 diabetes, it was recognized early on that the patients enrolled into the study had a very high prevalence of hypertension. The UKPDS steering group showed remarkable foresight in embedding a 'Hypertension in Diabetes Study' (HDS) within UKPDS that addressed a key question: would more intensive vs. less intensive blood pressure lowering improve clinical outcomes in people with type 2 diabetes? In so doing, it also addressed an important ancillary question, notably the tolerability and safety of BP lowering in this patient population [1].

The Hypertension in Diabetes Study in UKPDS—design and early data

Although UKPDS started in 1977, the HDS did not start until a decade later in 1987 and involved 20 of the 23 UKPDS study centres. Of the original 4297 patients recruited into UKPDS, 243 had either been lost to follow-up or had died by the time the HDS was commenced. Of the remaining 4097, 38% (1544) were hypertensive as defined by UKPDS criteria; of these, 1148 were eligible and entered the HDS study (Fig. 9.1; Table 9.1) [1]. The patients were allocated to treatment with either 'less tight control of BP', aiming for BP < 180/105 mmHg or 'tight control of BP', aiming for BP < 150/85 mmHg. These BP targets indicate where we were with regard to the general ignorance about the significance of BP as a risk factor in diabetes and the genuine uncertainty about the potential balance between benefit and harm when the study was designed. In fact, the original blood pressure target for the 'less tight control' group was 200/105 mmHg! This was reduced to < 180/105 mmHg by the steering committee of the HDS as data about the importance of BP-lowering began to emerge in the early 1990s. Nevertheless, the very fact that, in the early 1990s, it was considered reasonable to randomize people with diabetes to what is now considered Grade III hypertension, is testimony to the lack of evidence and, consequently, the low profile of BP control in the routine care of people with type 2 diabetes at the time.

Another intriguing aspect of the study was further randomization of the tight BP control group into two groups, one allocated to treatment with the angiotensin-converting enzyme (ACE) inhibitor captopril, the other allocated to treatment with the β-blocker atenolol [2]. Clearly, this was designed to deter-

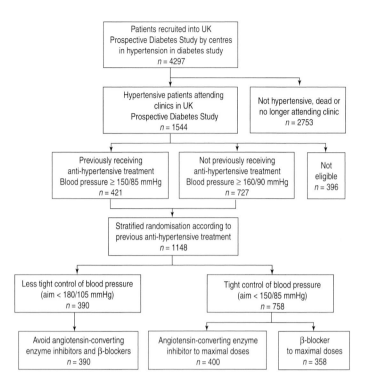

Figure 9.1 Design and allocation of patients to the treatment arms of the Hypertension in Diabetes Study–reproduced with permission from [1].

mine whether the choice of therapy mattered. Alas, in my view, this comparison was a mistake that looked hopelessly underpowered with only 758 patients assigned to 'tighter BP control' subsequently divided into two treatment groups. There was never a hope of a meaningful result and I will discuss it no further.

Even before the outcome of the BP intervention study reported in 1998, the HDS group were already generating some important findings. They reported a strikingly high prevalence of hypertension at 40% (defined at systolic BP≥160 mmHg and/or diastolic BP≥90 mmHg) at the time of diagnosis of type 2 diabetes, with a higher prevalence in women and increasing prevalence with age [3,4]. The threshold for diagnosis of hypertension used in the UKPDS was much higher than current thresholds, consequently, by modern criteria (BP≥140/90 mmHg) almost 80% would have been designated hypertensive. They also noted that the hypertensive patients were more likely to be obese and already had almost double the risk of established cardiovascular complications at the time of diagnosis of type 2 diabetes, when compared with those without hypertension. Alarmingly, most of the hypertension was unrecognized and untreated [3].

Table 9.1 Baseline characteristics of the patients in the Hypertension in Diabetes Study. Reproduced with permission from [1]

	Tight (n = 758)	Less tight (n = 390)
Mean (SD) age (years)	56.4 (8.1)	56.5 (8.1)
Male sex	410 (54)	227 (58)
Ethnic group:		
White	651 (86)	344 (88)
Afro-Caribbean	62 (8)	25 (6)
Asian Indian	39 (5)	17 (4)
Other	6 (1)	4 (1)
Mean (SD) body mass index (kg/m^2)	29.8 (5.5)	29.3 (5.5)
Median (interquartile range) fasting plasma glucose (mmol/l)	7.4 (6.1–9.2)	7.4 (6.2–9.8)
Mean (SD) glycated haemoglobin (%)	6.9 (1.7)	6.8 (1.5)
Mean (SD) blood pressure (mmHg):		
Systolic	159 (20)	160 (18)
Diastolic	94 (10)	94 (9)
Receiving anti-hypertensive treatment	286 (36)	145 (37)
Smoking:		
No. of patients	746	379
Non-smoker	281 (38)	142 (38)
Ex-smoker	294 (39)	152 (40)
Current smoker	171 (23)	85 (22)
Urinary albumin (mg/l)*:		
≥50	114 (18)	53 (16)
≥300	18 (3)	13 (4)
Retinopathy:		
No. of patients	617	312
20 20 or worse	143 (23)	89 (29)
35 35 or worse	45 (7)	32 (10)
Mean (SD) cholesterol (mmol/l):		
Total	5.5 (1.1)	5.6 (1.1)
HDL	1.10 (0.27)	1.10 (0.28)
LDL	3.6 (1.1)	3.6 (1.1)
Geometric mean (1 SD interval) triglyceride (mmol/l)	1.6 (0.9–2.6)	1.6 (0.9–2.8)
Median duration (interquartile range) of diabetes (years)	2.7 (1.0–4.2)	2.5 (1.0–4.4)
Treatment for diabetes:		
Diet	175 (29)	89 (29)
Sulphonylurea	200 (34)	103 (34)
Metformin	41 (8)	23 (7)
Combined oral hypoglycaemic agents	28 (5)	16 (5)
Insulin	144 (23)	70 (24)
Other	6 (1)	1 (1)

HDL, high-density lipoprotein
LDL, low-density lipoprotein
SD, standard deviation
*Corrected to urinary creatinine concentration of 8 mmol/l.

Although the Framingham heart study had already highlighted that diabetes was a major cardiovascular risk factor [5], the HDS was one of the first prospective evaluations of the association between BP and clinical outcomes in a major clinical outcomes trial. Within 5 years of commencing HDS, the strong association between BP and clinical outcomes was reported by the group for patients with type 2 diabetes [4]. After a median follow-up of only 4.6 years, it had become clear that hypertension was a major risk factor for cardiovascular morbidity and mortality in this population. The authors prophetically speculated that 'anti-hypertensive therapy may provide greater benefit in this high-risk group than in the general population…' [4].

The Hypertension in Diabetes Study in UKPDS—main results

The follow-up of patients with BP lowering in the HDS was for a median of 8.4 years. The mean blood pressure during follow-up was significantly reduced in the group assigned tight blood pressure control (144/82 mmHg) compared with the group assigned to less tight control (154/87 mmHg). The results were dramatic [1]. The 10/5 mmHg difference in BP was associated with a reduction in diabetes-related endpoints by one-quarter, reductions in death related to diabetes by almost one-third, a reduction in stroke by almost half and heart failure by more than half and a reduction in microvascular disease by approximately one-third (mainly delayed progression of retinopathy) (Fig. 9.2). The number needed to treat (NNT) to prevent one major complication over 10 years was only six patients, the NNT to prevent a diabetes-related death was only 15 patients. Whatever the endpoint, there was a tendency to improvement with improved BP control—everything got better and nothing got worse. The treatment strategy was safe and well tolerated and the result was unequivocal, indeed remarkable from such a small study.

The impact of the hypertension study in UKPDS

The phrase 'landmark study' is overused. However, it is difficult to overstate the importance of the HDS—this was undoubtedly a landmark study. Not because it was a mega-trial with a perfect design, but because it wasn't. It was a small study by modern standards and it asked a simple and important question. Apart from the aforementioned eccentricity of the subdivision of the tighter control group, it had a perfect design and studied a very high-risk population with a high number of events that afforded it the kind of statistical power that would be unattainable today because of the improvements in care. It also studied a younger population (mean age 56 years), with a good balance of male (56%) and female patients. However, perhaps most important of all, it was a study undertaken by diabetologists themselves, alongside an intervention, notably intensified glycaemic control, which they anticipated would be the most effective intervention of all. I doubt the result would have had quite

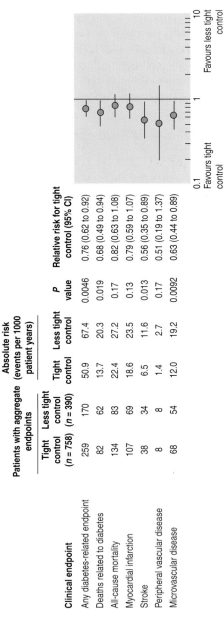

Clinical endpoint	Patients with aggregate endpoints		Absolute risk (events per 1000 patient years)		P value	Relative risk for tight control (95% CI)
	Tight control (n = 758)	Less tight control (n = 390)	Tight control	Less tight control		
Any diabetes-related endpoint	259	170	50.9	67.4	0.0046	0.76 (0.62 to 0.92)
Deaths related to diabetes	82	62	13.7	20.3	0.019	0.68 (0.49 to 0.94)
All-cause mortality	134	83	22.4	27.2	0.17	0.82 (0.63 to 1.08)
Myocardial infarction	107	69	18.6	23.5	0.13	0.79 (0.59 to 1.07)
Stroke	38	34	6.5	11.6	0.013	0.56 (0.35 to 0.89)
Peripheral vascular disease	8	8	1.4	2.7	0.17	0.51 (0.19 to 1.37)
Microvascular disease	68	54	12.0	19.2	0.0092	0.63 (0.44 to 0.89)

Figure 9.2 Numbers of patients who attained one or more clinical endpoints in aggregates representing specific types of clinical complications, with relative risks comparing tight control of blood pressure with less control. Reproduced with permission from [1].

the same impact had it been from a study undertaken by a group of cardio-vascular trialists. Indeed, just prior to publication of UKPDS and HDS in 1998, the diabetes subgroup ($n = 583$) from the Systolic Hypertension in the Elderly Programme (SHEP) had reported a reduction in cardiovascular events by half over 5 years of treatment in an elderly population experiencing a similar im-provement in BP control [6]. This impressive data from SHEP, unlike the HDS, had little impact on treatment strategies at the time.

The HDS changed clinical practice around the world and elevated the management of BP to the forefront of care for people with type 2 diabetes. The study had identified that hypertension was almost invariably present in these patients, rather than the exception. The study had demonstrated that hypertension was dangerous and markedly increased the risk of the prema-ture development of diabetes complications and that, untreated, ultimately contributed to premature mortality. The study showed for the first time that for BP 'lower was better' with regard to improving the outcomes for people with type 2 diabetes, and that lower was safe. The study also showed almost all patients would require multiple drugs in combination to achieve improved BP control and better clinical outcomes. The HDS prompted a revolution in the care of patients with type 2 diabetes and improved their outcomes, with the recognition that this was primarily a cardiovascular disease that responded best to treatment strategies that targeted cardiovascular risk factors. Strategies now involve intensified BP control and the widespread use of statins and anti-platelet therapies as exemplified and supported by the more recent publica-tions from the Steno study group [7,8].

Relative importance of blood pressure vs. glycaemic control in UKPDS

One of the key drivers for change resulting from UKPDS was recognition of the importance of BP control set in the context of improved glycaemic control. Glycaemic control was at the time the main focus of treatment for people with type 2 diabetes. The UKPDS was the first study to allow the relative impact of two different treatment strategies to be compared prospectively. The data clearly showed that intensified BP control was impressive at reducing major diabetes endpoints, including significant reduction in diabetes-related death, stroke and microvascular disease and trends to benefit in all endpoints, despite the relatively small size of the BP-lowering study. Moreover, these benefits ap-peared more impressive than those resulting from the intensified glycaemic control strategy (Table 9.2), even for microvascular endpoints, for which the latter had been strongly advocated. This comparison is not designed to show the relative merits of competing strategies, but rather to emphasize the huge psychological impact of demonstrating the power of BP reduction alongside the holy grail of diabetes management at the time.

Table 9.2 Numbers needed to treat (NNT) in UK Prospective Diabetes Study (UKPDS) to prevent one of the major endpoints analysed in the trial, stratified by intervention; i.e. intensified glycaemic control vs. intensified blood pressure (BP) control

UKPDS endpoint	NNT intensified glycaemic control	NNT intensified BP control
Any diabetes endpoint	200	61
Diabetes-related death	No benefit	152
All-cause death	No benefit	208
Myocardial infarction	370	204
Stroke	No benefit	196
Microvascular endpoint	357	138

Where are we now, 10 years on?

There are still many unanswered questions with regard to the optimal BP-lowering strategy and targets for people with type 2 diabetes, but there has also been much progress since the pioneering days of the HDS in the UKPDS. One key question has been: does it matter what drug we use to lower BP in people with type 2 diabetes? To some extent this is superfluous because of the likelihood that most patients will need a combination of drugs—a finding highlighted by the HDS [1]. A meta-analysis of trials that followed the UKPDS concluded that BP lowering per se is the dominant means of achieving macro- and microvascular benefits and that lower does appear to be better—even more so than in the non-diabetic hypertensive population [9]. This in part relates to the fact that people with diabetes are at much higher cardiovascular risk and thus stand to gain more absolute benefit from BP lowering. It may also relate to the fact that people with diabetes are especially vulnerable to hypertensive injury [10]. This vulnerability relates to a number of factors, especially in the microcirculation as a result of impaired autoregulation of blood flow. However, it is also because of higher 24-h BP loads (relating to early subtle autonomic dysfunction that impairs the usual nocturnal fall in BP) and as a result of premature stiffening of the abdominal aorta (because of glycation of elastic fibres) which impairs ventricular–vascular coupling, increases pulse-wave velocity and increases systolic pressure for any given stroke volume [10]. The latter might explain why β-blocker-based treatment is less effective at preventing cardiovascular events and mortality than other treatments in people with diabetes [11,12]. There has also been controversy about whether blockade of the renin–angiotensin system (RAS) 'adds value' over and above the BP lowering it produces in preventing cardiovascular events in people with diabetes. Some studies suggest these agents do [11,13], others have not confirmed this [14-17]. However, there does appear to be an advantage of RAS blockade on renal endpoints in patients with type 2 diabetes (albuminuria and progression of renal disease) [18-20], which has prompted international guidelines to conclude that RAS blockade should be part of the cocktail of treatments used to lower BP in people with type 2 diabetes. Thus, modern treatment strategies would usually include RAS blockade along with a calcium channel blocker and/or a thiazide-type diuretic.

The HDS confirmed that 'lower is better' with regard to BP control for patients starting treatment with overt hypertension—but how low is low enough? This remains a key question. The recent ADVANCE trial tested the 'lower is better' hypothesis by further lowering BP with an ACE-inhibitor (perindopril)/thiazide-type diuretic (indapamide) combination vs. placebo on top of conventional therapy on vascular events in 11 140 people with type 2 diabetes [21]. The BP-lowering combination therapy was added irrespective of baseline blood pressure levels or the use of other blood pressure-lowering drugs. Over a mean follow-up of 4.3 years, the active therapy was associated with a lower BP (−5.6/−2.2 mmHg) vs. placebo treatment. This modest BP reduction was associated a significant 9% risk reduction in major macrovascular and microvascular events, an 18% reduction in cardiovascular death and a 14% reduction in all-cause mortality. Importantly, there was no evidence that the benefits of additional BP-lowering therapy differed according to initial blood pressure level—in other words, even those within the lowest BP stratum at baseline experienced a similar relative risk reduction to those in the highest BP stratum. Moreover, the lowest BP stratum included patients whose BP was already below the currently recommended treatment target for type 2 diabetes (< 130/80 mmHg). It is also noteworthy that, unlike the HDS, the ADVANCE result was achieved in a population of patients with high concomitant use of statins, anti-platelet drugs, ACE inhibition and good glycaemic control, in both arms of the trial. This trial thus extends the original findings of the HDS and provides strong evidence to support the safety, tolerability and efficacy of a 'lower is better' philosophy for BP control in people with diabetes and that the modern treatment goal should perhaps be 'the lowest pressure the patient will tolerate without an adverse impact on function' [22]. Further information of the impact of a more intensive BP-lowering strategy will come from the Action to Control Cardiovascular Risk in Diabetes (ACCORD) study from the USA [23]. ACCORD is testing whether lowering BP to normal (< 120 mmHg systolic) will reduce stroke and heart disease risk better compared with a usually targeted level in current clinical practice; i.e. below the current definition of hypertension (< 140 mmHg systolic) in people with type 2 diabetes.

Conclusions

Quantitative and qualitative disturbances in BP are very common in people with type 2 diabetes. The optimal goal of therapy is now a moving target. The momentum began with the result of the HDS in the UKPDS. We now know much more about BP, its prevalence, its pathophysiology, its consequences and its treatment in people with type 2 diabetes. There is little doubt that the HDS was a catalyst for this spectacular growth in knowledge over the past 10 years.

A number of trials have followed that have incrementally shifted the evidence base and have impacted on treatment guidelines. The void of information and the myths and misconceptions have given way to a solid foundation for the treatment of BP in people with type 2 diabetes. There is more to do to consolidate guidance for clinicians and to define the optimal BP-lowering treatment strategy and targets. However, the millions of patients today and in the future with type 2 diabetes should be grateful to the 1148 patients enrolled into the HDS and the foresight of those who studied them.

Summary

Hypertension is now established as a major risk factor for premature cardiovascular morbidity and mortality in people with type 2 diabetes and all modern treatment guidelines recommend the routine treatment of hypertension in these patients. However, these developments have been relatively recent. Only a decade ago, outside of small studies in patients with nephropathy, there was little evidence with regard to the efficacy and safety of treating elevated blood pressure in people with type 2 diabetes. Consequently, for many patients, elevated blood pressure remained undetected and untreated. This changed with the publication of the Hypertension in Diabetes Study (HDS) in 1998. This study revealed that hypertension was very common in people with type 2 diabetes and demonstrated the dramatic benefits of blood pressure lowering in reducing their risk of major macrovascular and microvascular complications. The unequivocal evidence from this study provided a much-needed catalyst for change, propelling blood pressure measurement and its treatment to the forefront of risk management in these patients. Many studies have followed and many questions remain with regard to the preferred anti-hypertensive treatment strategy and optimal treatment targets for blood pressure. In the meantime, many millions of patients with type 2 diabetes worldwide have benefited and will continue to benefit from the therapeutic insights gained from the treatment of blood pressure in the 1148 patients enrolled in the Hypertension in Diabetes Study in the UK Prospective Diabetes Study.

References

1 UK Prospective Diabetes Study Group. Tight blood pressure control and risk of macrovascular and microvascular complications in type 2 diabetes: UKPDS 38. *Br Med J* 1998;317:703-713.

2 UK Prospective Diabetes Study Group. Efficacy of atenolol and captopril in reducing risk of macrovascular and microvascular complications in type 2 diabetes: UKPDS 39. *Br Med J* 1998;317:713-720.

3 Hypertension in Diabetes Study Group. HDS 1: Prevalence of hypertension in newly presenting type 2 diabetic patients and the association with risk factors for cardiovascular and diabetic complications. *J Hypertens* 1993;11:309-317.

4 Hypertension in Diabetes Study Group. HDS 2: Increased risk of cardiovascular complications in hypertensive type 2 diabetic patients. *J Hypertens* 1993;11:319-325.

5 Garcia MJ, McNamara PM, Gordon T, Kannel WP. Morbidity and mortality in diabetics in the Framingham population. Sixteen-year follow-up study. *Diabetes* 1974;23:105-111.

6 Curb JD, Pressel SL, Cutler JA, Savage P, Applegate WB, Black H *et al*. Effect of diuretic-based antihypertensive treatment on cardiovascular disease risk in older diabetic patients with isolated systolic hypertension. Systolic Hypertension in the Elderly Program Cooperative Research Group. *J Am Med Assoc* 1996;276:1886-1892.

7 Gaede P, Vedel P, Larsn N, Jensen GV, Parving HH, Pederson O. Multifactorial intervention and cardiovascular disease in patients with type 2 diabetes. *N. Eng J Med* 2003;348:383-393.

8 Gaede P, Lund-Andersen H, Parving HH, Pederson O. Effect of a multifactorial intervention on mortality in type 2 diabetes. *N Eng J Med* 2008; 358:580-591.

9 Turnbull F, Neal B, Algert C, Chalmers J, Chapman N, Cutler J *et al*. Effects of different blood pressure-lowering regimens on major cardiovascular events in individuals with and without diabetes mellitus: results of prospectively designed overviews of randomized trials. *Arch Intern Med* 2005;165:1410-1419.

10 Williams B. The unique vulnerability of diabetic subjects to hypertensive injury. In: Williams B, ed., *Hypertension in Diabetes*. London and New York: Martin Dunitz Publisher, 2003:99–108.

11 Lindholm LH, Ibsen H, Dahlöff B, Devereox RB, Beevers G, de Faire U *et al*. Cardiovascular morbidity and mortality in patients with diabetes in the Losartan Intervention For Endpoint reduction in hypertension study (LIFE): A randomised trial against atenolol. *Lancet* 2002;359:1004-1010.

12 Dahlöff B, Sever PS, Poulter NR, Wedel H, Beevers DG, Caulfield M *et al*. for the ASCOT Investigators. Prevention of cardiovascular events with an antihypertensive regimen of amlodipine adding perindopril as required versus atenolol adding bendroflumethiazide as required, in the Anglo-Scandinavian Cardiac Outcomes Trial-Blood Pressure Lowering Arm (ASCOT-BPLA): a multicentre randomised controlled trial. *Lancet* 2005;366:895–906.

13 Heart Outcomes Prevention Evaluation Study Investigators. Effects of ramipril on cardiovascular and microvascular outcomes in people with diabetes mellitus: results of the HOPE study and MICRO-HOPE substudy. *Lancet* 2000;355:253-259.

14 The ALLHAT Officers and Coordinators for the ALLHAT Collaborative Research Group. Major outcomes in high-risk hypertensive patients randomized to angiotensin-converting enzyme inhibitor or calcium channel blocker vs diuretic: the Antihypertensive and Lipid Lowering treatment to prevent Heart Attack Trial (ALLHAT). *J Am Med Assoc* 2002; 288:2981–2997.

15 Whelton PK, Barzilay J, Cushman WC, Davis BR, Iiamathi E, Kostis JB *et al*., for the ALLHAT Collaborative Research Group. Clinical outcomes in antihypertensive treatment of type 2 diabetes, impaired fasting glucose concentration, and normoglycemia. *Arch Intern Med* 2005;165:1401–1409.

16 Mahboob-Rahman M, Pressel S, Davis BR, Nwachuku C, Wright JT, Whelton PK *et al*. for the ALLHAT Collaborative Research Group. Renal outcomes in high-risk hypertensive patients treated with an angiotensin-converting enzyme inhibitor or a calcium channel blocker vs a diuretic. *Arch Intern Med* 2005;165: 936–946.

17 Zanchetti A, Julius S, Kjeldsen S, McInnes GT, Hua S, Weber M *et al*. Outcomes in subgroups of hypertensive patients treated with regimens based on valsartan and amlodipine: an analysis of findings from the VALUE trial. *J Hypertens* 2006; 24:2163–2168.

18 Parving HH, Lehnert H, Bröchner-Morteasen J, Gomis R, Andersen S, Arner P, for the Irbesartan in Patients with Type 2 Diabetes and Microalbuminuria Study Group. The effect of Irbesartan on the development of diabetic nephropathy in patients with type 2 diabetes. *N Eng J Med* 2001; 870:78.

19 Lewis EJ, Hunsicker LG, Clarke WR, Berl T, Pohl MA, Lewis JB *et al*. Renoprotective effect of the angiotensin–receptor antagonist Irbesartan in patients with nephropathy due to type 2 diabetes. *N Eng J Med* 2001; 345:851-860.

20 Brenner BM, Cooper ME, de Zeeuw D, Keane WF, Mitch WE, Parving HH *et al*. for the RENAAL Study Investigators. Effects of Losartan on renal and cardiovascular outcomes in patients with type 2 diabetes and nephropathy. *N Eng J Med* 2001; 345:861-869.

21 ADVANCE Collaborative Group. Effects of a fixed combination of perindopril and indapamide on macrovascular and microvascular outcomes in patients with type 2 diabetes mellitus (the ADVANCE trial): a randomised controlled trial. *Lancet* 2007; 370: 829–840.

22 Williams B. The year in hypertension. *J Am Coll Cardiol* 2008; 51:1803-1817.

23 Action to Control Cardiovascular Risk in Diabetes (ACCORD) Trial. Design and methods. *Am J Cardiol* 2007; 99:S21-S33.

10 | Microvascular disease: what does the UKPDS tell us about diabetic nephropathy?

Rudy Bilous

Newcastle University, Newcastle upon Tyne, UK

Introduction

Over the last 20 years, diabetes has become the leading cause of end-stage renal failure in the USA and other Western countries and most of these patients have type 2 diabetes [1]. Moreover, there is an over-representation from ethnic sub-groups such as Native Americans [1] and South Asians in the UK [2], for reasons that are not well understood. People with diabetes do not do well on dialysis: less than 20% are alive after 5 years, with most dying from cardiovascular disease [1]. It is therefore critical that we better understand the pathophysiology of nephropathy in type 2 diabetes and implement treatments that can prevent this terrible complication. This article will review the contribution of the UK Prospective Diabetes Study (UKPDS) to these aims.

The impact of the UKPDS on our understanding of nephropathy will be covered under three main headings: natural history, therapy and aetiology.

Study definitions

The UKPDS remains the largest study in type 2 diabetes with pre-specified renal endpoints, namely death from renal disease and/or renal failure defined as a plasma creatinine $>250\,\mu mol/l$ (not related to an acute clinical event) and/or the need for dialysis [3]. Fatal and non-fatal renal failure were also part of the composite microvascular endpoint, which also included retinopathy requiring photocoagulation and vitreous haemorrhage. Surrogate renal endpoints were microalbuminuria (UAC 50–299 mg/l); clinical grade proteinuria (UAC > 300 mg/l) and a twofold plasma creatinine increase [3]. These three endpoints were reported per triennium as a median of the year in question and the preceding and subsequent years' values. In the most recent paper, the investigators report estimated creatinine clearance (eCC) using the Cockroft–Gault formula, defin-

Originally published: Bilous R. Microvascular disease: what does the UKPDS tell us about diabetic nephropathy? *Diabetic Medicine* 2008; 25 (Suppl. 2): 25–29

ing renal impairment as either $<60\,\text{ml/min/1.73}\,\text{m}^2$ or a doubling of plasma creatinine[4].

Natural history

UKPDS was an open-label randomized controlled trial of glycaemic control, with several other studies embedded within it[3,5,6]. Furthermore, recruitment and observation took place over 20 years, from 1977 to 1997, during which time standards of treatment and targets changed dramatically. Thus, the observations of UKPDS 64 and 74 do not, strictly speaking, comprise studies of natural history.

At entry into the UKPDS, 4727 (92.7%) had no nephropathy, 333 (6.5%) had microalbuminuria and 37 (0.7%) had proteinuria. Median follow-up was 10.4 years and during this time a further 867 developed microalbuminuria, 264 proteinuria, 71 elevated plasma creatinine and 14 needed renal replacement therapy (RRT). There were 17 renal deaths[7]. Transition rates between stages ranged from 2.0 to 2.8% per annum, very similar to those published for type 1 diabetes. The prevalence of microalbuminuria and proteinuria combined 15 years after diagnosis was 28%, similar to ~30% for an inception cohort of 277 type 1 diabetic patients in Denmark[8]. The sequence of progression through the defined stages was remarkably consistent, with very small numbers (<0.3%) progressing by two or more stages per year (Fig. 10.1).

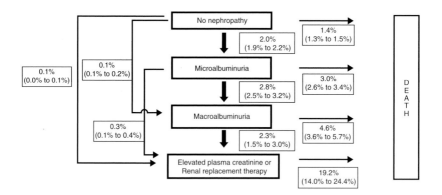

Figure 10.1 Progression through stages of nephropathy for the UK Prospective Diabetes Study cohort, taken from Adler *et al.* [7]. Here, the stages of diabetic nephropathy are defined as follows: no nephropathy [urinary albumin concentration (UAC) ≤ 50 mg/l, plasma creatinine < 175 μmol/l and not requiring dialysis]; microalbuminuria [UAC 51–299 mg/l on two consecutive annual samples or a single UAC value 51–99 mg/l followed by proteinuria or a plasma creatinine > 175 μmol/l or renal replacement therapy (RRT) or death]; proteinuria [UAC > 300 mg/l on two consecutive annual visits or a single value > 300 mg/l followed by a plasma creatinine > 175 μmol/l or RRT or death]; and elevated plasma creatinine or RRT [plasma creatinine > 175 μmol/l on two consecutive visits or a single value > 175 μmol/l followed by RRT, renal transplantation or death]. Rates are per cent progressing per annum.

There was an increasing annual death rate at each stage, ranging from 1.4% for those with no nephropathy to 19.2% for those with an elevated plasma creatinine or needing RRT; most deaths were secondary to cardiovascular disease. The greatly increased mortality in type 2 patients with renal impairment has since been confirmed by others [9]. These data confirmed that patients with macroalbuminuria and/or an elevated plasma creatinine were more likely to die in any year than require RRT. This finding may partly explain why the prevalence of UK dialysis patients with diabetes remains below 20% [2], which is relatively modest by international comparison [1]. The data also show that almost 94% of patients with microalbuminuria remain in this stage in any one year and the majority do not progress to RRT. The median time spent in microalbuminuria without progression to macroalbuminuria or worse is approximately 11 years.

During a median follow up of 15 years, 1449 of 5032 patients (29%) developed an eCC of <60 ml/min/1.73 m^2 (UKPDS 74) [4]. Of interest is the dislocation between albuminuria and creatinine clearance; 51% of those who develop an eCC <60 ml/min/1.73 m^2 never tested positive for albuminuria and a further 16% developed albuminuria subsequently. Only 169 (3.4%) doubled their plasma creatinine during the study, again underlining the relatively slow progression towards end-stage renal failure. It is now widely recognized that type 2 diabetic patients with albuminuria have a range of renal pathology [10]. Thus, there may be several pathological mechanisms causing a reduced eCC, some of which would not necessarily lead to proteinuria.

The relationship between glycaemia and blood pressure with the pre-defined endpoints of the UKPDS were described in UKPDS 35 and 36 [11,12], which looked at the associations between recorded glycaemia and blood pressure and outcome. From the renal standpoint, the combined microvascular endpoint of retinal photocoagulation and vitreous haemorrhage associated with fatal and non-fatal renal failure was used, but data for the surrogate albuminuria endpoint were not included. There was an almost tenfold increase in hazard ratio for this combined endpoint for a glycated haemoglobin (HbA$_{1c}$)$>9.0\%$, compared with $<6.0\%$. Each 1% reduction in HbA$_{1c}$ in UKPDS was associated with a 37% reduction in risk. The relationship with systolic blood pressure (SBP) was also significant, but not as striking, with an approximate twofold increase in hazard ratio at >160 mmHg compared with <120 mmHg. Each 10 mmHg reduction in SBP was associated with a 13% reduction in microvascular endpoints.

Therapy

There was no impact of glycaemic control on the pre-specified renal outcomes (see above). However, at 9 and 12 years there was a significant reduction in the numbers with both microalbuminuria (relative risk (RR) 0.76; 99% confidence interval 0.62–0.91, $P=0.00062$; and RR 0.67; 0.53–0.86, $P<0.0001$; respectively) and proteinuria (RR 0.67; 0.42–1.07, $P=0.026$ and RR 0.66; 0.39–1.10, $P=0.036$; respectively) in the intensively treated patients in the glycaemic control study.

This benefit is less than that seen in type 1 patients in the Diabetes Control and Complications Trial (DCCT) [13, 14], but this is probably a result of the smaller separation in HbA_{1c} between the intensive and conventional groups in the UKPDS (Table 10.1). There was also a significant reduction in the numbers of patients experiencing a doubling in plasma creatinine at 0 to 9 and 0 to 12 years, but the numbers were very small (0.71 vs. 1.76%, $P=0.027$; and 0.91 vs. 3.52%, $P=0.0028$; respectively).

The main UKPDS [3] had embedded within it a trial of anti-hypertensive therapy which randomized patients between 1987 and 1991 [5]. These patients were either on anti-hypertensive therapy with a SBP ≥ 150 mmHg and/or diastolic ≥ 85 mmHg or on no therapy with a SBP ≥ 160 mmHg and/or diastolic ≥ 90 mmHg. A total of 1148 patients were randomized to either tight blood pressure (BP) control ($n=758$, target BP 150/85 mmHg) or less tight BP control ($n=390$, initial target $<200/105$ mmHg, reduced in 1992 to $<180/105$ mmHg). The tight BP group were further randomized to an open-label regimen based upon captopril ($n=400$, 25 mg twice daily, increasing to 50 mg twice daily) or atenolol ($n=358$, 50 mg daily, increasing to 100 mg daily if required). The less tight group were treated with agents other than angiotensin-converting enzyme inhibitors (ACEI) or beta-blockers. The median follow-up was 8.4 years. Mean BP at 9 years was 144/82 mmHg in the 297 tight control patients and 154/87 mmHg in the 156 less tight control group (mean BP for other years with the respective numbers are not shown). Only 56% of patients in the tight control group were at target at 9 years, despite the majority being on two or more anti-hypertensive agents. There was an even balance of patients in both treatment groups in the different glycaemic therapy arms.

The BP study was of shorter duration and had smaller numbers [5]. As in the glycaemia study, there was no impact of tight BP control on the pre-specified renal outcomes. There was, however, a significant reduction in those developing microalbuminuria, but not proteinuria, in the tight control group at 6 years (RR 0.71; 99% confidence interval 0.51–0.99, $P=0.00085$; RR 0.61; 0.31–1.21, $P=0.061$; respectively). There was no significant impact on either endpoint at 9 years, nor for doubling of serum creatinine at any time.

There was no reported difference between captopril or atenolol in terms of any renal endpoint, but no details are provided [14]. The average dose of either captopril or atenolol is not stated. In the BENEDICT Trial of trandolapril vs. verapamil vs. both vs. placebo in hypertensive, normoalbuminuric patients, ACEI was associated with an approximate 50% reduction in new onset microalbuminuria compared with placebo at 3 years (5 vs. 10%). This contrasts with the UKPDS of 18.3% vs. 23.7% (tight vs. less tight BP, $P=0.052$) at 3 years [15]. The achieved mean BP was slightly lower in BENEDICT by 2/0 mmHg in the placebo group and 5/1 mmHg in the trandolapril-treated patients, which may explain part of the discrepancy.

The Irbesartan in MicroAlbuminuric Type 2 patients (IRMA2) study showed that 300 mg irbesartan for 24 months was associated with a 70% reduction in the hazard ratio for development of clinical nephropathy (urinary albumin

Table 10.1 Effect of intensive glycaemic control on cumulative incidence of micro- and macroalbuminuria at 9 years in the DDCT and UKPDS

	n	HbA$_{1c}$	Microalbuminuria	RRR	P	Macroalbuminuria	RRR	P
DCCT								
Primary prevention	346 I 378 C	7.2% I 9.2% C	16% I 27% C	34%	0.04	2.6% I 2.3% C	NS	NS
Secondary prevention	363 I 352 C	7.2% I 9.2% C	26% I 42% C	43%	<0.001	5.2% I 11.3% C	56%	<0.01
UKPDS	2408 I 994 C	7.0% I 7.9% C (10-year data)	19% I 25% C	24%	<0.001	4.4% I 6.5% C	33%	0.026

Microalbuminuria defined as urinary albumin excretion > 28 μg/min from a single timed 4-h sample in the DCCT and median urinary albumin concentration from random samples > 50 mg/l in the UKPDS. Macroalbuminuria defined as > 208 μg/min or > 300 mg/l, respectively.
C, conventional glycaemic therapy; I, intensive; DCCT, Diabetes Control and Complications Trial; HbA$_{1c}$, glycated haemoglobin; RRR, relative risk reduction; UKPDS, UK Prospective Diabetes Study.

excretion >300 mg/day, roughly equivalent to UKPDS definition of proteinuria) vs. placebo (approximately 5 vs. 15% incidence; $P<0.001$) [16]. Achieved
BP was more comparable with that in the UKPDS at 144/83 mmHg in the placebo and 141/83 mmHg in the irbesartan group. There were ~300 patients per
treatment group in BENEDICT and ~ 200 in IRMA2, so the discrepancy with
the captopril-treated patients in UKPDS is puzzling. Both trandolapril and
irbesartan are longer-acting drugs than captopril, so the lack of effect of the
ACEI in the UKPDS may reflect incomplete blockade of the renin–angiotensin
system.

Aetiology

Glycaemia/blood pressure

Both glycaemic [11] and blood pressure [12] control are clearly important for
nephropathy development, although the exponential relationship between
HbA_{1c} and microvascular disease is striking and underlines the greater importance of very poor glycaemic control in the development of retinopathy
(and, by inference, nephropathy). In contrast with type 1 diabetes, hypertension appears to be an early feature of type 2 diabetes (38% were hypertensive
at baseline) [5] and may drive nephropathy development. In type 1 patients,
blood pressure rises as albuminuria increases and may therefore be more of
an effect of renal damage, as well as being an accelerating factor, once nephropathy is developing [17]. SBP was a significant risk factor for both microalbuminuria and proteinuria and impaired renal function in univariate and multivariate models of nephropathy development, resulting in a 15% increased
hazard ratio per 10 mmHg for these endpoints [4].

Ethnicity

Nineteen per cent of patients in the UKPDS were of non-white Europid ethnicity, with the majority being South Asian [3]. There was a twofold hazard
ratio for microalbuminuria in the South Asian patients, but no impact on proteinuria or impaired renal function in either uni- or multivariate analysis [4].
This may reflect a higher mortality in this group, so they cannot be seen to
progress to worsening albuminuria or renal impairment. However, interpretation of these results may be unreliable because the Cockroft–Gault formula
based upon weight and plasma creatinine has not been validated as an accurate measure in this population.

Diet and lipids

There was a significant reduction in albuminuria after 3 months of diet treatment (microalbuminuria reduced from 28 to 17%) in 672 patients (UKPDS X)
[18]. This paper defined an abnormal UAC as >25 mg/l corrected to a urinary
creatinine concentration of 10 mmol/l. The baseline UAC was partly explained
by glycaemia and systolic blood pressure in multivariate analysis (approximately 6.0% of variance each), but only the UAC at baseline related to sub-

sequent reduction (7.9% variance explained). These data are consistent with other reports of short-term changes in albuminuria following diagnosis of type 2 diabetes and glycaemic correction, and probably result from haemodynamic changes secondary to reductions in glycaemia, but perhaps partly as a result of a reduced dietary protein intake.

The association between plasma lipid levels, albuminuria and impaired renal function was described in both early and more recent publications. A total of 585 patients on diet only for 3 years showed little change overall in albuminuria, but fasting plasma glucose, triglycerides and SBP together explained 10% of the variance [19]. Plasma triglycerides (and to a lesser extent total cholesterol) were also associated with the risk of developing microalbuminuria and proteinuria over the whole duration of the study [4]. However, only total and low-density lipoprotein (LDL) cholesterol were linked to a reduced estimated creatinine clearance. Others have described similar relationships between lipids and nephropathy. Meta-analysis of intervention trials in man suggest a benefit of plasma lipid lowering on rate of loss of glomerular filtration rate (GFR) and, to a lesser extent, albuminuria [20].

Genetics

The role of genetic polymorphisms of the angiotensin-converting enzyme (ACE) and angiotensinogen genes in patients with microalbuminuria was explored in 180 patients who had a median UAC of 74 mg/l (interquartile range 54-126) [21]. There was no significant link between microalbuminuria and either the insertion (I) or the deletion (D) polymorphism in the ACE gene, but UAC was higher in those who are homozygous for the DD genotype (88 vs. 67 mg/l, $P < 0.001$), suggesting a possible role in modifying but not initiating the nephropathic process. However, this study was too small to be conclusive.

Caveat

The UKPDS contribution to our understanding of diabetic nephropathy has been substantial. As with any large multi-centre trial, there are caveats and many of these are much easier to spot with hindsight. However, the single annual spot urine sample at a varying time point during the morning and the variation in reporting UAC (sometimes correcting for urinary creatinine and sometimes not); using renal failure and the co-aggregation of renal and retinal events into a joint microvascular endpoint; but most of all the reporting of data sometimes as survival curves and sometimes as rates per number examined at an individual time point can make interpretation of the study difficult. It is also important to remember that these were newly diagnosed type 2 diabetic patients followed for a median of 10.4 years, so conclusions about the effects of glycaemia and blood pressure during longer durations of diabetes have had to be deduced rather than directly observed.

Conclusion

The UKPDS has confirmed that hyperglycaemia and hypertension are the bad companions in our type 2 diabetic patients and their combination greatly increases the risk of developing diabetic nephropathy. This landmark study has demonstrated conclusively that glycaemic correction and tight blood pressure control are critical goals of management in our patients. Moreover, the long-term observation of the UKPDS cohort has shown that cardiovascular mortality increases dramatically as renal function declines. Vigorous correction of cardiovascular risk factors is therefore even more important in those type 2 patients developing renal complications.

Summary

The UK Prospective Diabetes Study is the largest study in type 2 diabetes with pre-specified renal outcomes. The study showed that the natural history of nephropathy in newly diagnosed type 2 diabetic patients was similar to that described previously in those with type 1 diabetes. Around 2% per annum progress from normo- to microalbuminuria [urinary albumin concentration (UAC) > 50 mg/l] and a further 2% from microalbuminuria to clinical grade proteinuria (UAC > 300 mg/l). Mortality rates for those with nephropathy are high, increasing from 1.4% per annum (normoalbuminuria) to 4.6% per annum (clinical grade proteinuria), and to 19.2% per annum for those with renal impairment.

More intensive blood glucose control resulted in both a 33% reduction in relative risk of development of microalbuminuria or clinical grade proteinuria at 12 years, and a significant reduction in the proportion doubling their plasma creatinine (0.91 vs. 3.52%, $P = 0.0028$).

Tighter blood pressure control also reduced microalbuminuria and clinical grade proteinuria; but at 6 years there was no effect on plasma creatinine levels.

These data underline the importance of glycaemic and blood pressure control in type 2 diabetes in order to prevent diabetic nephropathy. Those patients unlucky enough to develop nephropathy need intensive surveillance and correction of cardiovascular risk factors.

References

1 US Renal Data System. USRDS 2007. Annual Data Report. Bethesda, MD: NIH, NIDDK, 2007. Available at www.usrds.org Last accessed 2 September 2008.
2 Ansell D, Feehally J, Feest TG, Tomson C, Williams AJ, Warwick G. UK Renal Registry Report 2007. Bristol, UK: UK Renal Registry.
3 UK Prospective Diabetes (UKPDS) Group. Intensive blood glucose control with sulphonylureas or insulin compared with conventional treatment and risk of complications in patients with type 2 diabetes (UKPDS 33). *Lancet* 1998;352:837-853.

4 Retnakaran R, Cull CA, Thorne KI, Adler AI, Holman RR for the UKPDS Study Group. Risk factors for renal dysfunction in type 2 diabetes. UK Prospective Diabetes Study 74. *Diabetes* 2006;55:1832-1839.

5 UK Prospective Diabetes Study Group. Tight blood pressure control and risk of macrovascular and microvascular complications in type 2 diabetes: UKPDS 38. *Br Med J* 1998;317:703-713.

6 UK Prospective Diabetes Study Group. Efficacy of atenolol and captopril in reducing risk of macrovascular and microvascular complications in type 2 diabetes: UKPDS 39. *Br Med J* 1993;317:713-720.

7 Adler AI, Stevens RJ, Manley SE, Bilous RW, Cull CA, Holman RR on behalf of the UKPDS Group. Development and progression of nephropathy in type 2 diabetes: The United Kingdom Prospective Diabetes Study (UKPDS 64). *Kidney Int* 2003;63:225-232.

8 Hovind P, Tarnow L, Rossing P, Jensen BR, Graae M, Torp I *et al*. Predictors for the development of microalbuminuria and macroalbuminuria in patients with type 1 diabetes: inception cohort study. *Br Med J* 2004;328:1105-1109.

9 Nag S, Bilous R, Kelly W, Jones S, Roper N, Connolly V. All cause and cardiovascular mortality in diabetic subjects increases significantly with reduced estimated glomerular filtration rate (eGFR): 10 years data from the South Tees Diabetes Mortality Study. *Diabet Med* 2007;24:10-17.

10 Fioretto P, Mauer M, Brocco E, Velussi M, Frigato F, Muollo B *et al*. Patterns of renal injury in NIDDM patients with microalbuminuria. *Diabetologia* 1996;39:1569-1576.

11 Stratton IM, Adler AI, Neil AW, Matthews DR, Manley SE, Cull CA *et al*. Association of glycaemia with macrovascular and microvascular complications of type 2 diabetes (UKPDS 35): prospective observational study. *Br Med J* 2000;321:405-412.

12 Adler AI, Stratton IM, Neil AW, Yudkin JS, Matthews DR, Cull CA *et al*. Association of systolic blood pressure with macrovascular and microvascular complications of type 2 diabetes (UKPDS 36): prospective observational study. *Br Med J* 2000;321:412-419.

13 The Diabetes Control and Complications Trial Research Group. The effect of intensive treatment of diabetes on the development of progression of long term complications in insulin dependent diabetes mellitus. *N Engl J Med* 1993;329:977-986.

14 The Diabetes Control and Complications Trial (DCCT) Research Group. Effective intensive therapy on the development and progression of diabetic nephropathy in the Diabetes Control and Complications Trial. *Kidney Int* 1995;47:1703-1720.

15 Ruggenenti P, Fassi A, Ilieva AP, Bruno S, Iliev IP, Brusegan V *et al*. Preventing microalbuminuria in type 2 diabetes. *N Engl J Med* 2004;351:1941-1951.

16 Parving H-H, Lehnert H, Brochner-Motensen J, Gomis R, Andersen S, Arner P. The effect of Irbesartan on the development of diabetic nephropathy in patients with type 2 diabetes. *N Engl J Med* 2001;345:870-878.

17 Microalbuminuria Collaborative Study Group, UK. Risk factors for development of microalbuminuria in insulin dependent diabetic patients: a cohort study. *Br Med J* 1993;306:1235-1239.

18 UK Prospective Diabetes Study (UKPDS) IX: Relationships of urinary albumin and N-acetylglucosaminidase to glycaemia and hypertension at diagnosis of type 2 (non-insulin dependent) diabetes mellitus and after 3 months diet therapy. *Diabetologia* 1993;36:835-842.

19 UK Prospective Diabetes Study (UKPDS) X: Urinary albumin excretion over 3 years in diet-treated type 2 (non-insulin dependent) diabetic patients, and association with hypertension, hyperglycaemia and hypertriglyceridaemia. *Diabetologia* 1993:36:1021-1029.

20 Fried LF, Orchard TJ, Kasiske BL for the Lipids and Renal Disease Progression Meta-analysis Study Group. Effect of lipid reduction on the progression of renal disease: A meta-analysis. *Kidney Int* 2001;59:260-269.

21 Dudley CRK, Keavney B, Stratton IM, Turner RC, Ratcliffe PJ. UK Prospective Diabetes Study XV: Relationship of renin-angiotensin system gene polymorphisms with micro-albuminuria in NIDDM. *Kidney Int* 1995;48:1907-1911.

11   Microvascular disease: what does the UKPDS tell us about diabetic retinopathy?

Eva M. Kohner

Peninsula Medical School, Exeter, UK

Introduction

The first meeting dedicated to diabetic retinopathy was held in Airlie House in Virginia in 1968 [1]. It was an important meeting because it defined all the significant caveats which made the study of diabetic retinopathy possible. Thus, it indicated for the first time the importance of photographic recording and grading of features of retinopathy in contrast to description of observations seen using the monocular ophthalmoscope. It discussed the importance of control of blood glucose, although at that time assessment of control was not possible. Most importantly, consensus was reached on the need for randomized controlled clinical trials for assessing treatments for diabetic retinopathy.

The University Group Diabetes Program reported after this meeting, but both the design and duration of the study were inadequate for valid conclusions to be drawn regarding the role of glycaemic control in vascular complications [2]. In addition, the apparent increased mortality with sulfonylureas was disturbing [3]. It was the outstanding vision and organizing ability of Robert Turner, who realized the importance of quantifying the effect of improved glycaemic control in type 2 diabetes on macro- and microvascular complications and comparing the currently available therapies. He set up a glucose control study which included estimations of glycated haemoglobin (HbA_{1c}) [4, 5].

Retinopathy

The retinopathy component of the UK Prospective Diabetes Study (UKPDS) utilized triennial retinal photographs taken in stereo pairs of four overlapping fields (lateral to macula, macula, disc and nasal), which were graded by

Originally published: Kohner EM. Microvascular disease: what does the UKPDS tell us about diabetic retinopathy? *Diabetic Medicine* 2008; 25 (Suppl. 2): 20–24

trained graders using Early Treatment of Diabetic Retinopathy Study (ETDRS) standard photographs [6]. Microaneurysms were counted in each eye up to four, or as five or more. Photographs were masked to the graders and any disagreements were adjudicated by a senior grader. A computer program assigned ETDRS retinopathy scores based on the detailed findings. Ophthalmoscopy and visual acuity assessed with an ETDRS or Snellen chart were performed yearly. Laser treatment and cataract extraction were carried out in each centre by the consultant ophthalmologists when deemed clinically necessary. The predefined retinopathy endpoints were the occurrence of photocoagulation, vitreous haemorrhage and cataract extraction.

Retinopathy features and their importance

Of the 3709 patients who had retinal photographs taken when they entered the study, 2316 had no retinopathy. In these patients, only 2.6% underwent photocoagulation by 9 years, with a similar outcome for patients who only had microaneurysms in one eye [7]. Of those with five or more microaneurysms, >40% required laser treatment or had vitreous haemorrhage by 12 years [8]. There was an almost linear relationship between the initial number of microaneurysms and the risk of subsequent retinopathy endpoints.

Other retinopathic lesions, including retinal haemorrhages, cotton-wool spots and hard exudates, were less common at entry, but those having ETDRS grade 35 retinopathy at least in one eye had a significantly worse prognosis. Both cotton-wool spots and hard exudates occurred more frequently in patients with less tightly controlled blood pressure [9]. Of the retinopathic lesions assessed, hard exudates were of most interest as they were associated with macular oedema if they occurred in the macular field. At entry, 3.6% of the patients had macular hard exudates, increasing to over 8% by 6 years [10]. Higher blood pressure levels were associated with the presence of hard exudates, but interestingly there was no relationship to total cholesterol levels. More recent analyses have shown that the spatial distribution of macular hard exudates is also related to subsequent visual outcomes [11].

Of the 332 patients who underwent photocoagulation, 72% had laser treatment for maculopathy, 12% for proliferative or pre-proliferative retinopathy, 5.5% for combined maculopathy and pre-proliferative retinopathy and 10.5% for other causes, mainly retinal vein occlusion [7].

Prevention and treatment of diabetic retinopathy

A main aim of the UKPDS was to determine definitively the impact of improved blood glucose control on retinopathy, with cataract extraction included as a minor endpoint. The addition of the blood pressure control arm of the study in a factorial design in hypertensive patients with a mean duration of diabetes of 2.6 years permitted the detailed evaluation of the role of the two main risk factors for retinopathy seen in type 2 diabetic patients.

Glucose control

After the initial 3-month run-in period, patients whose fasting plasma glucose remained >6.0 mmol/l were randomized to a conventional glucose control policy, initially by diet only, or to an intensive glucose control policy by sulphonylurea or insulin, with metformin therapy also a possibility in overweight patients [12]. The median difference in HbA_{1c} achieved between the conventional and intensive groups throughout the study was 0.9%.

At entry to the trial, patients with higher glucose levels were more likely to have retinopathy, possibly reflecting a longer duration of diabetes before diagnosis. When patients were subdivided by tertile of HbA_{1c} at entry, both incidence and progression of retinopathy were significantly lower in the lowest third compared with the other two [13]. When microvascular endpoints were examined in relation to updated HbA_{1c}, there were only 20 per 1000 patient years for HbA_{1c} <6.0%, whereas they occurred in over 30% of patients with HbA_{1c} ≥9.0% by 3 years (Fig. 11.1).

Most importantly, glycaemic exposure over time was shown to be a major factor for the development of retinopathy, with a 31% lower risk of retinopathy for a 1% decrement in HbA_{1c} and no evidence of a U- or J-shaped curve [14]. Thus, reduction of an elevated HbA_{1c} is likely to be worthwhile irrespective of the initial level. In addition to reducing risk of retinopathy, a 1% decrement in HbA_{1c} was associated with a 19% reduced risk of cataract extraction [14].

The importance of total glycaemic exposure is further emphasized by the lower rate of photocoagulation seen in the patients allocated to the intensive

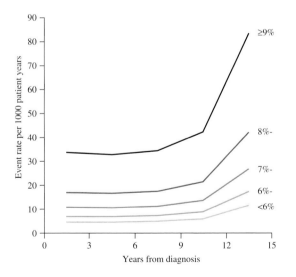

Figure 11.1 Microvascular endpoints and glycated haemoglobin (HbA_{1c}). Relationship between event rate/1000 patient years and HbA_{1c}. UK Prospective Diabetes Study (UKPDS) 35 [14], reproduced with permission. Illustration supplied by Irene Stratton.

control group compared with the conventional control group, although separation between the two groups was only evident after the first 9 years. Thus, not only is the level of glycaemia important, but the duration of exposure is an independent risk factor [15].

Blood pressure control

The blood pressure control study included those UKPDS patients who were already being treated for hypertension or whose blood pressure was over 160/90 mmHg. Patients were allocated at random to tight control with a beta blocker (atenolol) or an angiotensin-converting enzyme (ACE) inhibitor (captopril). Target levels were < 150/85 mmHg in the tight control group, and in the less tight control group initially < 180/105 mmHg, later reduced to < 180/95 mmHg. Unlike the glucose arm of the UKPDS, this was a treat-to-target study with additional anti-hypertensive agents added in a stepwise fashion if blood pressure targets were not met. Thus, many patients in the tight control group were on three or more hypotensive agents. The mean blood pressure in the tight controlled group over the study period was 144/82 mmHg, with little difference between those allocated to beta blocker or ACE inhibitor therapy, compared with 154/87 mmHg in the less tight control group. This 10/5 mmHg difference had a major effect on the risk of many complications.

By 9 years of follow-up, retinopathy levels deteriorated by over eight levels in ETDRS grading in 23% of 152 less tightly controlled patients compared with just under 10% of 384 of those who were tightly controlled, and twice as many reached the endpoint of laser treatment or vitreous haemorrhage. As the commonest cause for laser treatment was maculopathy (a condition associated with visual loss), it was not unexpected that, by 9 years, 20% of the less tight group lost three lines of visual acuity on the ETDRS chart (15 letters) compared with 10% of the tightly controlled patients.

The endpoint of photocoagulation was significantly related to the level of systolic blood pressure reached. For every 10 mm reduction of blood pressure there was an 11% reduction in endpoints. Importantly, there was no lower limit of blood pressure where the benefit was not noted [16].

Duration of high blood pressure was also conducive to reaching endpoints. Calculation of event rate in epidemiological parameters is presented in Fig. 11.2. This illustrates the endpoint or 'event rate' per 1000 patient years in relation to mean blood pressure over the years. Of those with a systolic pressure of less than 130 mmHg, only 10 per 1000 patient years reached an endpoint by 12 years and 20 per 1000 patient years deteriorated to such a level at 15 years. In contrast, in those with blood pressure ≥ 160 mmHg, 45 per 1000 patient years reached an endpoint after 5 years of follow-up. Cataract extraction, as expected, was not influenced by blood pressure control [16].

It is clear from these studies that both control of blood pressure and blood glucose are important in reducing the incidence and progression of diabetic retinopathy (and other microvascular diseases). The interaction of the two is shown in Fig. 11.3. It is important that both be adequately treated [17].

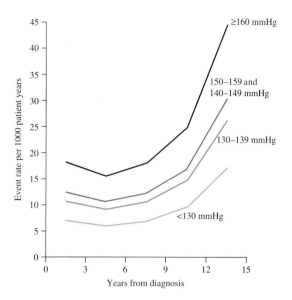

Figure 11.2 Microvascular endpoints and systolic blood pressure. Relationship between event rate/1000 patient years and systolic blood pressure. UK Prospective Diabetes Study (UKPDS) 36 [16], reproduced with permission. Illustration supplied by Irene Stratton.

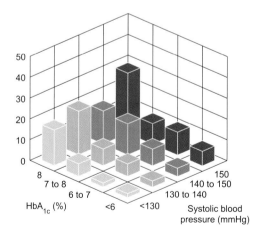

Figure 11.3 Modelled microvascular endpoints. Effect of blood pressure and glucose levels on microvascular complications. Reproduced with permission from UK Prospective Diabetes Study (UKPDS) 75 [17]. Note: Incidence of UKPDS composite endpoints in 4320 patients, as rate per 1000 person-years. Values are for 16 different combinations of updated mean HbA_{1c} and updated mean SBP. Unadjusted rates are shown.

Discussion

The UKPDS is a landmark study in type 2 diabetes, similar to the Diabetes Control and Complications Trial (DCCT) in type 1 patients, which has had a major impact on the management of diabetes [18]. It also established beyond doubt the importance of improving both blood glucose and blood pressure control in minimizing the risk of microvascular complications.

Since it reported in 1998, there have been further advances in the treatment of diabetes, building on the achievements of the UKPDS. With better understanding of the pathological mechanisms involved, targeted treatments for retinopathy are being developed, mostly for advanced forms of retinopathy needing photocoagulation. The demonstration that retinopathy is an inflammatory disease introduced the importance of the role of white blood cells in the evolution of lesions [19]. Ruboxistaurine, a protein kinase $\beta1/2$ inhibitor, was the first laboratory-to-bedside drug which was studied in clinical trials of severe non-proliferative diabetic retinopathy and macular hard exudates. Although there was no significant reduction of progression of retinopathy, there was a 40% reduction in sustained visual loss of three lines or more on the standard Logmar chart [20, 21]. As Ruboxistaurine inhibits Cor-2 enzyme activity (important in the leukocyte action in retinopathy [19]), it might have been more effective if given earlier in the development of diabetic retinopathy.

Evidence for the involvement of the renin–angiotensin system not only in the elevation of blood pressure, but also in regulating vascular permeability and angiogenesis [22], led to the DIRECT study which uses the angiotensin II receptor inhibitor Candesartan in a randomized clinical study of over 5000 patients, which will report at the European Association for the Study of Diabetes (EASD) meeting in 2008.

Lipid-lowering agents, especially statins, are widely used now to reduce macrovascular complications of diabetes. Their use has not yet been tested in a controlled study for retinopathy. As hard exudates and macular oedema are often associated with high lipid levels [23], they may be of benefit in preventing this complication. They are also important in the inhibition of white cell aggregation [24], thus influencing the inflammatory response.

Other drugs are now being studied or developed to prevent progression to sight-threatening retinopathy, such as benfotamine, newer aldose reductase inhibitors and, most importantly, anti-inflammatory agents.

The UKPDS paved the way for the reduction of severe retinopathy and resulted in further research with the ultimate goal of preventing retinopathy altogether.

Summary

The UK Prospective Diabetes Study (UKPDS) was a randomized controlled clinical study which looked at the effect of improved blood glucose and blood pressure control on macro- and microvascular complications in type 2 diabetes. Retinopathy was the commonest microvascular outcome and this article looks at this complication.

Newly diagnosed diabetic patients were randomized to intensive or conventional glycaemic control and a subset of hypertensive patients to tight or less tight blood pressure control. Patients were seen every 3 months in study clinics and retinopathy was assessed by adjudicated grading of triennial colour retinal photographs. Photocoagulation treatment, vitreous haemorrhage and cataract extraction were predefined UKPDS endpoints. Observational analyses of the data were used to examine the relationship of updated mean glycated haemoglobin (HbA$_{1c}$) and mean blood pressure levels to retinopathy outcomes.

The UKPDS showed that both improved glucose control and improved blood pressure control reduced the risk of retinopathy, with a linear relationship between the log hazard ratio for retinopathy and both updated mean HbA$_{1c}$ and updated mean blood pressure. A 1% decrement in HbA$_{1c}$ equated to a 31% reduction in retinopathy and a 10 mmHg decrement in systolic blood pressure equated to an 11% reduction in photocoagulation or vitreous haemorrhage. Evidence of retinopathy at diagnosis, including the presence of microaneurysms only, increased significantly the risk of progression to photocoagulation.

The UKPDS stands out as a landmark study in type 2 diabetes, emphasizing the crucial importance of controlling both blood glucose and blood pressure in order to minimize the risk of developing sight-threatening retinopathy.

References

1 Goldberg MF, Fine SL (Eds). Symposium on the Treatment of Diabetic Retinopathy. Goldberg MF and Fine S (Eds.): US Public Health Service, Arlington, VA, USA, 1969.

2 University Group Diabetes Program. A study of the effects of hypoglycemia agents on vascular complications in patients with adult-onset diabetes. *Diabetes* 1976;25:1129-1153.

3 Scott J, Poffenbarger PL. Pharmacogenetics of tolbutamide metabolism in humans. *Diabetes* 1979;28:41-51.

4 Koenig RJ, Peterson CM, Jones RL, Saudek C, Lehrman M, Cerami A. Correlation of glucose regulation and hemoglobin A$_{1c}$ in diabetes mellitus. *N Engl J Med* 1976;295:417-420.

5 Peterson CM, Jones RL, Dupuis A, Levine BS, Bernstein R, O'Shea M. Feasibility of improved blood glucose control in patients with insulin-dependent diabetes mellitus. *Diabetes Care* 1979;2:329-335.

6 Early Treatment of Diabetic Retinopathy Study Research Group (1991). Fundus photographic risk factors for progression of diabetic retinopathy: ETDRS 12. *Ophthalmology* 1991;98:823-833.

7 Kohner EM, Stratton IM, Aldington SJ, Holman RR, Matthews DR. Relationship between the severity of retinopathy and progression to photocoagulation in patients with type 2 diabetes mellitus in the UKPDS (UKPDS 52). *Diabet Med* 2001;18:178-184.

8 Kohner EM, Stratton IM, Aldington SJ, Turner RC, Matthews DR for the UK Prospective Diabetes Study (UKPDS) Group. Microaneurysms in the development of diabetic retinopathy (UKPDS 42). *Diabetologia* 1999;42:1107-1112.

9 Matthews DR, Stratton IM, Aldington SJ, Holman RR, Kohner EM for the UK Prospective Diabetes Study (UKPDS) Group. Risks of progression of retinopathy and vision loss related to tight blood pressure control in type 2 diabetes mellitus (UKPDS 69). *Arch Ophthalmol* 2004;122:1631-1640.

10 Stratton IM, Matthews DR, Aldington SJ, Holman RR. Risk factors for presence of hard exudates at diagnosis of type 2 diabetes and after 6 years. Abstract no. 116. Presented at the International Diabetes Federation (IDF) meeting in Paris, France, 24–28 August 2003. Also published in *Diabetologia* 2003;46(Suppl 2):A42.

11 Stratton IM, Scanlon PH, Holman RR, Lipinski SL, Aldington SJ. Visual loss related to the position of hard exudates in diabetic maculopathy in type 2 diabetes in the UKPDS. Presented at the Diabetes UK Meeting, Glasgow, UK, 16–18 March 2007. Also published in *Diabetice Medicine* 2007;24(Suppl 1):90.

12 UK Prospective Study Group. Intensive blood-glucose control with sulphonylureas or insulin compared with conventional treatment and risk of complications in patients with type 2 diabetes (UKPDS 33). *Lancet* 1998;352:837-853.

13 Stratton IM, Kohner EM, Aldington SJ, Turner RC, Holman RR, Manley SE *et al.* for the UKPDS Group. UKPDS 50: Risk factors for incidence and progression of retinopathy in type II diabetes over 6 years from diagnosis. *Diabetologia* 2001;44:156-163.

14 Stratton IM, Adler AI, Neil HAW, Matthews DR, Manley SE, Cull CA *et al.* on behalf of the UK Prospective Diabetes Study Group. Association of glycaemia with macrovascular and microvascular complications of type 2 diabetes (UKPDS 35): prospective observational study. *Br Med J* 2000;321:405-411.

15 Stevens RJ, Stratton IM, Holman RR. UKPDS 58: Modeling glucose exposure as a risk factor for photocoagulation in type 2 diabetes. *J Diabetes Complications* 2002;16:371-376.

16 Adler AI, Stratton IM, Neil HAW, Yudkin JS, Matthews DR, Cull CA *et al.* on behalf of the UK Prospective Diabetes Study Group. Association of systolic blood pressure with macrovascular and microvascular complications of type 2 diabetes (UKPDS 36): prospective observational study. *Br Med J* 2000;321:412-419.

17 Stratton IM, Cull CA, Adler AI, Matthews DR, Neil HAW, Holman RR. Additive effects of glycaemia and blood pressure exposure on risk of complications in type 2 diabetes: a prospective observational study (UKPDS 75). *Diabetologia* 2006;49:1761-1769.

18 Nathan DM, Buse JB, Davidson MB, Ferranini E, Holman RR, Sherwin R *et al.* Management of hyperglycemia in type 2 diabetes: a consensus algorithm for the initiation and adjustment of therapy. Update regarding thiazolidinediones: a consensus statement from the American Diabetes Association and the European Association for the Study of Diabetes. *Diabetes Care* 2008;31:173-175.

19 Chibber R, Ben-Mahmud BM, Chibber S, Kohner EM. Leukocytes in diabetic retinopathy. *Curr Diab Rev* 2007;3:3-14.

20 The PKC-DRS Study Group. The effect of ruboxistaurin on visual loss in patients with moderately severe to very severe non-proliferative diabetic retinopathy: initial results of the Protein Kinase C ß inhibitor Diabetic Retinopathy Study (PKC-DRS). *Diabetes* 2005;54:2188-2197.

21 Aiello LP, Davis MD, Girach A, Kles KA, Milton RC, Sheetz MJ *et al.* for the PKC-DRS 2 Group. Effect of ruboxistaurin on visual loss in patients with diabetic retinopathy. *Ophthalmology* 2006;113:2221-2230.

22 Sjølie AK, Porta M, Parving HH, Bilous R, Klein R: The DIRECT Programme Study Group. The DIabetic REtinopathy Candesartan Trials (DIRECT) Programme: baseline characteristics. *J Renin Angiotensin Aldosterone Syst* 2005;6:25-32.

23 Chew EY, Klein ML, Ferris FL 3rd, Remaley NA, Murphy RP, Chantry K *et al*. Association of elevated serum lipid levels with retinal hard exudate in diabetic retinopathy. Early Treatment Diabetic Retinopathy Study (ETDRS report 22). *Arch Ophthalmol* 1996;114:1079-1084.

24 Yamagishi S, Nakamura K, Matsui T, Sato T, Takeuchi M. Potential utility of statins, 3-hydroxy-3-methylglutaryl coenzyme A reductase inhibitors in diabetic retinopathy. *Med Hypotheses* 2006;66:1919-1921.

12 Ethnic diversity in type 2 diabetes

Timothy M. E. Davis

School of Medicine and Pharmacology, Fremantle Hospital, University of Western Australia, Perth, Australia

Introduction

Ethnicity is well recognized as a major influence on the risk and nature of diabetes. As the UK population is increasingly multi-ethnic [1], the UK Prospective Diabetes Study (UKPDS) has provided the opportunity to examine, from the time of diagnosis, the relationship between ethnicity and important aspects of type 2 diabetes, including glycaemic control, other vascular risk factors and complications [2-5]. These analyses have implications for clinical management as well as healthcare planning and community education.

Based on the 2001 Census, the main ethnic/racial groups in the UK general population are Whites (92%), Asians (4%) and Blacks (2%) [1]. The majority of the Asians are from India, Pakistan and Bangladesh, and most of the Blacks are from the Caribbean. These data were ascertained from self-identification, an approach that was also used to categorize ethnicity in the UKPDS. The percentages of White Caucasians (WC), Indian-Asians (IA) and Afro-Caribbeans (AC) in the 5098 patients recruited to the UKPDS were 82, 10 and 8%, respectively [2]. When considered against UK general population data [1], these figures suggest that the prevalence of type 2 diabetes in the main UK minorities is high compared with that in the majority WC group. Previous epidemiological studies show the same ethnicity-specific increased risk of diabetes [6-10]. These various observations provide evidence that the ethnic categories in the UKPDS cohort are broadly representative of diabetes in the UK population.

What does UKPDS add to what is already known?

Demographic and biophysical features

Demographic and biophysical characteristics of UKPDS patients are summarized by ethnic group in Table 12.1. The IA patients were a mean ≥2 years

Originally published: Davis TME. Ethnic diversity in type 2 diabetes. *Diabetic Medicine* 2008; 25 (Suppl. 2): 52–56

Table 12.1 Baseline characteristics of UK Prospective Diabetes Study (UKPDS) patients categorized by ethnicity

	Males			Females		
	White Caucasian	Indian-Asian	Afro-Caribbean	White Caucasian	Indian-Asian	Afro-Caribbean
Number	2425	362	219	1752	172	168
Age (years)	52±9	47±9**	52±7	53±9	48±9**	50±7**
Smoking (never/ex-/current; %)†	21/44/35	42/21/37**	36/31/33*	44/27/29	90/4/6**	85/7/8**
Alcohol (never/occasional/regular+heavy; %)†	15/56/29	47/36/17**	14/62/24	30/65/5	72/28/0**	39/57/4
Physical fitness (sedentary/moderate/active; %)†	17/32/51	40/32/28**	16/30/54	21/38/41	38/44/18**	14/41/45
Social class (I or II/III/IV or V; %)†	30/44/26	35/38/27	10/38/52**	21/45/34	24/34/42	19/28/53**
Height (cm)†	174±7	169±7**	171±7**	160±6	155±6**	160±6
Body mass index (kg/m^2)‡	28.2±4.8	25.9±3.8**	26.6±3.4**	30.7±6.6	28.4±4.8**	29.5±4.8*
Waist–hip ratio‡	0.94±0.06	0.95±0.05**	0.93±0.05	0.86±0.08	0.88±0.08*	0.86±0.07
Systolic blood pressure (mmHg)‡	134±19	123±16**	133±18	140±21	129±19**	139±20
Diastolic blood pressure (mmHg)‡	82±10	79±16*	84±10*	84±11	81±9*	86±11**
Treated for hypertension (%)†	13	5*	16	23	10*	25
Fasting plasma glucose (mmol/l)†	11.6±3.6	11.0±3.5	12.3±3.7*	12.4±3.8	11.9±3.4	12.8±3.7
HbA$_{1c}$ (%)†	9.2±2.2	9.0±2.2	9.9±2.5**	9.3±2.2	9.0±2.1	10.0±2.6**
Pancreatic β-cell function (%)‡	36 (17–74)	44 (21–90)**	27 (13–55)**	35 (17–71)	39 (20–75)*	28 (14–57)**
Insulin sensitivity (%)‡	24 (14–41)	22 (13–35)**	30 (18–51)**	21 (12–35)	20 (12–32)*	25 (16–40)**
Plasma total cholesterol (mmol/l)†	5.5±1.1	5.3±1.0	5.3±1.2	5.9±1.2	5.3±1.0**	5.6±1.3
Plasma LDL cholesterol (mmol/l)†	3.6±1.0	3.4±0.9	3.5±1.1	3.9±1.1	3.5±0.9**	3.8±1.3
Plasma HDL cholesterol (mmol/l)‡	1.01±0.24	1.00±0.24	1.13±0.26**	1.09±0.25	1.08±0.24	1.23±0.28**
Plasma triglycerides (mmol/l)‡	1.8 (1.0–3.2)	1.9 (1.1–3.2)	1.3 (0.8–2.1)**	1.8 (1.1–3.0)	1.7 (1.0–2.7)	1.3 (0.8–2.0)**

Data are, unless otherwise stated, mean±SD or geometric mean and (SD interval). Data taken from [2].
*$P<0.01$, **$P<0.001$ vs. White Caucasian group; P-values obtained †after adjustment for age; ‡after adjustment for age and body mass index.
HbA$_{1c}$, glycated haemoglobin; HDL, high-density lipoprotein; LDL, low-density lipoprotein; SD, standard deviation.

younger than WC and AC patients when categorized by gender [2]. They were also shorter but had a greater waist–hip ratio. This latter finding suggests that IA patients with type 2 diabetes are more prone to central obesity and this could reflect the more sedentary lifestyle found in this group [2]. However, IA patients were the least likely to smoke and consume alcohol. Compared with both WC and IA patients, those from an AC ethnic background were more likely to come from social classes IV and V.

Glycaemic control

At diagnosis, the WC and IA patients in the UKPDS had a similar mean fasting plasma glucose (FPG) and glycated haemoglobin (HbA_{1c}) [2] (see Table 12.1). However, the IA subjects were less insulin sensitive with a lower %S assessed from homoeostasis model assessment (HOMA) and had greater pancreatic β-cell function (higher HOMA %B) [2]. The AC patients had the highest FPG and HbA_{1c} of the three ethnic groups, with the lowest %B and highest %S [2]. The relative insulin resistance in IA and insulin sensitivity in AC patients reflected similar findings in other studies of type 2 diabetes [11, 12] and, in the case of IA subjects, a relatively sedentary lifestyle and central obesity. However, when examined longitudinally [4], there were no significant differences in the change in FPG or HbA_{1c} in the three groups over a period of 9 years. Overall, these data suggest that ethnicity does not play a role in the glycaemic progression seen in type 2 diabetes despite the group-specific differences in the initial underlying pathophysiology.

Non-glycaemic vascular risk factors

Blood pressure levels and the prevalence of hypertension were lowest in the IA subjects at baseline [2] (see Table 12.1). Mean systolic and diastolic blood pressure levels were ≥10 mmHg and ≥5 mmHg, respectively, below those in the other two groups regardless of gender. Diastolic blood pressure was significantly higher (by 2 mmHg) in the AC vs. the WC patients and there was electrocardiographic and radiological evidence that this was associated with a greater prevalence of left ventricular hypertrophy [2]. By contrast, available UK data at the time of publication of the baseline data in 1994 suggested that there were no differences in blood pressure between IA and WC [13, 14] or between WC and AC [15] diabetic patients. As with glycaemic control, there were no consistent between-group differences in the changes in blood pressure over the 9 years after UKPDS entry [4].

Plasma lipid profiles were similar in WC and IA patients at UKPDS entry, but AC patients had significantly higher mean plasma high-density lipoprotein (HDL) cholesterol concentrations (by ≥0.12 mmol/l) and lower mean plasma triglycerides (by ≥0.4 mmol/l) than the other two groups, regardless of gender [2] (see Table 12.1). These differences became more marked during the first 3 years of diabetes and then plateaued [4]. Baseline and follow-up plasma low-density lipoprotein (LDL) concentrations were similar across the three groups, except for a lower mean in IA females at UKPDS entry [2]. Although the results of other studies support the more favourable plasma lipid profile in AC vs. WC patients with type 2 diabetes seen in the UKPDS [15], and which parallels the relatively high insulin sensitivity in the AC group [12], available non-UKPDS data from IA patients suggest that both total and HDL cholesterol are lower than in WC patients [16].

Complications

Consistent with the UKPDS exclusion criteria, which included macroangio-pathy, nephropathy and severe retinopathy [17], relatively few patients had a complication at entry and there were no between-group differences [2]. Published UKPDS data relating to the subsequent development of complications in the three main ethnic groups are, however, restricted to myocardial infarction (in which a specific analysis of the relationship with ethnicity was performed [3]) and nephropathy (in which ethnicity was included as one of a range of potential independent associates [5]).

In the case of fatal or non-fatal myocardial infarction, an interim analysis performed more than 18 months before the UKPDS closed out, showed that AC patients had a substantial (70%) and highly statistically significant reduction in risk relative to WC patients after adjustment for the major cardiovascular risk factors [3] (see Table 12.2). While this finding paralleled results from other studies in the UK [15] and USA [18], the non-significant hazard ratio for IA vs. WC patients for the same endpoint (1.2 with 95% confidence intervals 0.9 to 1.7 after adjustment for baseline cardiovascular risk factors) appeared at odds with other UK studies suggesting an increased cardiovascular risk in IA patients [19, 20]. Because of this discrepancy and the lack of sufficient statistical power to reveal a modest increased risk, the UKPDS authors concluded that a larger and/or longer study was needed [3].

A recent analysis of complete UKPDS data examined predictors of the development of albuminuria (micro- and macroalbuminuria) and renal impairment (a reduction in creatinine clearance (CrCl) to $\leq 60\,ml/min/1.73\,m^2$ and a doubling of the serum creatinine) [5]. Apart from doubling of serum creatinine, an endpoint with limited numbers (see Table 12.2), IA ethnicity was associated with these outcomes independent of other variables including blood pressure [5]. The adjusted hazard ratios for microalbuminuria, macroalbuminuria and a CrCl $\leq 60\,ml/min/1.73\,m^2$ indicated that IA ethnicity was associated with twice the risk of each relative to WC ethnicity after adjustment for age, sex and other endpoint-specific explanatory variables [5] (see Table 12.2). This is consistent with the results of previous studies from UK communities with relatively large numbers of people from an IA ethnic background [21–23].

What is the overall status of this topic now?

Barnett and colleagues have recently highlighted features in IA individuals in the UK that might account for their increased risk of type 2 diabetes and premature vascular disease [24]. Some of these (younger age at presentation of

Table 12.2 Numbers of UK Prospective Diabetes Study (UKPDS) patients in the three main ethnic groups with fatal or non-fatal myocardial infarction (median follow-up 8.7 years) and four renal endpoints (median follow-up 15 years), together with incidence rates and hazard ratios adjusted for other age, sex and other explanatory variables

	Number of patients			Events per 1000 patient years			Hazard ratio (95% confidence interval)	
	White Caucasian	Indian-Asian	Afro-Caribbean	White Caucasian	Indian-Asian	Afro-Caribbean	Indian-Asian vs. White Caucasian	Afro-Caribbean vs. White Caucasian
Myocardial infarction analysis [3]	4101	490	383					
Fatal or non-fatal myocardial infarction	499	45	14	14.6	11.8	4.0	1.2 (0.9-1.7)	0.3* (0.2, 0.6)
Nephropathy analysis [5]	1834	184	149					
Microalbuminuria	620	88	48	33.3	48.0	30.6	2.0* (1.6, 2.6)	1.2 (0.9, 1.7)
Macroalbuminuria	178	28	13	9.5	15.3	8.3	2.1* (1.4, 3.2)	1.1 (0.6, 1.9)
CrCl ≤60 ml/min/1.73 m^2	496	44	44	26.6	24.0	28.0	1.9* (1.4, 2.7)	1.3 (0.9, 1.8)
Doubling of serum creatinine	51	5	2	2.7	2.7	1.3	1.5 (0.6, 3.9)	0.4 (0.1, 1.7)

*$P < 0.001$.

CrCl, creatinine clearance.

type 2 diabetes, central obesity and reduced physical activity), but not others (high levels of triglycerides and low levels of HDL cholesterol), were present in the UKPDS IA patients [2], while there was a relatively low prevalence of hypertension which persisted but did not worsen in longitudinal analyses [4] and which has been found subsequently by others [25]. Given this mix of favourable and unfavourable risk factors and concerns relating to the statistical power of interim analyses of the relationship between IA ethnicity and myocardial infarction [3], further assessment of data from longer follow-up of UKPDS patients would be valuable. Such analyses are given further credence by frequent reports that microalbuminuria is an important independent cardiovascular risk factor in type 2 diabetes [26] and the finding that IA ethnicity was an independent predictor of albuminuria in the UKPDS [5].

The reasons behind the strong association between IA ethnicity and both renal impairment and albuminuria remain unclear [5, 21-23]. This was also the case for the favourable coronary artery disease outcome in AC patients, which was present even after adjustment for the higher plasma HDL cholesterol and lower plasma triglycerides in this group. Chaturvedi and colleagues [15] have suggested that lower central obesity and the related greater insulin sensitivity may be responsible. However, hyperinsulinaemia did not independently predict vascular outcome in the UKPDS [17,27]. Other genetic, cultural, lifestyle or environmental influences may be responsible, perhaps underlying more favourable coagulation and/or lipoprotein particle size profiles in AC patients. Nevertheless, recent meta-analyses have emphasized the major contribution of established vascular risk factors (including hypertension, dyslipidaemia and smoking) to coronary heart disease, while questioning the significance of recently identified risk factors such as C-reactive protein, fibrinogen, lipoprotein(a) and homocysteine [28]. Whether these novel risk factors have a disproportionate impact in non-WC ethnic/racial groups remains to be established.

Conclusions

The UKPDS has provided a unique opportunity to assess ethnic differences in important aspects of type 2 diabetes. It is hoped that further analyses, such as of the relationship between ethnicity and other major complications such as stroke and retinopathy, will be published in future. Although the simple classification of ethnicity used in the UKPDS could be criticized because it does not take into account variables other than self-identification that could be important determinants of ethnic background [29], it has nevertheless revealed clinically significant differences in vascular risk and outcome between the main ethnic groups identified using the same methodology as that employed by the UK government [1]. These differences were seen when clinical management was standardized under the UKPDS protocol, but there is evidence that such uniformity does not exist in the context of usual diabetes care in the community, especially in the case of disadvantaged IA patients [30]. Such inequality could prove a strong barrier to improving the quality of life and outcome of all UK patients with type 2 diabetes.

Summary

The present review assesses published data relating to the main ethnic groups in the UK Prospective Diabetes Study (UKPDS), namely White Caucasians (WC; 82% of the cohort), Indian-Asians (IA; 10%) and Afro-Caribbeans (AC; 8%).

At entry, the IA patients were younger than WC and AC patients, had a greater waist–hip ratio and more sedentary lifestyle, but had the lowest prevalence of hypertension and current smoking. The AC patients had the poorest glycaemic control but the most favourable lipid profile. The differences in modifiable vascular risk factors did not change over 9 years of follow-up. Consistent with UKPDS exclusion criteria, few patients had complications at baseline and there were no between-group differences. An interim analysis of incident fatal/non-fatal myocardial infarction (median followup 8.7 years) showed that the AC patients had a 70% lower risk than WC after adjustment for explanatory variables and that IA patients had a similar risk to WC. An analysis of complete albuminuria and renal failure data (median follow-up 15 years) showed that IA ethnicity was independently associated with an increased risk.

There are sustained ethnic differences in the nature of diabetes, including vascular risk factors. AC patients had a substantially reduced risk of myocardial infarction that was not explained by their more favourable lipid profile, while IA patients were more likely to develop nephropathy than WC and IA patients. Longer follow-up is needed to determine whether the increased macrovascular risk observed in IA patients in other studies is replicated in the UKPDS cohort.

Acknowledgement

The author is grateful to Kerensa Thorne for providing the nephropathy data summarized in Table 12.2.

References

1 UK Government. National Statistics Online. Focus on ethnicity and identity. Available from http://www.statistics.gov.uk/focuson/ethnicity Last accessed 2 September 2008.
2 UK Prospective Diabetes Study Group. UK Prospective Diabetes Study. XII: Differences between Asian, Afro-Caribbean and white Caucasian Type 2 diabetic patients at diagnosis of diabetes. UK Prospective Diabetes Study Group. *Diabet Med* 1994;11:670-677.
3 UK Prospective Diabetes Study Group. Ethnicity and cardiovascular disease. The incidence of myocardial infarction in white, South Asian, and Afro-Caribbean patients with type 2 diabetes (UK Prospective Diabetes Study 32). *Diabetes Care* 1998;21:1271-1277.

4 Davis TM, Cull CA, Holman RR. Relationship between ethnicity and glycemic control, lipid profiles, and blood pressure during the first 9 years of type 2 diabetes: UK Prospective Diabetes Study (UKPDS 55). *Diabetes Care* 2001;24:1167-1174.

5 Retnakaran R, Cull CA, Thorne KI, Adler AI, Holman RR. Risk factors for renal dysfunction in type 2 diabetes: UK Prospective Diabetes Study 74. *Diabetes* 2006;55:1832-1839.

6 Mather HM, Keen H. The Southall Diabetes Survey: prevalence of known diabetes in Asians and Europeans. *Br Med J (Clin Res Ed)* 1985;291:1081-1084.

7 Forrest RD, Jackson CA, Yudkin JS. Glucose intolerance and hypertension in north London: the Islington Diabetes Survey. *Diabet Med* 1986;3:338-342.

8 Samanta A, Burden AC, Fent B. Comparative prevalence of non-insulin-dependent diabetes mellitus in Asian and white Caucasian adults. *Diabetes Res Clin Pract* 1987;4:1-6.

9 Pais P, Pogue J, Gerstein H, Zachariah E, Savitha D, Jayprakash S *et al*. Risk factors for acute myocardial infarction in Indians: a case–control study. *Lancet* 1996;348:358-363.

10 Nazroo JY. The Health of Britain's Ethnic Minorities. London: Policy Studies Institute, 1997.

11 Mohan V, Sharp PS, Cloke HR, Burrin JM, Schumer B, Kohner EM. Serum immunoreactive insulin responses to a glucose load in Asian Indian and European type 2 (non-insulin-dependent) diabetic patients and control subjects. *Diabetologia* 1986;29:235-237.

12 Chaiken RL, Banerji MA, Pasmantier R, Huey H, Hirsch S, Lebovitz HE. Patterns of glucose and lipid abnormalities in black NIDDM subjects. *Diabetes Care* 1991;14:1036-1042.

13 Nicholl CG, Levy JC, Mohan V, Rao PV, Mather HM. Asian diabetes in Britain: a clinical profile. *Diabet Med* 1986;3:257-260.

14 Samanta A, Burden AC, Jagger C. A comparison of the clinical features and vascular complications of diabetes between migrant Asians and Caucasians in Leicester, U.K. *Diabetes Res Clin Pract* 1991;14:205-213.

15 Chaturvedi N, Jarrett J, Morrish N, Keen H, Fuller JH. Differences in mortality and morbidity in African Caribbean and European people with non-insulin dependent diabetes mellitus: results of 20-year follow-up of a London cohort of a multinational study. *Br Med J* 1996;313:848-852.

16 Game FL, Jones AF. Ethnicity and risk factors for coronary heart disease in diabetes mellitus. *Diabetes Obes Metab* 2000;2:91-97.

17 UK Prospective Diabetes Study Group. Intensive blood-glucose control with sulphonylureas or insulin compared with conventional treatment and risk of complications in patients with type 2 diabetes (UKPDS 33). UK Prospective Diabetes Study (UKPDS) Group. *Lancet* 1998;352:837-853.

18 Folsom AR, Szklo M, Stevens J, Liao F, Smith R, Eckfeldt JH. A prospective study of coronary heart disease in relation to fasting insulin, glucose, and diabetes. The Atherosclerosis Risk in Communities (ARIC) Study. *Diabetes Care* 1997;20:935-942.

19 Chaturvedi N, Fuller JH. Ethnic differences in mortality from cardiovascular disease in the UK: do they persist in people with diabetes? *J Epidemiol Community Health* 1996;50:137-139.

20 Mather HM, Chaturvedi N, Fuller JH. Mortality and morbidity from diabetes in South Asians and Europeans: 11-year follow-up of the Southall Diabetes Survey, London, UK. *Diabet Med* 1998;15:53-59.

21 Burden AC, McNally PG, Feehally J, Walls J. Increased incidence of end-stage renal failure secondary to diabetes mellitus in Asian ethnic groups in the UK. *Diabet Med* 1992;9:641-645.

22 Mather HM, Chaturvedi N, Kehely AM. Comparison of prevalence and risk factors for microalbuminuria in South Asians and Europeans with Type 2 diabetes mellitus. *Diabet Med* 1998;15:672-677.

23 Fischbacher CM, Bhopal R, Rutter MK, Unwin NC, Marshall SM, White M *et al*. Microalbuminuria is more frequent in South Asian than in European origin populations: a comparative study in Newcastle, UK. *Diabet Med* 2003;20:31-36.

24 Barnett AH, Dixon AN, Bellary S, Hanif MW, O'Hare JP, Raymond NT *et al*. Type 2 diabetes and cardiovascular risk in the UK south Asian community. *Diabetologia* 2006;49:2234-2246.

25 Baskar V, Kamalakannan D, Holland MR, Singh BM. Does ethnic origin have an independent impact on hypertension and diabetic complications? *Diabetes Obes Metab* 2006;8:214-219.

26 Basi S, Lewis JB. Microalbuminuria as a target to improve cardiovascular and renal outcomes in diabetic patients. *Curr Diab Rep* 2007;7:439-442.

27 Turner RC, Millns H, Neil HA, Stratton IM, Manley SE, Matthews DR *et al*. Risk factors for coronary artery disease in non-insulin dependent diabetes mellitus: UK Prospective Diabetes Study (UKPDS 23). *Br Med J* 1998;316:823-828.

28 Canto JG, Iskandrian AE. Major risk factors for cardiovascular disease: debunking the 'only 50%' myth. *J Am Med Assoc* 2003;290:947-949.

29 Azuonye IO. Differences in mortality between African Caribbean and European people with non-insulin dependent diabetes. Authors' method of assigning ethnic group was wrong. *Br Med J* 1997;314:303-304; author reply 304-305.

30 Soljak MA, Majeed A, Eliahoo J, Dornhorst A. Ethnic inequalities in the treatment and outcome of diabetes in three English Primary Care Trusts. *Int J Equity Health* 2007;6:8.

13 UKPDS—modelling of cardiovascular risk assessment and lifetime simulation of outcomes

Amanda I. Adler

Institute of Metabolic Sciences, Addenbrooke's Hospital, Cambridge, UK

Introduction

The UK Prospective Diabetes Study (UKPDS), as a clinical trial (or experiment), tested whether allocated treatments for diabetes reduced the incidence of complications of type 2 diabetes. However, the UKPDS also contributed substantially to our understanding of how diabetic complications evolved by recording the characteristics, and then outcomes, of more than 5000 individuals with type 2 diabetes followed initially for up to 20 years, and now 30 years. Using epidemiological (observational) methods, UKPDS investigators described, in quantitative terms, the relationship between risk factors and the occurrence over time of diabetic complications. The resulting models estimated via numerical equations what might occur in populations or individuals with type 2 diabetes, based on what did occur in the UKPDS.

These models contributed in particular to the understanding of cardiovascular disease (CVD). At the start of the UKPDS, the reality that diabetes increased the risk of CVD was widely recognized, was the object of a major trial [1], but was understudied. By the end of the UKPDS trial, the US National Institutes of Health had cardiovascular disease in diabetes as a high priority [2] and epidemiological studies and trials existed [3–9] but many questions remained.

This paper summarizes, for the general reader, the substantial contribution of the UKPDS to modelling of coronary, cerebrovascular and peripheral arterial disease and death in type 2 diabetes. These models defined two main areas: the identification of risk factors and the development of mathematical models to simulate the incidence and consequences of diabetic complications.

Originally published: Adler AI. UKPDS—modelling of cardiovascular risk assessment and lifetime simulation of outcomes. *Diabetic Medicine* 2008; 25 (Suppl. 2): 41–46

Identification of risk factors

Coronary disease

UKPDS 23 [10] found risk factors for coronary artery disease (CAD) including angina, myocardial infarction (MI) and death. It documented that hyperglycaemia increased the risk of CAD independently of other risk factors, recognizing that individuals with hyperglycaemia might also have higher values of other risk factors. The magnitude of the risk increase—estimated at roughly 11% for each 1% (1 unit) increase in glycated haemoglobin (HbA_{1c})—therefore reflected the contribution of glycaemia itself. Although the UKPDS was limited to individuals with diabetes, as hyperglycaemia characterizes and defines diabetes, this important finding helped explain why individuals with diabetes experience disproportionately high rates of CVD.

The investigators modelled glycaemia in a natural, inherently easy-to-understand way as a continuous variable. Thus, the hazard ratio, as an estimation of relative risk, compared the risk associated with a given HbA_{1c} level (e.g. 9.0%) to the next lower integer level (e.g. 8.0%). This avoided the comparison of 'poor' vs. 'good' glycaemic control, a cruder categorization and one that invariably changes over time.

The paper proposed a quintet of potentially modifiable predictors, including high levels of low-density lipoprotein (LDL), low levels of high-density lipoprotein cholesterol (HDL), hypertension, hyperglycaemia and smoking. By estimating the hazard ratios for each variable, one could also estimate the theoretical benefit from altering these measures in trials and, if proven effective, in practice. For example, as a 1-mmol/l increase in LDL increased risk for MI by roughly one-third, trialists might expect an equivalent risk decrease from therapies that lowered LDL by this amount, all other things being equal.

This paper also showed that, compared with the general population of England and Wales, UKPDS participants were more likely to die earlier, a difference that was greater in women than in men, and confirmed findings elsewhere [11].

Meta-analysts have subsequently validated that the relationship between hyperglycaemia and CAD is of the magnitude documented in UKPDS 23 [12]. Trials have now proven that lowering LDL reduces the incidence of myocardial infarction and stroke [13, 14], lending credence to the causal role of LDL. The disproportionate decrease in life expectancy attributable to diabetes in women has, with other evidence, led to a women-centred government-sponsored international forum [15], publications [16] and public health initiatives [17]. Epidemiologists continue to test for new risk factors for CHD in diabetes [18].

Stroke

UKPDS 29 [19] identified risk factors for stroke. Measured at entry into the UKPDS, increasing age, male sex, elevated systolic blood pressure and presence of atrial fibrillation increased the risk of stroke, while glycaemia and albuminuria did not. These findings suggested that risk factors for stroke in the general population also increased risk in individuals with diabetes, in whom they were more common. Subsequent analyses evaluating HbA$_{1c}$ over time [20] found that glycaemia increased the incidence of stroke, but to a lesser degree than for other diabetic complications. Despite the size of the UKPDS cohort, the incidence of stroke may have been too small to identify all risk factors tested.

Peripheral vascular disease (PVD)

UKPDS 59 [21] identified predictors for peripheral vascular (arterial) disease, defined by combinations of low ankle–arm blood pressure indices, absent pulses and symptomatic claudication, and showed that peripheral and coronary artery disease shared risk factors. The paper proposed that hyperglycaemia was even more strongly associated with PVD than with CAD. In addition to glycaemia, dyslipidaemia, smoking, blood pressure and age, existing CVD increased risk. Male sex did not increase risk for PVD, unlike for coronary disease in diabetes, but similar to PVD in the general population [22].

Insulin resistance

UKPDS 47 and UKPDS 67 [23, 24] explored the role of insulin resistance in the occurrence of CVD. As the UKPDS measured fasting plasma insulin, one could estimate insulin resistance using the simple homeostatic model assessment (HOMA) or the simpler insulin level model. These papers found no association between insulin resistance measured at diagnosis of diabetes, or after a dietary run-in period, with subsequent CVD. If HOMA or insulin levels inaccurately reflected insulin resistance, then these papers may have failed to find a real difference. If insulin resistance, or hyperinsulinaemia per se, increases the risk of CVD in diabetes, then these studies did not find it. Of note, within the main UKPDS trial, the group randomized to insulin did not have a higher rate of myocardial infarction compared with other therapies [25].

Metabolic syndrome

Following the emergence of the metabolic syndrome (which grouped documented and potential risk factors for CVD) and following controversy surrounding its prognostic value [26], UKPDS 78 [27] tested whether patients with type 2 diabetes with metabolic syndrome developed complications more frequently than patients without metabolic syndrome, but with type 2 diabetes. The prevalence of metabolic syndrome, depending on definition, ranged from one-quarter to two-thirds of UKPDS patients. UKPDS 78 showed that, regardless of definition, the metabolic syndrome conferred a greater risk of macrovascular, but not microvascular disease. The probability that an individual with metabolic syndrome developed CVD over the approximate 10 years of follow-up did not exceed 20%, the level at which British guidelines of the time advocated treatment with lipid lowering. The investigators did not address whether a label of metabolic syndrome predicted CVD better than did a label of high (calculated absolute) risk. Whether the designation of metabolic syndrome predicted CVD more accurately than diabetes itself could not be addressed, as all patients in the UKPDS had diabetes.

Simulation of the incidence of diabetic complications

Mathematical models, as representations of reality, exist throughout all fields in science, engineering and finance and are now increasingly common in medicine. In chronic disease, modelling can simulate the clinical and economic implications of an intervention under a variety of scenarios. Modellers choose and vary the numerical parameters relating to epidemiological, therapeutic, economic and behavioural assumptions, amongst others. In diabetes, modelling provides an alternative when trials do not exist, when the duration of a trial is less than lifelong or when trials include participants markedly different in character from one's own patients. Modelling, with an aim of informing clinical decisions, guideline development and health spending, frees practitioners and decision makers from the frustrations of repeatedly collating and interpreting copious amounts of information.

Some physicians inherently distrust models as 'unreal', yet most likely use them routinely. Randomized clinical trials customarily employ modelling (e.g. proportional hazards modelling) to report treatment effects. Body mass index models adiposity. David Eddy has written 'Models use the same facts that physicians use ... the difference between the model and the physician's head is that the model is far more powerful and accurate...' [28].

In addition to the models identifying risk factors, the UKPDS investigators created models that forecast the incidence of complications. Equivalent to absolute risk and expressed as a rate, incidence reflects the probability of an event occurring within a period of time. Also, by estimating time free of complications under different circumstances, the model could estimate benefits of given treatments.

Life expectancy

UKPDS 46 [29] describes the methods used to estimate life expectancy attributable to lowering blood glucose or blood pressure. Ideal therapies prolong life and improve its quality. In the UKPDS, the trial of control of blood pressure increased time to death, but the main trial of blood glucose control did not [25, 30]. Clinical trials may not last long enough to detect a difference in mortality, even if one exists. As such, it is common for modellers to extrapolate beyond the period of the trial.

To determine life expectancy from study entry, the model estimated the probability of a patient of a given age and duration of diabetes dying in a given year (discrete-time modelling). As the UKPDS excluded relatively ill patients, the modellers minimized potential biases by excluding data from early in the trial. As people usually prefer benefits sooner rather than later, and as the costs related to therapies for diabetes accrue years before the benefits, the model employed discounting. To test the performance of the model (to validate it), the authors developed the model based on 8 years of follow-up and tested whether it predicted accurately the events in the subsequent 4 years. The authors calculated a range of plausible values (confidence intervals), thereby acknowledging that the anticipated life expectancies were estimates.

The difference in life expectancy associated with blood glucose and blood pressure control each ranged from approximately 6 months to 1 year. The UKPDS modellers assumed that once the trial has ended, both groups would experience a similar death rate. However, the difference in life expectancy may be even greater, as evidence from type 1 diabetes shows that similar assumptions may not hold [31].

In a separate paper, investigators studied case fatality from CVD [32]. Characteristics distinguishing those who died from those who survived after an MI included older age, duration of diagnosed diabetes, higher values of glycaemia, higher systolic blood pressure and the presence of albuminuria. Those who did not survive their strokes were more likely to be female, have higher values of HbA_{1c}, higher systolic blood pressure, higher white blood cell counts and were more likely to have had a previous stroke. All factors independently increased case fatality.

UKPDS Risk Engine

The UKPDS Risk Engine combined mathematical equations into a model that estimates the absolute risk of incident cardiovascular disease [29, 32–34] (Fig. 13.1). Models existed prior to the UKPDS Risk Engine, but differed; for instance, they may not have considered a measure of glycaemia [35]. A model may have derived estimates from small, localized populations, which might not have been appropriate for the populations to which it was ultimately applied [36]. The Risk Engine incorporates HbA_{1c} and values from the multi-ethnic UKPDS population, increasing its potential contribution to British (and similar) diabetic populations.

However, the generalizability of the models may be limited by the exclusion or under-representation in the UKPDS, as with other trials, of the very ill, those with recent myocardial infarctions, the very elderly and those who cannot or do not consent. Even so, the variables included in the Risk Engine probably increase risk equivalently in these groups. The Risk Engine does not include medications, which could bias estimates for individuals on treatments with beneficial effects unmeasured by variables in the Risk Engine.

There are myriad potential uses for the UKPDS Risk Engine. Modellers can incorporate it into other models (hence the metaphorical 'engine'). Clinical trialists can use it to help determine sample size. Actuaries and epidemiologists can use it to forecast disease distribution and health planners to direct scarce resources to high-risk patients. Clinicians can use it, relieving them of calculating intuitively the absolute risk of CVD in a given patient. Risk estimation permits a more defined estimate than 'high risk' and communicating risk to patients may itself encourage health [37].

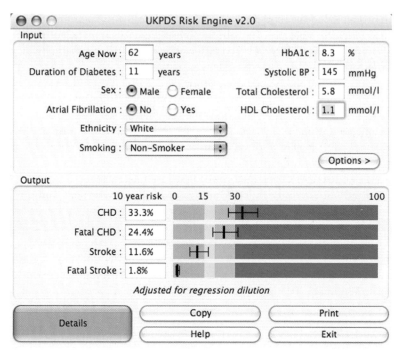

Figure 13.1 UKPDS Risk Engine (v2.0) for estimation of fatal and non-fatal coronary heart disease (CHD) and stroke risks. Available at www.dtu.ox.ac.uk/riskengine. Last accessed 2 September 2008.

In actuality, the UKPDS Risk Engine and the UKPDS Outcomes Model described below have been used extensively by modellers [38] to determine risk in individuals with diabetes [39] and to calculate cardiovascular risk as a primary outcome in interventional trials [40]. It has been used to assess the cost-effectiveness of screening for diabetes [41] as well as for treatments [42]. It has inspired, in part, the development of new risk equations for non-British populations [43, 44] and has forecast/confirmed results of clinical trials [38]. The development of models for cardiovascular disease in diabetes continues—some with increasing complexity [45], and others assess contributions of more-recently identified risk factors [46].

Outcomes Model

The UKPDS Outcomes Model [47] comprehensively models four functions: (i) the incidence and interdependence of complications; (ii) the changes in risk factors over time; (iii) the quality of life associated with each complication; and (iv) the costs associated with complications and therapies (Fig. 13.2). The Outcomes Model integrates proportional hazards equations to estimate the risk of developing one or more of seven diabetes-related complications. These include ischaemic heart disease (angina), MI (fatal or non-fatal), heart

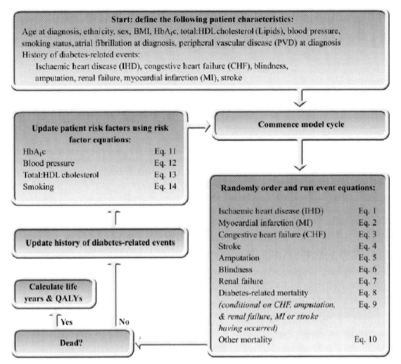

Figure 13.2 UKPDS Outcomes Model; reproduced with permission from Clarke et al. Diabetologia 2004 [47]. BMI, body mass index; HbA$_{1c}$, glycated haemoglobin; HDL, high-density lipoprotein; LDL, low-densitylipoprotein; QALYs, quality-adjusted life years.

failure, stroke (fatal or non-fatal), blindness, renal failure and lower extremity amputation. The model takes into account biochemical and demographic variables, as well as co-existing complications. The model can be used to measure quality of life (utility) for each complication by assigning a numerical value to each. Zero represents death and 1.0 full health. Standard values for a range of complications have been estimated based on a survey of UKPDS patients. Overall, the average utility for patients without complications was 0.78 while patients with complications reported lower values (UKPDS 62 [48]). The model combines length of life with quality of life numerically as quality-adjusted life years (QALYs).

The Outcomes Model simulates the burden of complications for a hypothetical population with type 2 diabetes. The model, which runs in 1-year cycles, predicts the series of events that unfold over time. Using the model, one can determine life expectancy, quality-adjusted life expectancy and cost-effectiveness, and calculate event rates. As a result, the model has particular value to health economists. Information about access to the UKPDS Outcomes Model and the Risk Engine is available on the Diabetes Trials Unit website [49].

In summary, taking advantage of the wealth of longitudinal data provided by the UKPDS, investigators used epidemiological, clinical, statistical, economic and computing expertise to build models and contribute to the understanding of the risks for, and incidence of, the cardiovascular complications of type 2 diabetes. These equations combine to simulate and predict the clinical and economic consequences of diabetes. In future, the need for modelling in type 2 diabetes will grow, along with the appreciation of the complexity of the disease and the decisions required to treat it successfully and economically.

Summary

Although known principally as a clinical trial, the UK Prospective Diabetes Study (UKPDS) provided longitudinal data which helped define the natural history of cardiovascular complications in type 2 diabetes. Using clinical, epidemiological, statistical and economics methods, UKPDS investigators developed mathematical models that helped define predictors (risk factors) for cardiovascular disease including angina, myocardial infarction, stroke, peripheral vascular disease and death in type 2 diabetes. The UKPDS made clearer the contributions to risk of age, hyperglycaemia, elevated blood pressure, adverse blood lipids and smoking. Equations were developed, combined and incorporated into the UKPDS Risk Engine and the UKPDS Outcomes models. For example, the UKPDS risk engine—version 2—estimates that a white 62-year-old man with 11 years of type 2 diabetes, a glycated haemoglobin of 8.3%, a systolic blood pressure of 145 mmHg and total and high-density lipoprotein cholesterol values of 5.8 and 1.1 mmol/l who did not smoke has a 33% chance of having overt coronary heart disease within 10 years. These models contribute to the estimation of risk and/or health outcomes adjusted for quality of life for use by, amongst others, clinicians, trialists, health planners, guideline developers and health economists.

References

1 Meinert C, Knatterud G, Prout T, Klimt C. A study of the effects of hypoglycemic agents on vascular complications in patients with adult-onset diabetes. *Diabetes* 1970;19:789-830.

2 Department of Health and Human Services National Institutes of Health National Heart Lung, and Blood Institute. Special emphasis panel on the prevention and treatment of cardiovascular disease in diabetes. Available at http://www.nhlbi.nih.gov/meetings/workshops/sepminfn.txt Last accessed 2 September 2008.

3 Kannel W, McGee D. Diabetes and cardiovascular disease. The Framingham study. *J Am Med Assoc* 1979;241:2035-2038.

4 Klein R. Hyperglycemia and microvascular and macrovascular disease in diabetes. *Diabetes Care* 1995;18:258-268.

5 Stamler J, Vaccaro O, Neaton JD, Wentworth D. Diabetes, other risk factors, and 12-year cardiovascular mortality for men screened in the Multiple Risk Factor Intervention Trial. *Diabetes Care* 1993;16:434-444.

6 Welborn T, Wearne K. Coronary heart disease incidence and cardiovascular mortality in Busselton with reference to glucose and insulin concentrations. *Diabetes Care* 1979;2:154-160.

7 Manson JE, Colditz GA, Stampfer MJ *et al.* A prospective study of maturity-onset diabetes mellitus and risk of coronary heart disease and stroke in women. *Arch Intern Med* 1991;151:1141-1147.

8 Haffner SM, Mitchell BD, Stern MP, Hazuda HP. Macrovascular complications in Mexican Americans wtih type II diabetes. *Diabetes Care* 1991;14:665-671.

9 Lehto S, Ronnemaa T, Haffner S, Pyorala K, Kallio V, Laakso M. Dyslipidemia and hyperglycemia predict coronary heart disease events in middle-aged patients with NIDDM. *Diabetes* 1997; 48:1354-1359.

10 Turner R, Millns H, Neil H *et al.* UK Prospective Diabetes Study. UKPDS 23: Risk factors for coronary artery disease in non-insulin dependent diabetes. *Br Med J* 1997;316:823-828.

11 Barrett-Connor E, Wingard DL. Sex differences in ischemic heart disease mortality in diabetics: A prospective population-based study. *Am J Epidemiol* 1983;118:489-496.

12 Selvin E, Marinopoulos S, Berkenblit G *et al.* Meta-analysis: glycosylated hemoglobin and cardiovascular disease in diabetes mellitus. *Ann Intern Med* 2004;141:421-431.

13 Collins R, Armitage J, Parish S, Sleigh P, Peto R. MRC/BHF Heart Protection Study of cholesterol-lowering with simvastatin in 5963 people with diabetes: a randomised placebo-controlled trial. *Lancet* 2003;361:2005-2016.

14 Colhoun HM, Betteridge DJ, Durrington PN *et al.* Primary prevention of cardiovascular disease with atorvastatin in type 2 diabetes in the Collaborative Atorvastatin Diabetes Study (CARDS): multicentre randomised placebo-controlled trial. *Lancet* 2004;364:685-696.

15 Alliance for European Diabetes Research. *Diabetes Research in Women 2007.* Available at http://www.cdc.gov/diabetes/pubs/women/ Last accessed 2 September 2008.

16 Centers for Disease Control and Prevention. *Diabetes and Women's Health Across the Life Stages: A Public Health Perspective.* Atlanta, GA: Centers for Disease Control and Prevention, 2001.

17 US Department of Health and Human Services. The National Agenda for Public Health Action: The National Public Health Initiative on Diabetes and Women's Health. Available at http://www.hhs.gov/news/press/2003pres/20030325.html Last accessed 2 September 2008.

18 Alssema M, Dekker JM, Kuivenhoven J *et al.* Elevated cholesteryl ester transfer protein concentration is associated with an increased risk for cardiovascular disease in women, but not in men, in Type 2 diabetes: the Hoorn Study. *Diabet Med* 2007;42:117-123.

19 Davis T, Millns H, Stratton I, Holman R, Turner R. Risk factors for stroke in type 2 diabetes. *Arch Intern Med* 1999;159:1097.

20 Stratton I, Adler A, Neil H *et al.* Association of glycaemia with macrovascular and microvascular complications of Type 2 diabetes (UKPDS 35). *Br Med J* 2000;321:405-411.

21 Adler A, Stevens R, Neil H, Holman R, Turner R. Hyperglycaemia and other potentially modifiable risk factors for peripheral vascular disease in Type 2 diabetes. *Diabet Med* 1999;16:16.

22 Selvin E, Erlinger T. Prevalence of and risk factors for peripheral arterial disease in the United States: results from the National Health and Nutrition Examination Survey, 1999–2000. *Circulation* 2004;100:738-743.

23 Adler A, Neil H, Manley S, Holman R, Turner R. Hyperglycemia and hyperinsulinemia at diagnosis of diabetes and their association with subsequent cardiovascular disease in the UK Prospective Diabetes Study (UKPDS 47). *Am Heart J* 1999;138:353-359.

24 Adler AI, Levy JC, Matthews DR, Stratton IM, Hines G, Holman RR. Insulin sensitivity at diagnosis of Type 2 diabetes is not associated with subsequent cardiovascular disease (UKPDS 67). *Diabet Med* 2005;22:306-311.

25 UKPDS Group. Intensive blood-glucose control with sulphonylureas or insulin compared with conventional treatment and risk of complications in patients with type 2 diabetes (UKPDS 33). *Lancet* 1998;352:837-853.

26 Gale EA. The myth of the metabolic syndrome. *Diabetologia* 2005;48:1679-1683.

27 Cull CA, Jensen CC, Retnakaran R, Holman RR. Impact of the metabolic syndrome on macrovascular and microvascular outcomes in type 2 diabetes mellitus: UK Prospective Diabetes Study 78. *Circulation* 2007;116:2119-2126.

28 Eddy DM. *Clinical Decision Making; From Theory to Practice*. Sudbury: Jones and Bartlett Publishers, 1996.

29 Stevens R, Adler A, Gray A, Briggs A, Holman R. Life-expectancy projection by modelling and computer simulation (UKPDS 46). *Diabetes Res Clin Pract* 2000;50:S5-13.

30 UKPDS Group. Tight blood pressure control and risk of macrovascular and microvascular complications in type 2 diabetes (UKPDS 38). *Br Med J* 1998;317:703-713.

31 The Epidemiology of Diabetes Interventions and Complications (EDIC) Research Group. Retinopathy and nephropathy in patients with Type 1 diabetes 4 years after a trial of intensive therapy. *N Engl J Med* 2000;342:381-389.

32 Stevens R, Coleman R, Adler A, Stratton I, Matthews D, Holman R. Risk factors for myocardial infarction case fatality and stroke case fatality in type 2 diabetes—UKPDS 66. *Diabetes Care* 2004;27:201-207.

33 Stevens R, Kothari V, Adler A, Stratton I, Holman R. The UKPDS Risk Engine: a model for the risk of coronary heart disease in type 2 diabetes (UKPDS 56). *Clin Sci* 2001;101:671-679.

34 Kothari V, Stevens RJ, Adler AI *et al*. UKPDS 60: risk of stroke in type 2 diabetes estimated by the UK Prospective Diabetes Study risk engine. *Stroke* 2002;33:1776-1781.

35 Anderson KM, Odell PM, Wilson PW, Kannel WB. Cardiovascular disease risk profiles. *Am Heart J* 1991;121:293-298.

36 Eastman RC, Javitt JC, Herman WH *et al*. Model of complications of NIDDM. I. Model construction and assumptions. *Diabetes Care* 1997;20:725-734.

37 Roach P, Marrero D. A critical dialogue: communicating with type 2 diabetes patients about cardiovascular risk. *Vasc Health Risk Manag* 2005;1:301-307.

38 The Mount Hood Modeling Group. Computer modeling of diabetes and its complications: a report on the Fourth Mount Hood Challenge Meeting. *Diabetes Care* 2007;30:1638-1646.

39 Ezenwaka CE, Nwagbara E, Seales D *et al*. Prediction of 10-year coronary heart disease risk in Caribbean type 2 diabetic patients using the UKPDS risk engine. *Int J Cardiol* 2008; 10.

40 Lauritzen T, Griffin S, Borch-Johnsen K, Wareham N, Wolffenbuttel B, Rutten G. The ADDITION study: proposed trial of the cost-effectiveness of an intensive multifactorial intervention on morbidity and mortality among people with Type 2 diabetes detected by screening. *Int J Obes Relat Metab Disord* 2000;24:6-11.

41 Glumer C, Yuyun M, Griffin S *et al*. What determines the cost-effectiveness of diabetes screening? *Diabetologia* 2006;49:1536-1544.

42 Shearer AT, Bagust A, Liebl A, Schoeffski O, Goertz A. Cost-effectiveness of rosiglitazone oral combination for the treatment of type 2 diabetes in Germany. *Pharmacoeconomics* 2006;24:35-48.

43 Folsom AR, Chambless LE, Duncan BB, Gilbert AC, Pankow JS. Prediction of coronary heart disease in middle-aged adults with diabetes. *Diabetes Care* 2003;26:2777-2784.

44 Yang X, So WY, Kong AP *et al.* Development and validation of a total coronary heart disease risk score in type 2 diabetes mellitus. *Am J Cardiol* 2008;101:596-601.

45 Eddy DM, Schlessinger L. Archimedes: a trial-validated model of diabetes. *Diabetes Care* 2003;11:3093-3101.

46 Ridker P, Buring J, Rifai N, Cook N. Development and validation of improved algorithms for the assessment of global cardiovascular risk in women: the Reynolds Risk Score. *J Am Med Assoc* 2007;297:611-619.

47 Clarke PM, Gray AM, Briggs A *et al.* A model to estimate the lifetime health outcomes of patients with type 2 diabetes: the UK Prospective Diabetes Study Outcomes Model (UKPDS 68). *Diabetologia* 2004;47:1747-1759.

48 Clarke P, Gray A, Holman R. Estimating utility values for health states of type 2 diabetic patients using the EQ-5D (UKPDS 62). *Med Decis Making* 2002;22:340-349.

49 Diabetes Trials Unit. Website. Available at http://www.dtu.ox.ac.uk Last accessed 2 September 2008.

14   The economic analyses of the UK Prospective Diabetes Study

Alastair M. Gray[1] and Philip Clarke[2]

[1] Health Economics Research Centre, Department of Public Health, University of Oxford, Oxford, UK
[2] School of Public Health, University of Sydney, New South Wales, Australia

Introduction

In the current era, it is common for large outcome trials to include in their protocol a planned economic analysis, including arrangements for the prospective collection of resource use and quality-of-life information during the study, and often including plans for extrapolating beyond the end of the study period by means of some form of modelling. Indeed, such analyses are frequently insisted upon by funding bodies such as the Medical Research Council (MRC) and NHS Health Technology Assessment programme. The UK Prospective Diabetes Study (UKPDS) was conceived and initiated in an earlier epoch and no explicit arrangements for economic analyses were made initially. However, in 1992 Robert Turner had the foresight to anticipate that such analyses could be fundamentally important to the study, and to the reception of its findings, and approached a small group of economists then at Wolfson College, Oxford (Alastair Gray, Alistair McGuire and Paul Fenn) to discuss how a full programme of economic analysis could be designed and funded. The group was later augmented at different stages by Maria Raikou, Rosa Legood, Andy Briggs and Philip Clarke.

It was quickly apparent that the UKPDS presented exceptional opportunities for economic analyses. Firstly, it would be possible to make the first reliable estimates of the cost-effectiveness of each of the main trial interventions by calculating the incremental costs of each intervention compared with the alternative (e.g. intensive vs. less intensive blood glucose control) in relation to the incremental effect. Secondly, it would be possible to look at the impact of the major diabetes-related complications on treatment costs and on quality of life, without many of the biases to which observational studies are prone. Thirdly, access to longitudinal data from such a large and carefully observed population would enable the development of longer-term models with applications far beyond the trial itself.

Originally published: Gray AM, Clarke P. The economic analyses of the UK Prospective Diabetes Study. *Diabetic Medicine* 2008; 25 (Suppl. 2): 47–51

It was also apparent that some additional information would have to be collected as soon as possible. In particular, a survey of all patients in the study would be required to obtain information on quality of life, using the kind of instrument useful to economists to estimate utility and hence quality-adjusted life years, the most obvious instrument being the EuroQol EQ-5D. A similar survey would be required on non-hospital resource use, particularly on use of primary care and domiciliary services.

A detailed economic analysis plan was developed and submitted to the MRC, but neither it, the Nuffield Provincial Hospitals Trust, the (then) British Diabetic Association nor the Department of Health could be persuaded to lend support. Eventually a package of funding was put in place via an unrestricted grant from a consortium of interested companies. Without this support, none of the many analyses described below would have been possible.

Data

The use of healthcare resources by patients was routinely collected during the UKPDS. For each patient, data were collected on the dose and duration of all main drug therapies, including anti-hypertensive drugs (captopril and atenolol and other anti-hypertensive therapies), all drugs used for treating diabetes (insulin, sulfonylureas, metformin), the number of home blood glucose tests and whether the patient was taking other therapies such as aspirin. Information on the date, duration and reasons for any hospital admission were also collected at each clinic visit.

This routine data collection was supplemented by information on use of non-inpatient healthcare resources collected by questionnaires distributed at routine clinic visits between January 1996 and September 1997 and by post to those who did not attend a clinic during that period. This questionnaire collected information from 3488 patients on all home, clinic and telephone contacts with general practitioners, nurses, chiropodists, opticians, dieticians and ophthalmic and other clinics over the previous 4 months.

A unit cost was then assigned to each type of resource use, using information from a variety of sources: for example, costing of drugs was based on the British National Formulary and hospital episodes were costed using the average cost per inpatient day across all hospitals in England, adjusted for specialty and length of stay. A cost per patient could then be calculated for any period during their participation in the study.

As the perspective of the economic evaluations was that of the healthcare purchaser, only direct health service costs were considered. Some adjustments were made to observed patterns of resource use, primarily to remove protocol-driven elements such as trial visits and replace them with estimated costs in a standard practice setting.

Initial cost-effectiveness studies

The first objective of the economic analyses was to estimate the incremental cost-effectiveness of the main study interventions: intensive vs. conventional blood glucose control and tight vs. less tight blood pressure control. These showed that tight blood pressure control had an incremental cost of approximately £800 per life year gained [1] and, similarly, that intensive blood glucose control would cost around £8000 for each additional year free of complications [2]. A subsequent analysis of metformin therapy showed that it not only significantly improved survival, but also produced net savings, as the cost of the drug, at least in the UK, was more than outweighed by savings from reduced complications [3]. Analysis of another study comparison, atenolol vs. captopril in hypertensive patients, indicated that captopril was significantly more expensive as a result of additional drug costs but also because of significantly more and longer hospitalizations, but provided no additional benefit [4].

To conclude this initial phase of work, a study was undertaken to estimate the total cost of implementing improved glycaemic and blood pressure control along the lines demonstrated by the UKPDS to the entire population of people with type 2 diabetes in England [5]. In part, this analysis was performed to assist the Department of Health in formulating and costing a National Service Framework for diabetes. The resulting estimate was that these interventions could be universally provided at an annual cost of around £100m, which would represent less than 1% of the planned incremental growth in UK healthcare spending over the period 2003–2008 and would be similarly affordable in other healthcare systems.

Estimating the quality of life and cost impact of diabetes-related complications

The initial UKPDS economic evaluations gave an estimate of likely cost-effectiveness, but had a number of limitations. They were either confined to the within-trial period, and therefore did not fully capture the longer-term costs and benefits of interventions, or did estimate overall remaining life expectancy (e.g. in UKPDS 40 [1]) but using a model (described in Stevens *et al.*, UKPDS 46 [6]) that predicted the future probability of three main types of event—coronary heart disease, stroke (either fatal or non-fatal) or other death—but not a full set of all main trial endpoints. There was, therefore, a need for a more comprehensive model. This created other needs: while life expectancy is widely recognized as a useful measure of benefit [7], it is also important to capture the effect complications have on quality of life. The quality-adjusted life year (QALY) is a favoured measure of health outcome amongst many health economists because it captures survival and quality of life and permits comparison of cost-effectiveness across the widest possible range of different interventions and disease areas [8]. The QALY is usually measured on a 'utility' scale in which 0 represents death and 1 represents full health in each year of life and hence the resulting cost-effectiveness studies are sometimes described as cost–utility analyses.

To proceed to a set of cost–utility analyses of UKPDS interventions, it was therefore necessary to have a comprehensive model and estimates of the quality of life and cost impact of all main diabetes complications.

The impact on utility of different diabetes-related complications was examined in UKPDS 62 [9] using a survey of 3192 patients still participating in the study in 1997. Although this survey was cross-sectional, detailed trial information existed on the occurrence and timing of complications amongst all patients and hence it was possible to estimate the immediate and longer-term impact of each type of complication on quality of life. The analyses showed that the mean utility for patients free of complications was 0.78 (i.e. 78% of full health). Patients with a history of complications had lower utility levels and the following decrements or reductions from the baseline utility were estimated: −0.055 for coronary heart disease (CHD); −0.090 for ischaemic heart disease (IHD); −0.164 for stroke; −0.108 for heart failure; −0.280 for amputation; and −0.074 for blindness in one eye.

A similar analysis was conducted to estimate the effect of these complications on costs [10]. This reported, for each complication, the observed effect on all healthcare costs in the 12 months following the event and in each subsequent year. This approach was not therefore an estimate simply of the immediate costs of a particular episode of care, but rather an estimate of the overall effect of a complication on the frequency and cost of all healthcare use, in the short and longer term. This type of 'event-based cost analysis' is ideally suited to many forms of economic modelling and, in response to widespread interest, a simple piece of complication-costs software was made available on the Internet (www.herc.ox.ac.uk).

The UKPDS Outcomes Model

Having derived estimates of the quality of life and cost impact of complications, it was then necessary to develop a comprehensive and reliable simulation model. Simulation models in diabetes are valuable tools as outcomes can take years and sometimes decades to eventuate (e.g. progression to renal failure), rendering it both costly and potentially unethical to undertake clinical trials of sufficient duration to obtain long-term outcomes on all patients. The primary purpose of these models is to estimate the future occurrence of diabetes-related complications and quantify outcomes in terms of mean life expectancy or mean quality-adjusted life expectancy and future healthcare costs. These simulation models can be used to inform cost-effectiveness analyses of different disease management strategies, especially when evidence of the impact of interventions on surrogate endpoints is limited or where evidence from clinical trials has to be extrapolated over patients' lifetimes [11].

The UK Prospective Diabetes Outcomes Model reported in UKPDS 68 [12] is a computer simulation model developed using patient level information from the UKPDS and has been developed as a tool to assist in the economic evaluation of any new intervention that alters the main risk factors of patients with type 2 diabetes.

The Outcomes Model involves probabilistic discrete-time computer simulation and is based on an integrated system of parametric proportional hazards risk equations. These were estimated from diagnosis of diabetes using individual patient data. The current version of the model includes both macrovascular (e.g. myocardial infarction, other ischaemic heart disease, congestive heart failure, stroke) and selected microvascular (e.g. blindness) complications.

Cost–utility analyses of UKPDS policies

An initial application of the UKPDS Outcomes Model was to provide a set of cost–utility estimates for all the main UKPDS interventions [13], in which both healthcare costs and expected QALYs were estimated for patients' remaining lifetimes.

A useful way of representing the combinations of cost-and-effect differences for each intervention is to plot the changes on a cost-effectiveness plane, which simultaneously represents the difference in the mean costs (on the y-axis) and life expectancy (on the x-axis) [14]. The origin on this plane represents the costs and outcomes associated with conventional therapy and so each intervention is measured relative to this point (Fig. 14.1). Based on the cost-effectiveness results reported in UKPDS72 [13], the discounted cost of an intensive blood glucose control policy with insulin or sulfonylureas was on average £884 more per patient and the discounted benefits gained were 0.15 QALYs, giving a cost:utility ratio of £6028 per QALY gained. The discounted cost of intensive blood glucose control policy with metformin in overweight patients was on average £1021 (95% confidence interval −4291, 2249) less than the conventional policy and had a longer discounted life expectancy of 0.55 QALYs, making this treatment strategy both cost saving and more effective. Finally, the discounted cost of tight blood pressure control policy was on average £108 more per patient and discounted life expectancy was 0.29 QALYs longer, giving a cost–utility ratio of £369 per QALY gained [13].

Based on these results, all three interventions have a cost per QALY gained that is very much lower than other accepted uses of healthcare resources. In the UK, interventions appear to have a high chance of acceptance by the National Institute for Clinical Excellence (NICE) if their cost-effectiveness is more favourable than the £20000–£30000 range per QALY, although this threshold is not universally accepted.

Further use of the UKPDS Outcomes Model

The Outcomes Model is now being used worldwide by a number of research groups to evaluate interventions in diabetes and for other applications. For example, it has been used to evaluate the cost-effectiveness of several diabetes

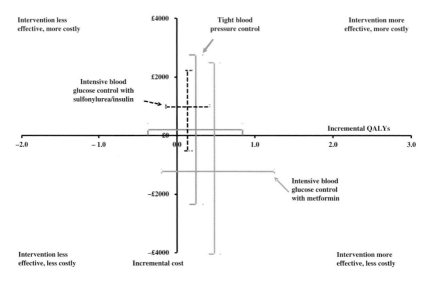

Figure 14.1 Costs and quality-adjusted life years (QALYs) gained (means and 95% confidence intervals) of intensive blood glucose control with metformin compared with no metformin, tight blood pressure control compared with less tight control and intensive blood glucose control with sulfonylurea/insulin compared with less intensive control. £UK 2004.

programmes for the Ontario Ministry of Health and Long-Term Care in Canada [15]. Other researchers have incorporated some or all of the set of reported risk equations that form the basis of the Outcomes Model in their own simulation models (e.g. Tilden *et al.* [16]). Such studies will allow the validity of the model to be assessed and compared. The UKPDS Outcomes Model performed well compared with other diabetes simulation models in one validation exercise predicting rates of cardiovascular disease for patients in the Collaborative Atorvastatin Diabetes Study (CARDS) [17] and was also able successfully to estimate the effects of therapies in the PROactive study [18].

Concluding remarks

The UKPDS economic analysis programme has been a highly productive collaborative enterprise. Few if any other large trials have resulted in such a range of peer-reviewed economic outputs. Nevertheless, some limitations should be noted. Firstly, had the analyses been designed prospectively from the start, some improvements could have been made in data collection: in particular, the EQ-5D and resource use questionnaires could have been administered at baseline and on an annual basis to generate panel data, rather than as a single cross-sectional survey, which may have resulted in under-recording of some resource use categories. Secondly, the trial commenced in the 1970s and was completed in the 1990s and some aspects of care have since changed: for example, angioplasty and coronary surgery have become much more common, lengths of stay for many conditions have fallen and new therapies have become common (statins were barely used by the UKPDS population but are now the standard of care). Thirdly, the patients recruited to the UKPDS—as in many trials—excluded patients with pre-existing complications, resulting in a study cohort that at least initially was not representative of newly diagnosed patients. Fourthly, despite the long follow-up period compared with most trials, comparatively few patients by the end had developed multiple complications, end-stage renal disease and the complex arrays of health problems found in patients in administrative datasets and routine practice.

Despite these limitations, the economic analyses derived from the UKPDS have produced relatively reliable new evidence to clinicians, policymakers and researchers on the consequences of diabetes and the cost-effectiveness of interventions, thereby assisting the development of treatment guidelines and improved standards of care. The analyses also provide good illustrations of a number of methodological innovations. Finally, the UKPDS Outcomes Model is gaining widespread acceptance as a validated tool for long-term economic and clinical prediction in diabetes and will be updated once UKPDS 10-year post-trial follow-up results are available. It is often said that the UKPDS is a trial that will never be repeated; equally, it is also a trial that will continue to provide valuable data to economists for many years to come.

Summary

An economic analysis was not initially included in the study design of the UK Prospective Diabetes Study (UKPDS). However, data were collected throughout the study on hospital drugs and medications used and these were supplemented near the end of the study by cross-sectional surveys of non-inpatient healthcare use and quality of life.

Evaluations of tight vs. less tight blood pressure control, intensive vs. less conventional blood glucose control and metformin showed that each was highly cost-effective and that all could be provided at modest total cost. Further analyses showed that amputations and stroke had particularly severe consequences for quality of life, and that amputations and non-fatal MI had high cost consequences. Finally, patient-level data were used to construct a diabetes outcomes model, which estimates the probability of longer-term complications from patient-specific risk factors and can be used in populations at different stages of diabetes progression.

The economic analyses arising from the UKPDS have provided new evidence to clinicians, policymakers and researchers on the consequences of diabetes and the cost-effectiveness of interventions, thereby assisting the development of treatment guidelines and improved standards of care. The analyses also illustrated a number of methodological innovations. Finally, the UKPDS Outcomes Model is gaining widespread acceptance as a validated tool for long-term economic and clinical prediction in diabetes.

References

1 UKPDS Group. Cost-effectiveness analysis of improved blood pressure control in hypertensive patients with type 2 diabetes: UKPDS 40. UK Prospective Diabetes Study Group. *Br Med J* 1998;317:720-726.

2 UKPDS Group. Cost-effectiveness of an intensive blood glucose control policy in patients with type 2 diabetes: economic analysis alongside a randomised controlled trial. UKPDS 41. UK Prospective Diabetes Study Group. *Br Med J* 2000;320:1373-1378.

3 Clarke P, Gray A, Adler A, Stevens R, Raikou M, Cull C *et al.* Cost-effectiveness analysis of intensive blood-glucose control with metformin in overweight patients with type II diabetes (UKPDS no. 51). *Diabetologia* 2001;44:298-304.

4 Gray A, Clarke P, Raikou M, Adler A, Stevens R, Neil A *et al.* An economic evaluation of atenolol vs. captopril in patients with type 2 diabetes (UKPDS 54). *Diabet Med* 2001;18:438-444.

5 Gray A, Clarke P, Farmer A, Holman R. Implementing intensive control of blood glucose concentration and blood pressure in type 2 diabetes in England: cost analysis (UKPDS 63). *Br Med J* 2002;325:860.

6 Stevens R, Adler A, Gray A, Briggs A, Holman R. Life-expectancy projection by modelling and computer simulation (UKPDS 46). *Diab Res Clin Pract* 2000;50:S5-S13.

7 Wright JC, Weinstein MC. Gains in life expectancy from medical interventions—standardizing data on outcomes. *N Engl J Med* 1998;339:380-386.

8 Torrance GW. Measurement of health state utilities for economic appraisal: a review. *J Health Econ* 1986;5:1-30.

9 Clarke P, Gray A, Holman R. Estimating utility values for health states of type 2 diabetic patients using the EQ-5D (UKPDS 62). *Med Decis Making* 2002;22:340–349.

10 Clarke P, Gray A, Legood R, Briggs A, Holman R. The impact of diabetes-related complications on healthcare costs: results from the UK Prospective Diabetes Study (UKPDS no. 65). *Diabet Med* 2003;20:442-450.

11 American Diabetes Association Consensus Panel (Philip Clarke). Guidelines for computer modeling of diabetes and its complications. *Diabetes Care* 2004;27:2262-2265.

12 Clarke PM, Gray AM, Farmer AJ, Fenn P, Stevens RJ, Matthews DR *et al.* A model to estimate the lifetime health outcomes of patients with type 2 diabetes: the UK Prospective Diabetes Study (UKPDS) Outcomes Model (UKPDS no. 68). *Diabetologia* 2004;47:1747-1759.

13 Clarke PM, Gray AM, Briggs A, Stevens RJ, Matthews DR, Holman RR. Cost–utility analyses of intensive blood glucose and tight blood pressure control in type 2 diabetes (UKPDS 72). *Diabetologia* 2005;48:868-877.

14 Van Hout B, Al MJ, Gordon GS, Rutten FF. Costs, effects and C/E ratios alongside a clinical trial. *Health Econ* 1994;3:309-319.

15 O'Reilly D, Hopkins R, Blackhouse G, Clarke P, Hux J, Tarride JE *et al.* Long-term cost–utility analysis of a multidisciplinary primary care diabetes management program in Ontario. *Can J Diabetes* 2007;31:205-214.

16 Tilden DP, Mariz S, O'Bryan-Tear G, Bottomley J, Diamantopoulos A. A lifetime modelled economic evaluation comparing pioglitazone and rosiglitazone for the treatment of type 2 diabetes mellitus in the UK. *Pharmacoeconomics* 2007;25:39-54.

17 Palmer AJ, Roze S, Valentine WJ, McEwan P, Gillett M, Holmes M *et al.* Computer modeling of diabetes and its complications—a report on the Fourth Mount Hood Challenge Meeting. *Diabetes Care* 2007;30:1638-1646.

18 Holman RR, Retnakaran R, Farmer A, Stevens R. PROactive study. *Lancet* 2006;367:25-26.

15 Impact of the UKPDS—an overview

Philip Home

Newcastle University and Newcastle Diabetes Centre, Newcastle upon Tyne, UK

Introduction

Assessing the impact of a clinical research study needs to address several domains. Information scientists will often try to use bibliographic measures, such as the number of primary and secondary publications referencing the source paper(s), influenced by supposed measure of the quality of the journals in which the original and citing papers appear [1]. However, for a study designed to have clinical impact, the real judgement should be on the effect on health outcomes or on the process of clinical care, both of which are more nebulous outcomes to measure [2]. Impact might also be measured as effects on the careers of the investigators, on the development of new medications and other technologies coming on to the market, on education materials and on awareness of the medical condition concerned [2].

This mini-review will attempt a global overview of the impact of the UK Prospective Diabetes Study (or studies) (UKPDS) by the 10th year after publication of the core papers (Tables 15.1 and 15.2). This landmark study randomized over 4200 people with newly diagnosed type 2 diabetes who failed to achieve a clinic fasting plasma glucose level < 6.1 mmol/l on lifestyle advice alone. Median follow-up was 10.0 years, the major studies being of glucose-lowering therapies, including metformin in the overweight, and blood pressure-lowering therapies.

Publications

The listed publications on the UKPDS website run to 85 full papers, excluding letters, comments and reviews [3]. Perhaps unusually for a major clinical trial, many of these (32 (38%)) were published before the core result papers appeared in September 1998. The proportion of papers appearing in either a

Originally published: Home P. Impact of the UKPDS—an overview. *Diabetic Medicine* 2008; 25 (Suppl. 2): 2–8

Table 15.1 Core UK Prospective Diabetes Study (UKPDS) publications

Reference	Core content and type	Journal
13	Clinical trial: active glucose lowering with sulfonylurea/insulin	*Lancet*
16	Clinical trial: active glucose lowering in the overweight (metformin)	*Lancet*
33	Clinical trial: active blood pressure lowering	*British Medical Journal*
26	Epidemiological analysis of effect of baseline characteristics	*British Medical Journal*
17	Within-study epidemiological analysis: blood glucose lowering	*British Medical Journal*
34	Within-study epidemiological analysis: blood pressure lowering	*British Medical Journal*
5	Cost-effectiveness analysis: blood glucose lowering	*British Medical Journal*
4	Cost-effectiveness analysis: blood pressure lowering	*British Medical Journal*

Table 15.2 Some areas in which the UK Prospective Diabetes Study (UKPDS) has had notable impact

Domain of impact	Site of impact
Natural history of diabetes	Clinical guidelines
Islet β-cell function	Educational resources
Targets of glucose and blood pressure control	Health economic models
Choice of glucose-lowering therapies	Follow-on research studies
Hypertension therapy	Clinical outcomes
Health economics	New drug developments
Cardiovascular risk engine	Pathophysiological understanding

major medical weekly (14 (16%)) or in *Diabetes, Diabetologia, Diabetes Care* or *Diabetic Medicine* (52 (61%)) is extraordinarily high at 78%, with *Diabetologia* being the key 'beneficiary' (18) by a short head over *Diabetic Medicine* (17). Few appear in less-prominent diabetes journals, in general metabolism or cardiovascular journals or in other journals.

Papers can be loosely classified as those of clinical interest (defined as those that might be read by a health professional interested in diabetes and/or cardiovascular disease, but without an interest in the science underlying their pathogenesis), those of more basic scientific interest, those of a public health interest (notably disease and economic modelling) and others. Papers of clinical interest dominate (58, 68%), with basic science (14, 16%) and public health (13, 15%) as minorities.

The surprising number of papers in the public health domain largely reflects economic modelling and it is to the credit of the UKPDS Group that use of the clinical trial data has gone beyond mere clinical endpoints [4,5]. This is reflected in the guidelines (see below), but it can also be noted that the American Centers for Disease Control and Prevention performed an economic analysis based on the UKPDS blood glucose and blood pressure arms, while the CORE economic model gives prominence to the UKPDS papers in validating its output predictions [6,7].

UKPDS influence on guidelines

In determining the influence of the UKPDS on clinical behaviour, it is necessary to distinguish specific effects from the general momentum of change. This can be examined by the use of publications in clinical guidelines, ideally in evidence-based guidelines utilizing systematic searches and literature reviews to avoid publication bias by familiarity [2]. The target here would be guidelines on the management of type 2 diabetes (or on glucose-lowering and/or blood pressure management within type 2 diabetes) published since the core papers in 1998. However, there must be a distinction between the use of UKPDS papers just as prime source material or whether they resulted in changes in guideline recommendations. This presents some difficulties as guidelines developed prior to 2000 were often not as methodologically rigorous as those that followed, although multidisciplinary, multiply funded, literature-based guidelines were developed by the International Diabetes Federation (IDF) (Europe) immediately prior to publication of the core UKPDS papers [8].

Even this evidence-based guideline approach to assessing impact has its problems. In the current version of the National Institute for Clinical Excellence (NICE) UK guidelines for the management of type 2 diabetes [9], UKPDS is mentioned 103 times and 12 papers are cited: this is, however, somewhat misleading as this current version is an update of the 2002 guideline [10] and, as a result, the core papers are scarcely mentioned or are contained within other referenced systematic reviews and meta-analyses, which are given citation preference. Furthermore, of the 103 references to UKPDS, 39 relate to the UKPDS risk engine for prediction of cardiovascular events and a further 37 to the UKPDS-derived health economic model used for making judgements on the cost-effectiveness of newer glucose-lowering therapies. Thus, while the glucose-lowering and blood pressure-lowering results of the UKPDS underpin the recommendations made in their respective areas, the more unusual contributions come from the areas of risk estimation and the health economic findings and modelling. Also notable are the use of the trial and epidemiological findings as the basis of the recommendations on glucose targeting (nine mentions) and, to a lesser extent, for blood pressure targeting. Nevertheless, the papers referenced in the guideline update cover a range of topics, including, in addition to the above, papers specifically on retinopathy, on hypoglycaemia and on the progression of islet β-cell failure. In the parent guideline on glucose-lowering published in

2002, UKPDS is mentioned once in a recommendation, eight times in evidence statements and 19 times in the narrative [10].

The impact of the UKPDS on diabetes guidelines has been worldwide. The IDF Global Guideline covers 19 areas of care management for people with type 2 diabetes [11]. The approach here was to use quality systematic reviews published by others, but 10 chapters reference UKPDS articles 19 times, an impressive 14% of all references in these chapters, covering a range of topics, including diagnosis, lifestyle interventions, targets and control monitoring, glucose- and blood pressure-lowering therapies and eye and kidney care. As with the UK guidelines, it is the strength of the large population studied over a considerable period of time which leads to much of the impact of the UKPDS and thus its ability to contribute to areas such as diagnosis, control levels, risk estimation and outcome modelling.

The Canadian diabetes guidelines cover type 1 and type 2 diabetes and gestational diabetes, so it is more difficult to put their citation of UKPDS in context [12]. Nevertheless, citation of UKPDS papers does occur some 17 times across eight chapters, the major impacts here occurring more predictably under oral medications (six of 49 cited papers). Indeed, the main UKPDS glucose-lowering paper [13] is recurrently cited in a number of chapters.

The UKPDS is also extensively cited outside diabetes guidelines. Literature searches of 'UKPDS' and 'guidelines' pick up hundreds of papers, amongst which are notably guidelines in the cardiovascular and renal areas.

Educational and research impacts

The UKPDS has had a considerable impact on available educational material. An analysis performed in 2005 showed that UKPDS data was the main subject of 18 of 183 slides (10%) on the Council for the Advancement of Diabetes Research and Education (CADRE) website and 29 of 95 (31%) slides on the website of the WorldWIDE initiative [14,15]. While the UKPDS core results do appear in these slides, they are more likely to include information derived from the longitudinal description of the study or from epidemiological analyses (Fig. 15.1). Thus, CADRE had four UKPDS slides on therapy, eight on metabolic control and five on epidemiological data. Both CADRE and WorldWIDE have similar illustrations of deteriorating blood glucose control over the course of time, perhaps the iconic slide of UKPDS, and of the epidemiological analyses of rates of microvascular complications and myocardial infarction with time (Fig. 15.1). More recently, the interest in glucagon-like peptide-1 (GLP-1) mimetics and enhancers has led to further study of the prevention of progression of insulin secretory inadequacy and to greater need for data on the change of homeostatis model assessment (HOMA) β-cell function with time (Fig. 15.1).

Although the core glucose-lowering study (sulfonylureas and insulin) and the overweight study (including metformin) maintained glucose control to an average glycated haemoglobin (HbA_{1c}) of around 6.5% over the first 5 years in the active treatment arms, and at least to some extent improved vascular

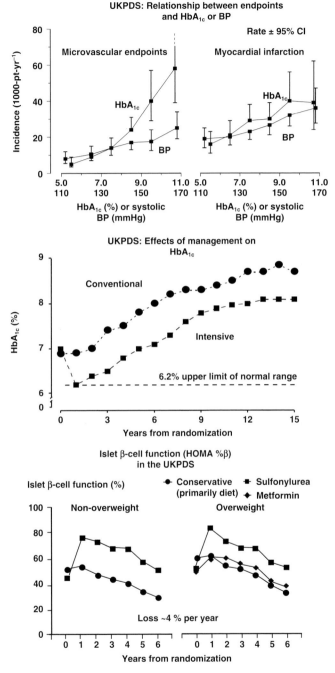

Figure 15.1 Three of the most commonly seen slides based on UKPDS data, here taken from the WorldWIDE slide resource. Reproduced with permission from [15]. Upper panel, the epidemiological data of vascular risk against blood glucose and blood pressure control; middle, the time course of change of glycated haemoglobin (HbA$_{1c}$) during the study; lower panel, the homeostasis model assessment (HOMA) islet β-cell function analysis for the non-insulin-treated groups. Attributions have been deleted in this figure for clarity—see text.

outcomes, the epidemiological data, particularly for myocardial infarction, suggested further gains from even lower HbA_{1c} levels, or perhaps from maintaining HbA_{1c} at this level for a longer period of time [13,16,17]. These issues seeded studies designed partly to replicate and extend the UKPDS (notably the Veterans Affairs Diabetes Trial (VADT) which enrolled people with established diabetes) and partly to extend the findings to tighter levels of control, and thus also hoping to improve study power (Action to Control Cardiovascular Risk in Diabetes (ACCORD) and ADVANCE) [18–20]. Results from all of these studies were presented in the summer of 2008 [21]. By contrast, the blood pressure findings of the UKPDS have in general been followed by studies aimed more at promoting the benefits of particular agents, and often with emphasis on renal rather than eye or cardiovascular outcomes, with some exceptions [22].

Specific impacts

Role of glycated haemoglobin

Fasting plasma glucose was once widely promoted as a useful clinical measure of blood glucose control through the 1980s and 1990s, not least by the UKPDS group themselves [23]. Since about 1980, however, there has been a shift to plasma glucose self-monitoring and glycated haemoglobin measurement as they became more practical and precise, a move vindicated for people with type 1 diabetes by the findings of the Diabetes Control and Complications Trial (DCCT) study in 1993 [24].

The UKPDS tracked the development of glycated haemoglobin assays and at least three were used during the study, the familiar results (expressed as HbA_{1c}) being partly arithmetic transformations of measures from earlier assays to the standard used in the DCCT [25]. In the course of time, UKPDS found glycated haemoglobin—and not fasting glucose—performed equivalently to low-density lipoprotein (LDL) and high-density lipoprotein (HDL) cholesterol and blood pressure as a predictor of measures of cardiovascular events [26].

The UKPDS design was predicated on the validity of fasting plasma glucose (FPG) as a measurement. It was thus the core measurement for inclusion (the participants did not have to have diabetes), the measure used to determine whether a participant would be randomized and the measure which, throughout the study, was used to monitor individual progress and, in some cases, determine therapy and therapy dose [27]. Logically then, the study outcomes would have been described in terms of FPG, but both the outcome and epidemiological papers give emphasis to HbA_{1c}, and that is the measure which has cascaded into clinical targets. It is also the measure used nearly universally by others in presentations of the UKPDS results ever since.

Metformin

One of the major 'beneficiaries' of the UKPDS has been the use of metformin. The principal study embedded in the UKPDS group of studies which examined the use of metformin was the overweight, primary-therapy study, comparing low-intensity management (initially lifestyle only) to active therapy with metformin, glibenclamide, chlorpropamide and insulin (five arms) [16]. By excluding people with less than 120% of ideal body weight (corresponding to a body mass index (BMI) of around 26.0 kg/m^2), the cohort has an average BMI of around 31.5 kg/m^2, similar to many current middle-aged populations with type 2 diabetes. The study might, however, be regarded as underpowered.

The finding of statistically significant reductions in the primary endpoints, mainly achieved by a reduction in myocardial infarction, has confirmed metformin's place as the only glucose-lowering therapy whose role in macrovascular protection is difficult to challenge (see below). This, combined with its neutral effects on body weight and lack of hypoglycaemia, removed most of the stigma attached to metformin after the metabolic studies of the late 1970s showing worsening of levels of blood lactate and pyruvate [28].

These observations have led to clear-cut effects on guidelines and clinical behaviour. In the pre-UKPDS 1998 European IDF guideline, metformin is given some prominence but is not promoted as first-line therapy [8]. In every guideline since then it appears as usual first-line therapy. Further understandings regarding safety followed the launch of metformin in the USA in the 1990s. Indeed, the consensus algorithm of the American Diabetes Association (ADA)/European Association for the Study of Diabetes (EASD), provocatively and perhaps wrongly, places metformin alongside lifestyle intervention from the time of diagnosis [29].

Perhaps, however, the case for metformin is overstated. The headline result of a –39% (95% CI –11% to –59%) reduction in myocardial infarction (MI) is not statistically different from the finding in the sulfonylurea–insulin group (–21% (+5% to –40%)) [16]. The Kaplan–Meier curves show little difference in MI even by 9 years from randomization, beyond which total participant numbers decrease—perhaps the finding applies to a sub-population? Subsequently, results from the Diabetes Outcome Progression Trial (ADOPT) study have made further contributions to these issues [30,31].

Sulfonylureas and insulin

The results of the main glucose study of the UKPDS, by contrast with the metformin study, left sulfonylureas and insulin in some cloud of uncertainty, the principal beneficiaries of which until 2007 have been the thiazolidinediones. The findings for reduction in microvascular disease were conclusive, with reductions of –25% (–7% to –40%) in microvascular endpoints [13]; welcome but in many minds just a confirmation of results to be expected after the DCCT findings in people with type 1 diabetes [24]. Reduction of macrovascular events was, however, statistically equivocal, with no difference for diabetes-related deaths (predominantly from MI) and the upper confidence interval of relative risk tantalizingly reaching 1.00 for myocardial infarction (risk reduction –16% (0% to –29%)).

Adopting the conventional statistical approach of a sharp cut-off around a significant P-value of 0.050, this is not confirmatory of a beneficial effect for active therapy against lifestyle-based therapy. Such an approach is beloved of rigid-thinking evidence-based medicine operatives, both in clinical and public health, but makes no sense to statisticians or to logical thinking. Ultimately, the Bayesian approach of a strong prior probability of reduction of arterial events would simply conclude that the UKPDS findings add to that probability and set a likely risk reduction in the order of 10–15% (and approximately the same per 1.0% of HbA_{1c}) with some confidence [17].

The results do, however, confirm the safety of sulfonylurea and insulin therapy and largely debunked the theories of damage from ion channel preconditioning and hyperinsulinaemia respectively. As a result, sulfonylurea therapy has retained its position as a second-line option, reinforced following the ADOPT results (with ADVANCE to come in the summer of 2008), and insulin therapy has increasingly secured a place as more than a salvage therapy of last resort [9,32].

Blood pressure control

The blood pressure control results of the UKPDS in some ways echoed those of the main glucose control study [33]. Thus, there were very useful reductions in microvascular endpoints (by −37% (−11% to −66%)) and consequently in all diabetes-related endpoints, but here myocardial infarction was definitely not shown to be improved (−21% (−41% to +7%)), although diabetes-related deaths decreased (−32% (−6% to −51%)), perhaps with contributions from heart failure and stroke. Judged by current standards, the study was again underpowered (429 total diabetes events), although the difference in reduction in blood pressure achieved, at 10/5 mmHg, is rather higher than in many current studies. Other features which account for the relative lack of clinical impact were the use of captopril and atenolol as the two first-line agents, both now unfashionable, while the studies of other blood pressure-lowering drugs which followed, in particular of the renin–angiotensin blockers, often showed benefits on renal outcomes. Furthermore, unlike blood glucose control, there was no deterioration in control of blood pressure with time or need for further intensification of therapy [33].

Although the level of blood pressure control in the tight treatment group (144/82 mmHg) was not that expected by 2008 standards, the UKPDS has contributed considerably to the debate over the target levels to be used for modern therapy. Perhaps it is all too easily forgotten that, back in the 1980s, achievement of blood pressure control below 160/95 mmHg was often considered too difficult. However, the epidemiological analyses of the UKPDS blood pressure data have proved more acceptable than those in the area of glucose control in suggesting targeting of tighter levels for people with type 2 diabetes, including of < 130/80 mmHg, even although the 'gain' per 10 mmHg is no better than per 1.0% HbA_{1c} for improvement in clinical outcomes (Fig. 15.1) [17,34]. Another area of impact is the continued endorsement of angiotensin-converting enzyme (ACE) inhibitors as first-line therapy in people with diabetes, in contrast to recommendations for older people without diabetes, in part because the evidence for microvascular protection against retinopathy provided by the UKPDS is not available for calcium channel blockers and thiazide diuretics.

Lastly, the lack of argument about titration and use of multiple-drug therapy for blood pressure control, in contrast to blood glucose control, is supported by the economic analysis from the UKPDS in this area and assisted again by the evidence of the extra benefit to microvascular protection [4,33].

Secular trends in blood glucose control and islet β-cell function

The most popular illustration from the UKPDS is that of the deterioration of blood glucose control over the course of the study in all treatment groups, a graph that appears in the core papers (Fig. 15.1). The rate of deterioration is ~1.5% HbA_{1c} per 10 years [13,16]. Early versions of this trend had been published 3 years before the outcome results papers and have had a very large effect on practice [35]. The concept that the intensity of therapy needed to be increased with time was already understood [8], but its graphical illustration turned worthy guideline statements into a firm concept more acceptable to prescribing physicians.

The observation that the progressive nature of type 2 diabetes appeared to be related to deterioration of islet β-cell function had further impact. Notably, the concept that insulin insensitivity contributes to the pathogenesis of hyperglycaemia is explained more readily with the understanding that the progressive decline of islet β-cell function compound a failure to compensate for decreasing insulin action [35]. Furthermore, as the rate of deterioration was shown to be independent of therapy [35], some formerly favoured concepts, such as secondary sulfonylurea failure, drug induced β-cell exhaustion and resting the islet β-cells with insulin, have faded from prominence. The concept of diabetes as a condition of failure of insulin delivery has also enhanced the therapeutic role of insulin therapy and thus its acceptability.

Conclusions

The UKPDS has excelled in the sheer breadth of its impact. This review has not, however, included a comparison of the UKPDS with other major studies, such as landmark clinical trials, including the DCCT and the 4S study, or key epidemiological studies such as the Framingham Study and the British doctors' smoking study, which have had a large but seemingly more focused influence on health practice (and thus outcomes). The effects of the UKPDS on outcomes of people with diabetes are impossible to quantify—a major study often accelerates trends in health care already in progress—and new diagnostic technologies and medications in the last 10 years have undoubtedly changed medical practice and perhaps improved outcomes as well, so impressively seen in multiple intervention studies like the Steno 2 [36]. In Newcastle secondary care, HbA_{1c} fell by 0.5% between 1998 and 2003, certainly an acceleration of past trend. Quite how much this will have contributed to improved vascular outcomes, alongside better eye screening, statin use and foot care, cannot be known, but all concerned, professionals and people with diabetes alike, must be grateful to Robert Turner and the UKPDS Group for their persistence in seeing this study through while maintaining its high quality.

Summary

The UK Prospective Diabetes Study (UKPDS) is a group of clinical trials, epidemiological analyses and health-modelling studies with an influence which can be assessed across a broad range of health domains.

Original publications (n=85) are notable for being mainly published in the key weekly or diabetes journals (78%) and being mainly in the clinical arena (68%). Notable reference to the publications can be found in UK National Institute for Clinical Excellence (NICE) guidelines, but also in evidence-based international guidelines, where UKPDS papers form a significant fraction of the citations. In educational materials UKPDS-derived slides remain popular (10 and 30% of some international slide sets), again as much for the epidemiological findings as for the core trial results. Slides of the deterioration in blood glucose control with time, and evidence that this is as a result of progressive decline of pancreatic islet β-cell function, are used particularly often. The UKPDS enhanced the promotion of glycated haemoglobin to its core role in clinical monitoring, through understanding of the quantitative relationship of vascular complications to glucose control, and thus to target setting. Notably, metformin therapy was promoted by the UKPDS findings on macrovascular disease in the overweight study, although controversy remains regarding the significance of the effect on macrovascular disease of the core glucose-lowering study, promoting the development of further studies reporting in 2008. The effects of decreasing blood pressure on microvascular disease have had an important impact on guidelines and health economic analyses, together with other evidence on the value of renin–angiotensin system blockers.

The UKPDS has evidently been unusually influential in the development of treatment guidelines, clinical education and the thinking of healthcare professionals. By inference it must be responsible for a significant part of the improvement in health outcomes in people with type 2 diabetes over the last decade.

References

1 Buxton M, Hanney S. How can payback from health services research be assessed? *J Health Serv Res Policy* 1996;1:35-43.
2 Hanney SR, Home PD, Frame I, Grant J, Green P, Buxton MJ. Identifying the impact of diabetes research. *Diabet Med* 2006;23:176-184.
3 Diabetes Trials Unit. UK Prospective Diabetes Study publications. Available at http://www.dtu.ox.ac.uk/ukpds/ Last accessed 2 September 2008.

4 UKPDS Group. Cost effectiveness analysis of improved blood pressure control in hypertensive patients with type 2 diabetes. *Br Med J* 1998;317:720-726.

5 UKPDS Group. Cost-effective analysis of intensive blood glucose control with metformin in overweight patients with type 2 diabetes. *Br Med J* 2000;320:1373-1378.

6 The CDC Diabetes Cost-effectiveness Group. Cost-effectiveness of intensive glycemic control, intensified hypertension control, and serum cholesterol level reduction for type 2 diabetes. *J Am Med Assoc* 2002;287:2542-2551.

7 Palmer AJ, Roze S, Valentine WJ, Minshall ME, Foos V, Lurati F *et al.* Validation of the CORE Diabetes Model against epidemiological and clinical studies. *Curr Med Res Opin* 2004;20:S27-S40.

8 European Diabetes Policy Group 1999. A desktop guide to type 2 diabetes mellitus. *Diabet Med* 1999;16:716-730.

9 The National Collaborating Centre for Chronic Conditions. Type 2 Diabetes (Update). London: Royal College of Physicians, 2008. Available at http://www.rcplondon.ac.uk/pubs/Specialty.aspx Last accessed 2 September 2008.

10 McIntosh A, Hutchinson A, Home PD, Brown F, Bruce A, Damerell A *et al*. Clinical guidelines and evidence review for type 2 diabetes: management of blood glucose. Sheffield: ScHARR, University of Sheffield, 2001. Available at http://www.nice.org.uk Last accessed 2 September 2008.

11 IDF Clinical Guidelines Task Force. Global guideline for type 2 diabetes. Brussels: International Diabetes Federation, 2005. Available at www.idf.org Last accessed 2 September 2008.

12 Canadian Diabetes Association Clinical Practice Guidelines Expert Committee. Canadian Diabetes Association 2003 Clinical Practice Guidelines for the Prevention and Management of Diabetes in Canada. *Can J Diabetes* 2003;27:S1-S152.

13 UKPDS Group. Intensive blood glucose control with sulphonylureas or insulin compared with conventional treatment and risk of complications in patients with type 2 diabetes. *Lancet* 1998;352:837-853.

14 Council for the advancement of diabetes research and education (CADRE). Core slide kit. Available at http://www.cadre-diabetes.org/r_core_slide_kit.asp Last accessed 2 September 2008.

15. Worldwide Initiative for Diabetes Education. Slide resources. Available at http://www.worldwidediabetes.org/slide_resources/slide_resources.htm Last accessed 2 September 2008.

16 UKPDS Group. Effect of intensive blood-glucose control with metformin on complications in overweight patients with type 2 diabetes. *Lancet* 1998;352:854-865.

17 Stratton IM, Adler AI, Neil HAW, Matthews DR, Manley SE, Cull CA *et al*. Association of glycaemia with macrovascular and microvascular complications of type 2 diabetes (UKPDS 35): prospective observational study. *Br Med J* 2000;321:405-412.

18 Abraira C, Duckworth W, McCarren M, Emanuele N, Arca D, Reda D *et al*. Design of the cooperative study on glycemic control and complications in diabetes mellitus type 2: Veterans Affairs Diabetes Trial. *J Diabetes Complications* 2003;17:314-322.

19 The Action to Control Cardiovascular Risk in Diabetes Study Group. Effects of intensive glucose lowering in type 2 diabetes. *N Engl J Med* 2008;358:2545-2559.

20 The ADVANCE Collaborative Group. Intensive blood glucose control and vascular outcomes in patients with type 2 diabetes. *N Engl J Med* 2008;358:2560-2572.

21 Home P. Safety of very tight blood glucose control in type 2 diabetes. *Br Med J* 2008;336:458-459.

22 ADVANCE Collaborative Group. Effects of a fixed combination of perindopril and inda-pamide on macrovascular and microvascular outcomes in patients with type 2 diabetes mellitus (the ADVANCE trial): a randomised controlled trial. *Lancet* 2007;370:829-840.

23 Holman RR, Turner RC. The basal plasma glucose: a simple relevant index of maturity-onset diabetes. *Clin Endocrinol (Oxf)* 1981;14:279-286.

24 The Diabetes Control and Complications Trial Research Group. The effects of intensive treatment of diabetes on the development and progression of long-term complications in insulin-dependent diabetes mellitus. *N Engl J Med* 1993;329:977-986.

25 Manley S. Haemoglobin A_{1c}—a marker for complications of type 2 diabetes: the experience from the UK Prospective Diabetes Study (UKPDS). *Clin Chem Lab Med* 2003;41:1182-1190.

26 Turner RC, Millns H, Neil HAW, Stratton IM, Manley SE, Matthews DR *et al*. UK Prospective Diabetes Study (UKPDS 23). Risk factors for coronary artery disease in non-insulin dependent diabetes mellitus: *Br Med J* 1998;316:823-828.

27 UK Prospective Diabetes Study Group. UK Prospective Diabetes Study (UKPDS). VIII. Study design, progress and performance. *Diabetologia* 1991;34:877-890.

28 Nattrass M, Todd PG, Hinks L, Lloyd B, Alberti KGMM. Comparative effects of phen-formin, metformin and glibenclamide on metabolic rhythms in maturity-onset diabetics. *Diabetologia* 1977;13:145-152.

29 Nathan DM, Buse JB, Davidson MB, Ferrannini E, Holman RR, Sherwin R *et al*. Management of hyperglycaemia in type 2 diabetes: a consensus algorithm for the initiation and adjustment of therapy. A consensus statement from the American Diabetes Association and the European Association for the Study of Diabetes. *Diabetologia* 2006;49:1711-1721.

30 Kahn SE, Haffner SM, Heise MA, Herman WH, Holman RR, Jones NP *et al*. Glycemic durability of rosiglitazone, metformin, or glyburide monotherapy. *N Engl J Med* 2006;355:2427-2443.

31 GlaxoSmithKline. Advisory committee briefing document cardiovascular safety of rosiglitazone, FDA Endocrinologic and Metabolic Drugs Advisory Committee and Drug Safety and Risk Management Advisory Committee. King of Prussia: GlaxoSmithKline, 2007. Available at www.fda.gov/ohrms/dockets/ac/07/briefing/2007-4308b1-01-sponsor-backgrounder.pdf Last accessed 2 September 2008.

32 Al-Ozairi E, Sibal L, Home P. Counterpoint: A Diabetes Outcome Progression Trial (ADOPT): good for sulfonylureas? *Diabetes Care* 2007;30:1677-1680.

33 UKPDS Group. Tight blood pressure control and risk of macrovascular and microvascular complications in type 2 diabetes. *Br Med J* 1998;317:703-713.

34 Adler AI, Stratton IM, Neil HAW, Yudkin JS, Matthews DR, Cull CA *et al*. Association of systolic blood pressure with macrovascular and microvascular complications of type 2 diabetes (UKPDS 36): prospective observational study. *Br Med J* 2000;321:412–419.

35 UK Prospective Diabetes Study Group. UKPDS 16. Overview of 6 years' therapy of type II diabetes: a progressive disease. *Diabetes* 1995;44:1249-1258.

36 Gæde P, Lund-Andersen H, Parving H-H, Pedersen O. Effect of a multifactorial intervention on mortality in type 2 diabetes. *N Engl J Med* 2008;358:580-591.

16 What do the critics say? A personal view

Peter J. Watkins

King's College Hospital, London, UK (retired)

Some criticisms of a study involving more than 5000 patients and conducted over 20 years would be almost inevitable, and indeed they came during the years after publication of the major results in 1998. Nor were critics gentle in their opinions. 'UKPDS is not a cohort study and analysis is misleading … investigators potentially render their analyses invalid … withdrawal might be considered' [1]. It has also been suggested that exaggeration of the benefits of UKPDS may be an example of 'groupthink … in which a group makes an overconfident and perhaps even irrational decision which it then defends fiercely …' [2]. Or, 'the debate on the nature of the relation between diabetes and hyperglycaemia and cardiovascular disease has a long history and the UKPDS has not resolved it' [3]. Considered responses to these and other criticisms [4,5] were subsequently published [5–7].

Some critics objected to what they considered the 'spin' given to the results. While the benefits of tight blood glucose control on microvascular events were generally acknowledged, critics expressed disquiet at possible exaggeration of the magnitude of this benefit [2] which might result in inappropriate advice to patients. Even more widespread criticism was levelled at the evident failure to obtain a statistically significant reduction in macrovascular events and mortality over a decade [2,8–10]. If this could not be achieved given that cardiovascular disease is the chief cause of death in type 2 diabetes, is tight glucose control really worthwhile, they ask, with its inherent problems of weight gain and hypoglycaemia [1,2], especially when insulin is used?

Yet, the very demonstration of the scale of cardiovascular deaths led to the perception of type 2 diabetes as a 'vascular disease', and has influenced physicians' entire approach to the treatment of this condition, with a vast increase in application of effective preventive measures whose potency outweighs that of tight glucose control alone. In particular, the critical role of blood pressure control has been demonstrated, not just in lessening some cardiovascular events, but also in its benefit on microvascular disease, both in preserving visual acuity as well as delaying the onset and evolution of nephropathy. And the importance of metformin as a cardiovascular protective agent, perhaps independently of its hypoglycaemic action [11], has attracted huge interest and altered the priorities in treatment. Although Nathan in his own critical review once considered that 'this finding should be accepted cautiously' [10], he had, by 2006, led the authorship on the first joint ADA/EASD consensus guidelines on the management of type 2 diabetes, recommending metformin as first-line therapy [12].

The progression of type 2 diabetes has long been recognized by practising physicians. Now the graphic description of its inexorable nature in the UKPDS has greatly influenced physicians' understanding of their patients, with the ever increasing frustration at attempts to improve blood glucose control regardless of the means of doing so. It was important therefore, that in sharp contrast to the earlier Universities Group Diabetes Program, the study demonstrated 'the absence of a pernicious effect of either insulin or sulphonylureas on cardiovascular outcomes' [10]. That perception at least was laid to rest, even if some uncertainty remains as to which combinations of treatment might after all be the best.

The bottom line of UKPDS must be its translation into patient care. Its influence, well described in the review by Home [13], has been felt worldwide. Physicians undoubtedly understand the nature of type 2 diabetes better than before, and new perceptions underlie new approaches to treatment. In particular, its nature as a progressive vascular disease has led to radical shifts in its management.

No-one would quibble with the advice to *improve* blood glucose control as contributing to reduction of microvascular events, and perhaps over the longer term to macrovascular events as well, bearing in mind that type 2 diabetes is diagnosed now at an ever younger age. But in response to the critics, what advice should be given to patients regarding initiation of *tight* blood glucose control? The suggestion has been made that 'informed choice should require that patients be provided with full explanations of the likely level of benefit expressed as an absolute, and not relative, risk reduction' [3]. Perhaps this is wise counsel. Use of the UKPDS Risk Engine [14] makes this possible. It is a truly remarkable tribute to this colossal study that we are able to offer such choices to our patients.

So the voices of the critics have been heard and considered. Headlines such as that from McCormack and Greenhalgh, pointing to 'versions and perversions of UKPDS' [2] with its accusations of interpretation bias, leave readers with the feeling that some critics at least show evidence of interpretation bias themselves.

References

1 Cruikshank JK. UKPDS is not a cohort study and analysis is misleading. Letter. *Br Med J* 2001;322:1246.

2 McCormack J, Greenhalgh T. Seeing what you want to see in randomised controlled trials: versions and perversions of UKPDS data. *Br Med J* 2000;320:1720–1723.

3 Jarrett RJ. Relation between diabetes and hyperglycaemia and cardiovascular disease has not been resolved. Letter. *Br Med J* 2001;322:1246–1247.

4 Ewart RM. The UKPDS: what was the question? Letter. *Lancet* 1999;353:1882.

5 Rapid responses. www.bmj.com/cgi/content/full/320/7251/1720#responses Last accessed 2 September 2008.

6 Stratton IM, Cull CA, Manley SE, Adler AI, Neil, HAW, Matthews DR, Holman RR. Authors reply. Letter. *Br Med J* 2001;322:1247.

7 Turner R, Holman R, Butterfield J. Authors reply. Letter. *Lancet* 1999;354:600.

8 Budenholzer B. Glycaemia and vascular effects of Type 2 diabetes. *Br Med J* 2001;322:1245-1246.

9 Yudkin J. Very tight glucose control may be high-risk, low benefit. Letter. *Br Med J* 2008;336:683.

10 Nathan DM. Some answers, more controversy, from UKPDS. *Lancet* 1998;352:832-833.

11 UK Prospective Diabetes Study (UKPDS) Group. Effect of intensive blood glucose control with metformin on complications in overweight patients with Type 2 diabetes (UKPDS 34). *Lancet* 1998;352:854-865.

12 Nathan DM, Buse JB, Davidson MB, Heine RJ, Holman RR, Sherwin R, Zinman B. Management of hyperglycaemia in Type 2 diabetes: a consensus algorithm for the initiation and adjustment of therapy. *Diabetes Care* 2006;29:1963-1972.

13 Home P. Impact of UKPDS—an overview. *UKPDS: the first 30 years.* Oxford: Blackwell Publishing, 2008; 125.

14 Adler AI. UKPDS—modelling of cardiovascular risk assessment and lifetime simulation of outcomes. *UKPDS: the first 30 years.* Oxford: Blackwell Publishing, 2008; 105.

17 Letters of congratulation on presentation of 20-year results: September 1998

Dear Robert
'It has been a very great project and a great achievement. You can be truly proud.'

Lord Butterfield of Stechford, Cambridge

'I am writing to congratulate you on your splendid achievement of bringing the UKPDS to completion. It was a privilege for me to hear from you over the years about the struggle to keep the study going. Thanks to your personal perseverance, you have created new information that should have a major impact on the treatment of this disease.'

Professor Gordon C. Weir, Joslin Diabetes Center, Boston, USA

'Congratulations on the spectacular UKPDS. The study is obviously an outstanding piece of work that will always be remembered as the definitive study in type 2 diabetes. The fact that you were able to complete the trial notwithstanding the various obstacles that were placed along the way is certainly a testimonial to the skills of yourself and your colleagues.'

Professor Lawrence A. Leiter, St Michael's Hospital, Toronto, Canada

'Just a note to congratulate you on your astonishing achievement in bringing the UKPDS to such a successful conclusion after commencing it so many years ago. I was fortunate to attend your triumph in Barcelona, and felt I was witnessing a historic event. There are very few occasions in medicine where clinical practice is irrevocably changed by one study—perhaps the 4S, ISIS 2 and DCCT trial are the best previous examples—what a feat! I can only liken the overall scale of your work, and eventual triumph against insuperable odds, to that of Wagner and his Ring cycle!'

Dr Hugh Mather, London

'It has been a privilege to have been involved in the UKPDS. I am full of admiration for the vision you displayed at its inception and the enormous stamina in seeing it through to such important conclusions. The diabetic professional community and patients owe you a great debt of gratitude.'

Dr John Tooke, Exeter

'The presentation of the UKPDS data at the EASD meeting in Barcelona was the scene of two triumphant afternoon sessions in the Sports Hall. The final product was incredibly hard hitting. Many people from the UK have told me how emotional they felt during the presentation. Sally Marshall said to me "I have not had a scrap to do with the UKPDS but it makes me very proud to be British".

'One of the great spin-offs of the UKPDS has been the group of friendly (most of them anyway) diabetologists who now feel privileged to be team members in this great enterprise. Many of us have developed our own research interests and teams on the back of the UKPDS and British diabetes would be a lot poorer without it.

'To quote Jorn Nerup in the closing words of his farewell address: "when in years to come we tell our grandchildren about the UKPDS, we will be able to say—I was there".'

Dr Charles Fox, Northampton

Figure 17.1 Barcelona 1998, EASD Investigators Meeting.

'Congratulations to you and all the fantastic team in Oxford for your work with UKPDS. In addition to having the vision to start the study, the tenacity to continue and fund it, you have also shown great skills in getting the message over.'

Professor Andrew Hattersley, Exeter

'After returning from Barcelona last week, I thought I really must write to congratulate you personally on bringing the UKPDS to such a successful conclusion. More than that, I would like to thank you for what has been an invaluable contribution to our specialty. From my perspective it does seem that this is one of the most important studies in diabetes that have been done in my professional lifetime.'

Professor John Saunders, Abergavenny, Wales

'Congratulations on a truly extraordinary achievement. I can honestly say that your study will have a major impact on both how I care for these patients and what I am able to tell them by way of encouragement as I do so. All other clinical diabetologists around the globe as well as the patients owe you and your team a similar debt.'

Dr Peter C. Butler, Edinburgh

'A personal note of congratulations on the UKPDS. We very much appreciate your marathon of foresight, dedication and sheer effort. Our best wishes to yourself, Jennie (behind every etc.) and your colleagues in what artistically might now be the postmodern period of the UKPDS.'

Drs Cliff and Caroline Bailey, Aston University, Birmingham

'It must be rare for a single study to dominate both the *Lancet* and the *BMJ* in the same week. You did it! And I mean you personally because I know that you provided the drive and leadership which kept up the enthusiasm of your many collaborators.'

Professor Richard Himsworth, Cambridge

'The main purpose of this note is to congratulate you and all the DRL on the successful completion of the UKPDS. Of course I know that the study will not be fully completed for a long time to come but I thought the *Lancet*/*BMJ* publications were magnificent, and everyone tells me that Barcelona was a triumph.'

Professor Jim Mann, University of Otago, New Zealand

'Twenty years has been a long time to wait—it has been worth it.'

'The Lister Lot', Lister Hospital, Stevenage

'We always knew that UKPDS wouldn't show anything—congratulations on proving us wrong!'

All in Norwich

'Robert, the man who has never taken no as a definitive answer; the man who has more files devoted to a single study stored at the MRC Head Office than any other. UKPDS is now a listed acronym in the MRC staff code.'

The MRC

'I attended your symposium at the last EASD conference in which your team presented the results of the historical UKPDS which in my opinion will be the reference study in diabetes management for decades to come, just the same way that the Framingham Study was to modern cardiology. Only an Englishman would undertake such a colossal task. BRAVO!'

Dr Raef M. Botros, Ain-Shams University, Cairo, Egypt

18 Reminiscences from the centres: February 2008

'The "Oxford Study" was unique in the camaraderie that developed not only between medical staff and patients but between patients themselves. Clinics became social gatherings enhanced by the cookery demonstrations that took place in the waiting room each week. The patients felt as if they belonged to an exclusive club and were privileged to be members.

'The summer meetings in Oxford helped to put our individual efforts in perspective and the punting and rounders which followed provided much hilarity and enjoyment. All in all the UKPDS was an experience which evokes happy memories and a sense of fulfilment'.

Ms Judy Tyrell and Dr Steve Hyer, The Doreen Kouba Diabetes Centre,
St Helier Hospital, Carshalton, Surrey

Figure 18.1 UKPDS Clinical Centres Meeting.

'Recollections of the Test Match commentator, the jeweller, the jazz musi-cian/fundraiser, the Roman Catholic priest who transferred from Oxford and whose blessings on all were appreciated, and above all the annual gift of a wonderful Caribbean iced rum chocolate Christmas cake baked in a house just alongside Aston Villa football ground. One patient was withdrawn from the study as unsuitable having spent some time in custody.'

Figure 18.2 Robert Turner as seen by Centre 17 (Scarborough).

'Robert Turner gave such enthusiastic leadership that inspired everyone with optimism and confidence—nothing was considered an obstacle—and there was the excellent annual bonding conference in Oxford'.

'The end of the study saw the awful cutting of the umbilical cord for most patients who enjoyed the value of individualized care and the consistency of staff.'

Dr David Wright, General Hospital, Birmingham

'I told a newly diagnosed gentleman to come to the clinic starving. When I saw him at the clinic the following week, he told me he hadn't eaten for the last three days (one of those days had been his birthday) but he still wasn't starving so thought he may not be included in the study.'

'One of the questions in the annual Quality of Life questionnaire asked about mood and depression "always/sometimes/never". One of our patients circled "always" which was a surprise until I read what he had written by the side "but I am a City fan".'

Dr Timothy Dornan, Manchester

'One lady seemed to think that being in a study entitled her to extra benefits, and asked Dr Whitehead to support her request for a new double bed. When told we couldn't do that she refused to come any longer.'

'We are still seeing approximately 115 UKPDS patients. Sadly now ageing, two had their 90th birthdays last year. UKPDS patients were usually willing to participate in our studies, and appreciated seeing the same staff.'

Mary Anderson, St Georges Healthcare NHS Trust, London

'Northampton joined the UKPDS in 1982. In our hospital, there was little infrastructure for diabetes and none for research. The Cripps family, in 1976, had built a lavish postgraduate centre with an attached research unit, although there was no research going on at that time. So we took over the building for UKPDS, which reinforced the idea for our patients that they were helping in research. By the time Julia Lawton, medical anthropologist, came to interview patients at the end of the study, most of them simply regarded UKPDS as their standard diabetes care. By 1987, after much expansion of the work, the building became our Diabetes Centre. Our research unit has also grown beyond expectation, and now operates from purpose-built premises. So Northampton diabetes and research owe a great debt to the UKPDS.'

Charles and Anna Fox, Northampton

'When the study clinic began at our much loved local hospital, none of us could have imagined the vicissitudes of three location changes which would later bring us to near-refugee status! Our worry had been that we would lose patients—all were older now, some more infirm, but the majority were able to continue to the end of the study.'

Gwen Taylor, General Hospital, Birmingham

'I remember with special fondness the quite extraordinary skills demonstrated by Robert and his team in bringing together such a large group of physicians, nurses and others to keep us "on board" for such a long period of time. This was undoubtedly helped by the universally friendly atmosphere even when discussing some of the difficult issues, for example, the hypertensive arm. We visited Oxford so often that I almost regard myself having become a postgraduate student! It was great fun to take part in the annual social event which I remember usually involved our somewhat pathetic attempts at learning how to punt, in which those of us who had not formally attended Oxbridge, struggled to compete!'.

Dr John Scarpello, University Hospital of North Staffordshire, Stoke-on-Trent

Figure 18.3 Punting after a UKPDS Centres Meeting.

19 Reminiscences from the UKPDS Biochemistry Laboratory

Susan Manley

Clinical Biochemistry, University Hospital Birmingham NHS Foundation Trust from Selly Oak, Birmingham, UK

Biochemistry played a central role in the UKPDS, just as in the DCCT, with 25 people working in the laboratory when the study was at its height. Not only were blood and urine samples analysed, but DNA was extracted and stored for future use, together with the plasma and urine samples. Many trips to the laboratory at the Radcliffe Infirmary were made in the early hours of the morning in high summer when the freezer alarms sounded. Thanks are due to the porters and switchboard, and of course all the staff who worked in the laboratory over the duration of the study.

The work began in a small research laboratory which grew to the size of a district general hospital laboratory. Quality control within the laboratory, quality assurance from comparisons with results in other hospitals, and accreditation were all introduced. Our external consultant, Dr Iain Ross from Aberdeen, visited annually. On one occasion, he parked his car in front of the Radcliffe Infirmary by the fountain where another of the same make but different colour was seen on television driven by Inspector Morse! Iain's work was meticulous: he expected assay performance to be in the top 10% of laboratories in the country.

A bespoke Laboratory Information Management System (LIMS) was designed and developed in-house by Ian Kennedy and Rury Holman to track receipt of samples, quality control assays and transfer approved results directly to the UKPDS Clinical Trials Management System (CTMS). Equipment was updated regularly to give the best possible performance for each assay. The necessity to detect small changes in measurements throughout the length of the study led us to publish, with Iain's help, a novel paper [1] in *Clinical Chemistry* on how to maintain comparability of biochemical data during long-term clinical trials. Dr Carole Cull arranged binding of several copies of this internal report with 'UKPDS BIOCHEMISTRY' in gold lettering on the spine. This tome can still be found on many bookshelves.

The need to obtain relevant results for global use prompted Dr Sue Manley and Mrs Irene Stratton to contact the Centers for Disease Control and Prevention (CDC) in Atlanta regarding a reference method for determining plasma glucose, and to discover more about the National Cholesterol Education

Program (NCEP). We received an invitation from Dr Gary Myers for a visit during the American Diabetes Association (ADA) meeting in 1995, when refurbishment for the Olympic Games in Atlanta was also in progress. While at the CDC, we were invited to meet Dr Randie Little and Mrs Hsiao-Mei Wiedmeyer from the DCCT! This meeting led to certification of the HbA$_{1c}$ measurement in our laboratory by the National Glycohemoglobin Standardization Program (NGSP). We also forged a professional relationship which continues to this day through membership of the US NGSP Advisory Committee which meets annually at the ADA. We were even able to offer Hsiao-Mei and her husband accommodation in Oxford when they found themselves stranded in the UK after the terrorist attacks of 11 September when attending the Diabetes UK professional meeting in Glasgow in 2001.

Numerous papers and abstracts were published on laboratory aspects of the UKPDS in journals for biochemistry, diabetes and medicine. Topics included ranges for biochemical risk factors in normoglycaemic subjects [2] and for patients with type 2 diabetes categorized by ethnic group [3]. One patient was identified as having hyperproinsulinaemia [4], leading the genetics team to the discovery of a novel point mutation, presented by Dr Margaret Warren-Perry in a poster at the president's session of the ADA in 1996. But most rewarding of all proved to be the graphic illustration relating the incidence of complications to updated HbA$_{1c}$ [5] which Dr Richard Eastman had predicted, before the EASD meeting in 1998, would be an icon of the study. And so it proved to be (Fig. 19.1).

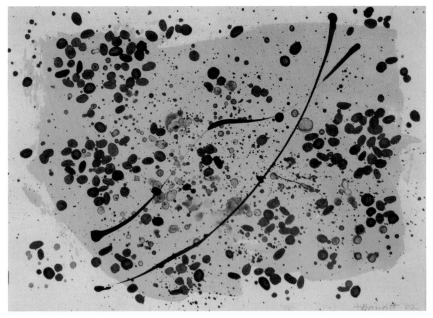

Figure 19.1 HbA$_{1c}$ representation in a painting by Alison Barrett presented to Mr Richard (Dick) Jelfs, who measured HbA$_{1c}$ throughout the study, on the occasion of his retirement.

Both research literature and textbooks are populated with papers from the UKPDS. In the current edition (4th) of Tietz [6] *Textbook of Clinical Chemistry and Molecular Diagnostics* from the US, Dr David Sacks states that 'Analogous correlations between HbA$_{1c}$ and complications (*with DCCT*) were observed in patients with type 2 diabetes in the UKPDS trial [7]. To ensure that the HbA$_{1c}$ results in the UKPDS were comparable to the DCCT, the same ion-exchange HPLC method was used … Based on the DCCT and UKPDS, the ADA recommends aiming for "near-normal" glycemia with a HbA$_{1c}$ less than 7%.'

Now, even after completion of the UKPDS, some of us are continuing to work in the laboratory translating the results of the clinical trial into practice [8–12].

References

1 Cull CA, Manley SE, Stratton IM, Neil HAW, Ross IS, Holman RR, Turner RC, Matthews DR. Approach to maintaining comparability of biochemical data during long-term clinical trials. *Clin Chem* 1997;43:1913-1918.

2 UK Prospective Diabetes Study Group. UKPDS XI: Biochemical risk factors in Type II diabetic patients at diagnosis compared with age-matched normal subjects. *Diabetic Med* 1994;11:534-544.

3 UK Prospective Diabetes Study Group. UKPDS XII: Differences between Asian, Afro-Caribbean and white Caucasian Type 2 diabetic patients at diagnosis of diabetes. *Diabetic Med* 1994;11:670-677.

4 Warren-Perry MG, Manley SE, Ostrega D, Polonsky K, Mussett S, Brown P, Turner RC. A novel point mutation in the insulin gene giving rise to hyperproinsulinemia. *J Clin Endocrinol Metabol* 1997;82:1629-1631.

5 UK Prospective Diabetes Study Group. UKPDS 35: Association of glycaemia with macrovascular and microvascular complications of type 2 diabetes: prospective observational study. *Br Med J* 2000;321:405-412.

6 Tietz. *Textbook of Clinical Chemistry and Molecular Diagnostics.* Ed Burtis, Ashwood & Bruns. Elsevier Saunders 2006; 4th edition: p880, column 2, paragraph 2.

7 UK Prospective Diabetes Study Group. UKPDS 33: Intensive blood-glucose control with sulphonylureas or insulin compared with conventional treatment and risk of complications in patients with type 2 diabetes. *Lancet* 1998;352:837-853.

8 Manley SE. Haemoglobin A$_{1c}$—a marker for complications of type 2 diabetes: the experience from the UK Prospective Diabetes Study (UKPDS). *Clin Chem Lab Med* 2003;41:1182-1190.

9 National Diabetes Support Team. Use of IFCC Reference method for calibration of HbA1c: implications for clinical care in the UK. *NHS Modernisation Agency Clinical Governance Support Team* 2004; Fact Sheet 6: 1-4.

10 IDF Clinical Guidelines Task Force. Global Guideline for Type 2 Diabetes. *Brussels: International Diabetes Federation* 2005; 26-28.

11 Manley SE, Round RA, Smith JM. Calibration of HbA$_{1c}$ and its measurement in the presence of haemoglobinopathies: report on a questionnaire to manufacturers. *Ann Clin Biochem* 2006;43:135-145.

12 Manley SE. Estimated average glucose derived from HbA$_{1c}$ (eAG): report from European Association for the Study of Diabetes (EASD), Amsterdam 2007. *Diabetic Med* 2008;25:126-128.

20 Views from participants

This study lasting 30 years is unique, and some of those participating over several decades commented on their involvement. Sentiments often expressed were 'the privilege and pleasure' of taking part, while some described the 'hope that this study helps everyone'. There are comments on the helpfulness of doctors and nurses during the study, such that it gave the participants 'confidence' and 'safety' by being 'only a phone call away'.

> 'It has always been comforting that you were in the background keeping an eye on me'.

> 'I would like to thank the Oxford study group for their care and attention especially in the early days/months when my diabetes came to light in 1983.'

The end of UKPDS was met with dismay by many participants, not surprisingly perhaps given that their confidence was always boosted by the intense support of the staff working during the study.

> 'I am sorry I won't be hearing from you again.'

> 'One visit a year to the clinic is not enough when in UKPDS we were seen every three months—we were spoilt.'

> 'I'm sorry the study is ending, and enjoyed the contact.'

Several participants commented on the adverse change in their care after the end of the study.

> 'I deplore the transfer of diabetic care from hospital to GP.'

> 'I had every confidence in the Hammersmith Hospital, but the new PCT, I feel, is more of a lottery.'

'It was a sad day when I was moved from the hospital to my own doctors'. I looked forward to my hospital visits and care I received.'

Comments on general health problems and ageing were no surprise in a study lasting 30 years, but in spite of sometimes severe ailments including stroke, arthritis, cancer and declining vision, a certain optimism prevails, no doubt an important tribute to the devoted care they received over so many years.

'The arthritis is worsening, my eyesight is worsening, the left leg is still paralysed from a stroke, but taking all things considered, I am a pretty healthy corpse now in my 80s.'

'I am now registered blind, but keeping a smile.'

'I have been in your study from 1984, I have exercised mostly by walking in my early years anything from 10 to 15 miles a day, although in the last year I walk five miles a day.'

Such positive attitudes and insights should be heard by all. They represent important and generally unspoken sentiments which should inform the future organization of diabetes care.

'Dear Professor Turner:
You have my sincere thanks for taking such good care of one over the last 11 years. I really enjoyed the extra attention and took great comfort knowing that my eyes, heart, feet, etc. were constantly being monitored. Call on my co-operation at any time, I am feeling a little lost at the moment.'

21 Most cited UKPDS papers

The seven most-cited UKPDS papers to date are:

Cited 6974 times

Turner R. Intensive blood-glucose control with sulphonylureas or insulin compared with conventional treatment and risk of complications in patients with type 2 diabetes: UKPDS 33. *Lancet* 1998; 352:837–853.

Cited 3157 times

Turner R, Holman R, Stratton I, Cull C, Frighi V, Manley S, Matthews D, Neil A, McElroy H, Kohner E, Fox C, Hadden D, Wright D. Tight blood pressure control and risk of macrovascular and microvascular complications in type 2 diabetes: UKPDS 38. *Brit Med J* 1998; 317:703–713.

Cited 1714 times

Stratton IM, Adler AI, Neil HAW, Matthews DR, Manley SE, Cull CA, Hadden D, Turner RC, Holman RR. Association of glycaemia with macrovascular and microvascular complications of type 2 diabetes: prospective observational study: UKPDS 35. *Brit Med J* 2000; 321:405–412.

Cited 1163 times

Holman R, Turner R, Stratton I, Cull C, Frighi V, Manley S, Matthews D, Neil A, Kohner E, Wright D, Hadden D, Fox C. Efficacy of atenolol and captopril in reducing risk of macrovascular and microvascular complications in type 2 diabetes: UKPDS 39. *Brit Med J* 1998; 317:713–720.

Cited 831 times

Turner RC, Millns H, Neil HAW, Stratton IM, Manley SE, Matthews DR, Holman RR. Risk factors for coronary artery disease in non-insulin dependent diabetes mellitus: United Kingdom prospective diabetes study: UKPDS 23. *Brit Med J* 1998; 316:823–828.

Cited 718 times

Turner RC, Cull CA, Frighi V, Holman RR. Glycemic control with diet, sulfonylurea, metformin, or insulin in patients with type 2 diabetes mellitus.
Progressive requirement for multiple therapies: UKPDS 49. *J Am Med Assoc*
1999; 281:2005–2012.

Cited 611 times

Adler AI, Stratton IM, Neil HAW, Yudkin JS, Matthews DR, Cull CA, Wright
AD, Turner RC, Holman RR. Association of systolic blood pressure with
macrovascular and microvascular complications of type 2 diabetes: UKPDS
36. Prospective observational study. *Brit Med J* 2000; 321:412–419.

22 UKPDS publications

UKPDS numbered papers

UKPDS I   UK Prospective Study of Therapies of Maturity-Onset Diabetes. Effect of diet, sulphonylurea, insulin or biguanide therapy on fasting plasma glucose and body weight over one year. R.C. Turner, R.R. Holman, C.A. Cull, I.M. Stratton, D.R. Matthews, V. Frighi, S.E. Manley, A. Neil, H. McElroy, A.D. Wright, E.M. Kohner, C.J. Fox, D.R. Hadden, Writing Committee for UKPDS group. *Diabetologia* (1983) **24**: 404–411.

UKPDS II   Reduction in HbA_{1c} with basal insulin supplement, sulphonylurea or biguanide therapy in maturity-onset diabetes. R.C. Turner, R.R. Holman, C.A. Cull, I.M. Stratton, D.R. Matthews, V. Frighi, S.E. Manley, A. Neil, H. McElroy, A.D. Wright, E.M. Kohner, C.J. Fox, D.R. Hadden, Writing Committee for UKPDS group. *Diabetes* (1985) **34**: 793–798.

UKPDS III Prevalence of hypertension and hypotensive therapy in patients with newly diagnosed diabetes. R.C. Turner, R.R. Holman, C.A. Cull, I.M. Stratton, D.R. Matthews, V. Frighi, S.E. Manley, A. Neil, H. McElroy, A.D. Wright, E.M. Kohner, C.J. Fox, D.R. Hadden, Writing Committee for UKPDS group. *Hypertension* [Suppl. II] (1985) **7**: 8–13.

UKPDS IV   Characteristics of newly presenting type 2 diabetic patients: male preponderance and obesity at different ages. R.C. Turner, R.R. Holman, C.A. Cull, I.M. Stratton, D.R. Matthews, V. Frighi, S.E. Manley, A. Neil, H. McElroy, A.D. Wright, E.M. Kohner, C.J. Fox, D.R. Hadden, Writing Committee for UKPDS group. *Diabetic Medicine* (1988) **5**: 154–159.

UKPDS V   Characteristics of newly presenting type 2 diabetic patients: estimated insulin sensitivity and islet β-cell function. R.C. Turner, R.R. Holman, C.A. Cull, I.M. Stratton, D.R. Matthews, V. Frighi, S.E. Manley, A. Neil, H. McElroy, A.D. Wright, E.M. Kohner,

C.J. Fox, D.R. Hadden, Writing Committee for UKPDS group. *Diabetic Medicine* (1988) **5**: 444–448.

UKPDS VI   Complications in newly diagnosed type 2 diabetic patients and their association with different clinical and biochemical risk factors. J. Howard-Williams, Z. Nugent, S.E. Manley, J. Mann, R.C. Turner. *Diabetes Research* (1990) **13**: 1–11.

UKPDS VII   Response of fasting plasma glucose to diet therapy in newly presenting type 2 diabetic patients. J. Howard-Williams, Z. Nugent, E. Eeley, D. Hadden, M. Lean, R.C. Turner. *Metabolism* (1990) **39**: 905–912.

UKPDS VIII Study design, progress and performance. R.C. Turner, R.R. Holman, D.R. Matthews, S.F. Oakes, P.A. Bassett, I.M. Stratton, C.A. Cull, S.E. Manley, V. Frighi. *Diabetologia* (1991) **34**: 877–890.

UKPDS IX   Relationships of urinary albumin and N-acetyl-glucosaminidase to glycaemia and hypertension at diagnosis of type 2 (non-insulin-dependent) diabetes mellitus and after 3 months' diet therapy. S.E. Manley, C.A. Cull, M.E. Burton, K.E. Fisher, R.C. Turner. *Diabetologia* (1993) **36**: 835–842.

UKPDS X   Urinary albumin excretion over 3 years in diet-treated type 2 (non-insulin-dependent) diabetic patients, and association with hypertension, hypoglycaemia and hypertriglyceridaemia. C.A. Cull, S.E. Manley, V. Frighi, R.R. Holman, R.C. Turner. *Diabetologia* (1993) **36**: 1021–1029.

UKPDS XI   Biochemical risk factors in type 2 diabetic patients at diagnosis compared with age-matched normal subjects. S.E. Manley, L.C. Meyer, H.A.W. Neil, I.S. Ross, R.C. Turner, R.R. Holman. *Diabetic Medicine* (1994) **11**: 534–544.

UKPDS XII   Differences between Asian, Afro-Caribbean and white Caucasian type 2 diabetic patients at diagnosis of diabetes. L.C. Meyer, S.E. Manley, V. Frighi, F. Burden, H.A.W. Neil, R.R. Holman, R.C. Turner. *Diabetic Medicine* (1994) **11**: 670–677.

UKPDS 13   Relative efficacy of randomly allocated diet, sulphonylurea, insulin or metformin in patients with newly diagnosed non-insulin dependent diabetes followed for three years. R.R. Holman, C.A. Cull, C.J. Fox, R.C. Turner. *British Medical Journal* (1995) **310**: 83–88.

UKPDS 14   Association of angiotensin-converting enzyme insertion/deletion polymorphism with myocardial infarction in NIDDM. B.D. Keavney, C.R.K. Dudley, I.M. Stratton, R.R. Holman, D.R. Matthews, P.J. Ratcliffe, R.C. Turner. *Diabetologia* (1995) **38**: 948–952.

UKPDS 15   Relationship of renin-angiotensin system gene polymorphisms with microalbuminuria in NIDDM. C.R.K. Dudley, B. Keavney, I.M. Stratton, R.C. Turner, P.J. Ratcliffe. *Kidney International* (1995) **48**: 1907–1911.

UKPDS 16 Overview of 6 years' therapy of type II diabetes: a progressive disease. R.C. Turner, C.A. Cull, I.M. Stratton, S.E. Manley, E.M. Kohner, D.R. Matthews, H.A.W. Neil, J.C. Levy, R.R. Holman. *Diabetes* (1995) **44**: 1249–1258.

UKPDS 17 A 9-year update of a randomized, controlled trial on the effect of improved metabolic control on complications in non-insulin-dependent diabetes mellitus. R.C. Turner, C.A. Cull, R.R. Holman. *Annals of Internal Medicine* (1996) **124**: 136–145.

UKPDS 18 Estimated dietary intake in type 2 diabetic patients randomly allocated to diet, sulphonylurea or insulin therapy. E.A. Eeley, I.M. Stratton, D.R. Hadden, R.C. Turner, R.R. Holman. *Diabetic Medicine* (1996) **13**: 656–662.

UKPDS 19 Heterogeneity in NIDDM: separate contributions of IRS-1 and beta 3-adrenergic-receptor mutations to insulin resistance and obesity respectively with no evidence for glycogen synthase gene mutations. Y. Zhang, N. Wat, I.M. Stratton, M.G. Warren Perry, M. Orho, L. Groop, R.C. Turner. *Diabetologia* (1996) **39**: 1505–1511.

UKPDS 20 Plasma leptin, obesity and plasma insulin in type 2 diabetic subjects. A. Widjaja, I.M. Stratton, R. Horn, R.R. Holman, R.C. Turner, G. Brabant. *Journal of Clinical Endocrinology & Metabolism* (1997) **82**: 654–657.

UKPDS 21 Low prevalence of the mitochondrial transfer RNA gene (tRNA $^{Leu(UUR)}$) mutation at position 3243bp in UK Caucasian type 2 diabetic patients. P.J. Saker, A.T. Hattersley, B. Barrow, M.S. Hammersley, V. Horton, M.D. Gillmer, R.C. Turner. *Diabetic Medicine* (1997) **14**: 42–45.

UKPDS 22 Effects of age at diagnosis on diabetic tissue damage during the first 6 years of NIDDM. T.M.E. Davis, I.M. Stratton, C.J. Fox, R.R. Holman, R.C. Turner. *Diabetes Care* (1997) **20**: 1435–1441.

UKPDS 23 Risk factors for coronary artery disease in non-insulin dependent diabetes mellitus. R.C. Turner, H. Millns, H.A.W. Neil, I.M. Stratton, S.E. Manley, D.R. Matthews, R.R. Holman. *British Medical Journal* (1998) **316**: 823–828.

UKPDS 24 A 6-year, randomized, controlled trial comparing sulfonylurea, insulin and metformin therapy in patients with newly diagnosed type 2 diabetes that could not be controlled with diet therapy. A. Wright, C.A. Cull, R.R. Holman, R.C. Turner. *Annals of Internal Medicine* (1998) **128**: 165–175.

UKPDS 25 Autoantibodies to islet-cell cytoplasm and glutamic acid decarboxylase for prediction of insulin requirement in type 2 diabetes. R.C. Turner, I.M. Stratton, V. Horton, S.E. Manley, P. Zimmet, I.R. Mackay, M. Shattock, G.F. Bottazzo, R.R. Holman. *Lancet* (1997) **350**: 1288–1293.

UKPDS 26 Sulphonylurea failure in non-insulin dependent diabetic patients over six years. D.R. Matthews, C.A. Cull, I.M. Stratton, R.R. Holman, R.C. Turner. *Diabetic Medicine* (1998) **15**: 297–303.

UKPDS 27 Plasma lipids and lipoproteins at diagnosis of NIDDM by age and sex. S.E. Manley, V. Frighi, I.M. Stratton, D.R. Matthews, R.R. Holman, R.C. Turner, H.A.W. Neil. *Diabetes Care* (1997) **20**: 1683–1687.

UKPDS 28 A randomised trial of efficacy of early addition of metformin in sulphonylurea-treated type 2 diabetes. A.D. Wright, C.A. Cull, R.R. Holman, R.C. Turner. *Diabetes Care* (1998) **21**: 87–92.

UKPDS 29 Risk factors for stroke in type 2 diabetes mellitus. T.M.E. Davis, H. Millns, I.M. Stratton, R.R. Holman, R.C. Turner. *Archives of Internal Medicine* (1999) **159**: 1097–1103.

UKPDS 30 Diabetic retinopathy at diagnosis of non-insulin-dependent diabetes mellitus and associated risk factors. E.M. Kohner, S.J. Aldington, I.M. Stratton, S.E. Manley, R.R. Holman, D.R. Matthews, R.C. Turner. *Archives of Ophthalmology* (1998) **116**: 297–303.

UKPDS 31 Hepatocyte nuclear factor-1 alpha (the MODY3 gene) mutations in late onset type II diabetic patients in the United Kingdom. R.D. Cox, L. Southam, Y. Hashim, V. Horton, Z. Mehta, J. Tahghavi, M. Lathrop, R.C. Turner. *Diabetes* (1999) **42**: 120–121.

UKPDS 32 Ethnicity and cardiovascular disease: the incidence of myocardial infarction in whites, south Asian and Afro-Caribbean patients with type 2 diabetes. A.I. Alder, H.A.W. Neil, I.M. Stratton, R.R. Holman, R.C. Turner. *Diabetes Care* (1998) **21**: 1271–1277.

UKPDS 33 Intensive blood-glucose control with sulphonylureas or insulin compared with conventional treatment and risk of complications in patients with type 2 diabetes. R.C. Turner, R.R. Holman, C.A. Cull, I.M. Stratton, D.R. Matthews, V. Frighi, S.E. Manley, H.A.W. Neil, H. McElroy, D. Wright, E. Kohner, C.J. Fox, D. Hadden. *Lancet* (1998) **352**: 837–853.

UKPDS 34 Effect of intensive blood-glucose control with metformin on complications in overweight patients with type 2 diabetes. R.C. Turner, R.R. Holman, I.M. Stratton, C.A. Cull, D.R. Matthews, S.E. Manley, V. Frighi, D. Wright, H.A.W. Neil, E. Kohner, H. McElroy, C.J. Fox, D. Hadden. *Lancet* (1998) **352**: 854–865.

UKPDS 35 Association of glycaemia with macrovascular and microvascular complications of type 2 diabetes. I.M. Stratton, A.I. Adler, H.A.W. Neil, D.R. Matthews, S.E. Manley, C.A. Cull, D. Hadden, R.C. Turner, R.R. Holman. *British Medical Journal* (2000) **321**: 405–412.

UKPDS 36 Association of systolic blood pressure with macrovascular and microvascular complications of type 2 diabetes. A.I. Adler, I.M. Stratton, H.A.W. Neil, J.S. Yudkin, D.R. Matthews, C.A. Cull, A.D.

Wright, R.C. Turner, R.R. Holman. *British Medical Journal* (2000) **321**: 412–429.

UKPDS 37   Quality of life in type 2 diabetic patients is affected by complications but not by intensive policies to improve blood glucose or blood pressure control. Z. Mehta, C.A. Cull, I.M. Stratton, J. Yudkin, C. Jenkinson, A. Fletcher, C. Battersby, R.R. Holman, R.C. Turner. *Diabetes Care* (1999) **22**: 1125–1136.

UKPDS 38   Tight blood pressure control and risk of macrovascular and microvascular complications in type 2 diabetes. R.C. Turner, R.R. Holman, I.M. Stratton, C.A. Cull, V. Frighi, S.E. Manley, D.R. Matthews, H.A.W. Neil, H. McElroy, E. Kohner, C.J. Fox, D. Hadden, D. Wright. *British Medical Journal* (1998) **317**: 703–713.

UKPDS 39   Efficacy of atenolol and captopril in reducing risk of macrovascular and microvascular complications in type 2 diabetes. R.R. Holman, R.C. Turner, I.M. Stratton, C.A. Cull, V. Frighi, S.E. Manley, D.R. Matthews, H.A.W. Neil, E. Kohner, D. Wright, D. Hadden, C.J. Fox. *British Medical Journal* (1998) **317**: 713–720.

UKPDS 40   Cost effectiveness analysis of improved blood pressure control in hypertensive patients with type 2 diabetes. M. Raikou, A. Gray, A. Briggs, R.J. Stevens, C.A. Cull, A. McGuire, P. Fenn, I.M. Stratton, R.R. Holman, R.C. Turner. *British Medical Journal* (1998) **317**: 720–726.

UKPDS 41   Cost-effectiveness of an intensive blood glucose control policy in patients with type 2 diabetes: economic analysis alongside randomised controlled trial. A. Gray, M. Raikou, A. McGuire, P. Fenn, R. Stevens, C.A. Cull, I.M. Stratton, A.I. Adler, R.R. Holman, R.C. Turner. *British Medical Journal* (2000) **320**: 1373–1378.

UKPDS 42   Microaneurysms in the development of diabetic retinopathy. E.M. Kohner, I.M. Stratton, S.J. Aldington, R.C. Turner, D.R. Matthews. *Diabetologia* (1999) **42**: 1107–1112.

UKPDS 43   Genetic heterogeneity of autoimmune diabetes: age of presentation in adults is influenced by HLA DRB1 and DQB1 genotypes. V. Horton, I.M. Stratton, G.F. Bottazzo, M. Shattock, I. Mackay, P. Zimmet, S.E. Manley, R.R. Holman, R.C. Turner. *Diabetologia* (1999) **42**: 608–616.

UKPDS 44   A randomised double-blind trial of acarbose in type 2 diabetes shows improved glycemic control over 3 years. R.R. Holman, R.C. Turner, C.A. Cull. *Diabetes Care* (1999) **22**: 960–964.

UKPDS 45   Effects of three months' diet after diagnosis of type 2 diabetes on plasma lipids and lipoproteins. S.E. Manley, I.M. Stratton, C.A. Cull, V. Frighi, E.A. Eeley, D.R. Matthews, R.R. Holman, R.C. Turner, H.A.W. Neil. *Diabetic Medicine* (2000) **17**: 518–523.

UKPDS 46   Life-expectancy projection by modelling and computer simulation. R.J. Stevens, A.I. Adler, A. Gray, A. Briggs, R.R. Holman. *Diabetes Research and Clinical Practice* [Suppl.] (2000) **50**: S5–S13.

UKPDS 47   Hyperglycaemia and hyperinsulinaemia at diagnosis of diabetes and their association with subsequent cardiovascular disease in the United Kingdom Prospective Diabetes Study. A.I. Adler, H.A.W. Neil, S.E. Manley, R.R. Holman, R.C. Turner. *American Heart Journal* (1999) **138**: S353–S359.

UKPDS 48   Sequence variants of the sarco(endo)plasmic reticulum Ca^{2+}-transport ATPase 3 gene (SERCA3) in Caucasian type II diabetic patients. A. Varadi, L. Lebel, Y. Hashim, Z. Mehta, S.J.H. Ashcroft, R.C. Turner. *Diabetologia* (1999) **42**: 1240–1243.

UKPDS 49   Glycaemic control with diet, sulphonylurea, metformin, or insulin in patients with type 2 diabetes mellitus: progressive requirement for multiple therapies. R.C. Turner, C.A. Cull, V. Frighi, R.R. Holman. *Journal of the American Medical Association* (1999) **281**: 2005–2012.

UKPDS 50   Risk factors for incidence and progression of retinopathy in type II diabetes over 6 years from diagnosis. I.M. Stratton, E.M. Kohner, S.J. Aldington, R.C. Turner, R.R. Holman, S.E. Manley, D.R. Matthews. *Diabetologia* (2001) **44**: 156–163.

UKPDS 51   Cost-effectiveness analysis of intensive blood-glucose control with metformin in overweight patients with type II diabetes. P. Clarke, A. Gray, A.I. Adler, R.J. Stevens, M. Raikou, C.A. Cull, I.M. Stratton, R.R. Holman. *Diabetologia* (2001) **44:** 298–304.

UKPDS 52   Relationship between the severity of retinopathy and progression to photocoagulation in patients with type 2 diabetes mellitus in the UKPDS. E.M. Kohner, I.M. Stratton, S.J. Aldington, R.R. Holman, D.R. Matthews. *Diabetic Medicine* (2001) **18**: 178–184.

UKPDS 53   Association studies of variants in promotor and coding regions of beta-cell ATP-sensitive K-channel genes SUR1 and Kir6.2 with type 2 diabetes mellitus. A.L. Gloyn, Y. Hashim, S.J.H. Ashcroft, R. Ashfield, S. Wiltshire, R.C. Turner. *Diabetic Medicine* (2001) **18**: 206–212.

UKPDS 54   An economic evaluation of atenolol vs. captopril in patients with type 2 diabetes. A. Gray, P. Clarke, M. Raikou, A.I. Adler, R.J. Stevens, H.A.W. Neil, C.A. Cull, I.M. Stratton, R.R. Holman. *Diabetic Medicine* (2001) **18**: 438–444.

UKPDS 55   Relationship between ethnicity and glycemic control, lipid profiles and blood pressure during the first 9 years of type 2 diabetes. T.M.E. Davis, C.A. Cull, R.R. Holman. *Diabetes Care* (2001) **24**: 1167–1174.

UKPDS 56   The UKPDS Risk Engine: a model for the risk of coronary heart disease in type II diabetes. R.J. Stevens, V. Kothari, A.I. Adler, I.M. Stratton, R.R. Holman. *Clinical Science* (2001) **101**: 671–679.

UKPDS 57   Efficacy of addition of insulin over 6 years in patients with type 2 diabetes in the U. K. Prospective Diabetes Study. A. Wright,

A.C.F. Burden, R.B. Paisey, C.A. Cull, R.R. Holman. *Diabetes Care* (2002) **25**: 330–336.

UKPDS 58   Modeling glucose exposure as a risk factor for photocoagulation in type 2 diabetes. R.J. Stevens, I.M. Stratton, R.R. Holman. *Journal of Diabetes and its Complications* (2002) **16**: 371–376.

UKPDS 59   Hyperglycemia and other potentially modifiable risk factors for peripheral vascular disease in type 2 diabetes. A.I. Adler, R.J. Stevens, H.A.W. Neil, I.M. Stratton, A.J.M. Boulton, R.R. Holman. *Diabetes Care* (2002) **25**: 894–899.

UKPDS 60   Risk of stroke in type 2 diabetes estimated by UKPDS risk engine. V. Kothari, R.J. Stevens, A.I. Adler, I.M. Stratton, S.E. Manley, H.A.W. Neil, R.R. Holman. *Stroke* (2002) **33**: 1776–1781.

UKPDS 61   Are lower fasting plasma glucose levels at diagnosis of type 2 diabetes associated with improved outcomes? S. Colagiuri, C.A. Cull, R.R. Holman. *Diabetes Care* (2002) **25**: 1410–1417.

UKPDS 62   Estimating utility values for health states of type 2 diabetic patients using EQ-5D. P. Clarke, A. Gray, R.R. Holman. *Medical Decision Making* (2002) **4**: 340–349.

UKPDS 63   Implementing intensive control of blood glucose concentration and blood pressure in type 2 diabetes in England: cost analysis. A. Gray, P. Clarke, A. Farmer, R.R. Holman. *British Medical Journal* (2002) **325**: 860–865.

UKPDS 64   Development and progression of nephropathy in type 2 diabetes: The United Kingdom Prospective Diabetes Study. A.I. Adler, R.J. Stevens, S.E. Manley, R.W. Bilous, C.A. Cull, R.R. Holman. *Kidney International* (2003) **63**: 225–232.

UKPDS 65   The impact of diabetes-related complications on healthcare costs: results from the United Kingdom Prospective Diabetes Study. P. Clarke, A. Gray, R. Legood, A. Briggs, R.R. Holman. *Diabetic Medicine* (2003) **20**: 442–450.

UKPDS 66   Risk factors for myocardial infarction case fatality and stroke case fatality in type 2 diabetes. R.J. Stevens, R.L. Coleman, A.I. Adler, I.M. Stratton, D.R. Matthews, R.R. Holman. *Diabetes Care* (2004) **27**: 201–207.

UKPDS 67   Insulin sensitivity at diagnosis of type 2 diabetes is not associated with subsequent cardiovascular disease. A.I. Adler, J.C. Levy, D.R. Matthews, I.M. Stratton, G. Hines, R.R. Holman. *Diabetic Medicine* (2004) **22**: 306–311.

UKPDS 68   A model to estimate the lifetime health outcomes of patients with type 2 diabetes: The United Kingdom Prospective Diabetes Study (UKPDS) Outcomes. P.M. Clarke, A.M. Gray, A. Briggs, A.J. Farmer, P. Fenn, R.J. Stevens, D.R. Matthews, I.M. Stratton, R.R. Holman. *Diabetologia* (2004) **47**: 1747–1759.

UKPDS 69   Risks of progression of retinopathy and vision loss related to tight blood pressure control in type 2 diabetes mellitus. D.R.

Matthews, I.M. Stratton, S.J. Aldington, E. Kohner. *Archives of Ophthalmology* (2004) **122**: 1631–1637.

UKPDS 70 Islet autoantibodies in clinically diagnosed type 2 diabetes: prevalence and relationship to metabolic control. T.M.E. Davis, A.D. Wright, Z.M. Mehta, C.A. Cull, I.M. Stratton, G.F. Bottazzo, E. Bosi, I.R. Mackay, R.R. Holman. *Diabetologia* (2005) **48**: 695–702.

UKPDS 71 IA-2 antibody prevalence and risk assessment of early insulin requirement in subjects presenting as type 2 diabetes. G.F. Bottazzo, E. Bosi, C.A. Cull, E. Bonifacio, M. Locatelli, P. Zimmet, I.R. Mackay, R.R. Holman. *Diabetologia* (2005) **48**: 703–708.

UKPDS 72 Cost utility analysis of intensive blood glucose and tight blood pressure control in type 2 diabetes. P.M. Clarke, A.M. Gray, A. Briggs, R.J. Stevens, D.R. Matthews, R.R. Holman. *Diabetologia* (2005) **48**: 868–877.

UKPDS 73 Hypoglycaemia in type 2 diabetic patients randomised to and maintained on monotherapy with diet, sulphonylurea, metformin or insulin for 6 years from diagnosis. A.D. Wright, C.A. Cull, K.M. Macleod, R.R. Holman for the UKPDS Group. *Journal of Diabetes and its Complications* (2006) **20**: 402–408.

UKPDS 74 Risk factors for renal dysfunction in type 2 diabetes. R. Retnakaran, C.A. Cull, K.I. Thorne, A.I. Adler, R.R. Holman for the UKPDS Group. *Diabetes* (2006) **55**: 1832–1839.

UKPDS 75 Additive effects of glycaemia and blood pressure exposure on risk of complications in type 2 diabetes: a prospective observational study. I.M. Stratton, C.A. Cull, A.I. Adler, D.R. Matthews, H.A.W. Neil, R.R. Holman. *Diabetologia* (2006) **49**: 1761–1769.

UKPDS 76 Paraoxonase 2 (PON2) polymorphisms and development of renal dysfunction in type 2 diabetes. R. Calle, M.I. McCarthy, P. Bannerjee, E. Zeggini, C.A. Cull, K.I. Thorne, S. Wiltshire, S. Terra, D. Meyer, J. Richmond, J. Mancuso, P. Milos, D. Freyburg, R.R. Holman. *Diabetologia* (2006) **49**: 2892–2899.

UKPDS 77 GAD autoantibodies and epitope reactivities persist after diagnosis in latent autoimmune diabetes in adults but do not predict disease progression. M. Desai, C.A. Cull, V.A. Horton, M.R. Christie, E. Bonifacio, V. Lampasona, P.J. Bingley, J.L. Levy, I.R. Mackay, P. Zimmet, R.R. Holman, A. Clark. *Diabetologia* (2007) **50**: 2052–2060.

UKPDS 78 Impact of the metabolic syndrome on macrovascular and microvascular outcomes in type 2 diabetes mellitus. C.A. Cull, C.C. Jensen, R. Retnakaran, R.R. Holman. *Circulation* (2007) **116**: 2119–2126.

Further UKPDS publications

L'etude UKPDS sur le controle de la glycemie et de l'hypertension arterielle dans le diabete de type 2: objectifs, structure et resultats preminiaires. J.C. Levy, C.A. Cull, I.M. Stratton, R.R. Holman, R.C. Turner. *Journ Annu Diabetol Hotel Dieu* (1993) 123–137.

Lessons from UK Prospective Diabetes Study. R.C. Turner, R.R. Holman. *Diabetes Research and Clinical Practice* (1995) **28**: S151–S157.

UK Prospective Diabetes Study: 3-year update. R.R. Holman for the UKPDS Group. *New Horizons in Diabetes Mellitus and Cardiovascular Disease, Current Science Press.* Ed Born GVR, Schwartz J. (1995) 183–186.

UK Prospective Diabetes Study. R.C. Turner, C.A. Cull, R.R. Holman. *Diabetes Care* (1996) **19**: 2: 182–183.

UK Prospective Diabetes Study. R.C. Turner, R.R. Holman. *Annals of Medicine* (1996) **28**: 439–444.

Progressive hyperglycaemia: the UKPDS Experience. R.R. Holman. *Consultant* (Supp) (1997) **37**: 530–536.

UKPDS: What was the question? UK Prospective Diabetes Study. R.C. Turner, R.R. Holman, J. Butterfield. *Lancet* (1999) **354**: 600.

Seeing what you want to see in randomised controlled trials. Authors' choice of study was ill informed (letter). R.R. Holman. *British Medical Journal* (2000) **321**: 1078–1079.

Underestimation of the importance of homocysteine as a risk factor for cardiovascular disease in epidemiological studies. R. Clarke, S. Lewington, A. Donald, C. Johnston, H. Refsum, I.M. Stratton, P. Jacques, M.M.B. Breteler, R.R. Holman. *Journal of Cardiovascular Risk* (2001) **8**: 363–369.

The UKPDS: implications for the dyslipidaemic patient. R.R. Holman. *Acta Diabetologica* (2001) **38**:(Suppl. 1)(5): S9–S14.

Butyrylcholinesterase K variant on chromosome 3q is associated with type II diabetes in white Caucasian subjects. Y. Hashim, D. Shepherd, S. Wiltshire, R.R. Holman, J.C. Levy, A. Clark *et al. Diabetologia* (2001) **44**: 2227–2230.

Standardization of glycated haemoglobin. S.M. Marshall, P.D. Home, S.M. Manley, J.H. Barth, W.G. John. *Annals of Clinical Biochemistry* (2002) **39**: 77–79.

Calculation of coronary risk in type 2 diabetes: another cause for concern: authors' reply (letter). R.R. Holman, S.E. Manley, R.J. Stevens on behalf of the UKPDS Study Group. *Clinical Science* (2002) **103**: 217–219.

Analysis of the United Kingdom Prospective Diabetes Study. R.R. Holman. *Endocrine Practice* (2002) **8**: 33–34.

Poor pregnancy outcome for women with type 2 diabetes. D.R. Hadden, C.A. Cull, D.J. Croft and R.R. Holman. *Diabetic Medicine* (2003) **20**: 506–507.

Autoantibodies to the islet cell antigen SOX-13 are associated with duration but not type of diabetes. T.M.E. Davis, Z. Mehta, I.R. Mackay, C.A. Cull, D.G. Bruce, S. Fida, M.J. Rowley, R.R. Holman. *Diabetic Medicine* (2003) **20**: 198–204.

Changing aspirin use in patients with type 2 diabetes in the UKPDS. C.A. Cull, H.A.W. Neil, R.R. Holman. *Diabetic Medicine* (2004) **21**: 1368–1371.

Reporting of diabetes on death certificates using data from the UK Prospective Diabetes Study. M.J. Thomason, J.P. Biddulph, C.A. Cull, R.R. Holman. *Diabetic Medicine* (2005); **22**: 1031–1036.

The variable number of tandem repeats upstream of the insulin gene is a susceptibility locus for latent autoimmune diabetes in adults. M. Desai, E. Zeggini, V.A. Horton, K.R. Owen, A.T. Hattersley, J.C. Levy, G.A. Hitman, M. Walker, R.R. Holman, M.I. McCarthy, A. Clark. *Diabetes* (2006) **55**: 1890–1894.

Long-term efficacy of sulfonylureas. R.R. Holman. *Metabolism Clinical and Experimental* (2006) **55** (Suppl. 1): S2–S5.

Is there a need for a clinical screening tool for autoimmune diabetes in adults? (letter). T.M.E. Davis, C.A. Cull, R.R. Holman. *Diabetes Care* (2006) **11**: 2560.

An association analysis of the HLA gene region in latent autoimmune diabetes in adults. M. Desai, E. Zeggini, V.A. Horton, K.R. Owen, A.T. Hattersley, J.C. Levy, M. Walker, K.M. Gillespie, P. Bingley, G.A. Hitman, R.R. Holman, M.I. McCarthy, A. Clark. *Diabetologia* (2007) **50**: 68–73.

Hypertension in Diabetes Study (HDS) papers

HDS1   Prevalence of hypertension in newly presenting type 2 diabetic patients and the association with risk factors for cardiovascular and diabetic complications. R.C. Turner, I.M. Stratton, V. Frighi, R. Holman, S.E. Manley, C.A. Cull. *Journal of Hypertension* (1993) **11**: 309–317.

HDS2   Increased risk of cardiovascular complications in hypertensive type 2 diabetic patients. V. Frighi, I.M. Stratton, R.R. Holman, D.R. Matthews, H.A.W. Neil, R.C. Turner. *Journal of Hypertension* (1993) **11**: 319–325.

HDS3   Prospective study of therapy of hypertension in type 2 diabetic patients: efficacy of ACE inhibitor and β-blockade. R.C. Turner, R.R. Holman, I.M. Stratton, S.E. Manley, V. Frighi. *Diabetic Medicine* (1994) **11**: 773–782.

HDS4   Therapeutic requirements to maintain tight blood pressure control. I.M. Stratton, S.E. Manley, R.R. Holman, R.C. Turner. *Diabetologia* (1996) **39**: 1554–1561.

23 Acknowledgements

Coordinating Centre

Chief Investigators: Holman RR, Turner RC. *Additional Investigators*: Matthews DR, Neil HAW. *Statisticians*: Cull CA, McElroy H, Mehta Z, Meyer L, Millns H, Morris R, Nugent Z, Owen R, Roberts S, Smith A, Stratton IM. *Biochemists*: Manley S, McVittie J, Moore J. *Consultant Biochemist*: Ross I. *Research Associate*: Frighi V. *Consultant Statistician*: Peto R. *Epidemiologists*: Adler AI, Mann JI. *Administrators*: Bassett P, Carpenter JR, Lodge S, Oakes S. *Dietician*: Eeley EA. *Biochemistry laboratory staff*: Ayres A, Benfield L, Bowen T, Brown J, Brownlee SM, Burnett M, Burton M, Carter RD, Christopher P, Dailey P, Draisey I, Eddy R, Evans MA, Fisher KE, Groves C, Islam K, Jelfs R, Kennedy I, Lawrence L, Logie LJ, Lovatt C, Mair R, Mitchiner J, Mullins R, Naylor B, Payne MJ, Powrie R, Stowell LA, Sutton P, Sutton PJ, Uren C, Williams FA, Williams PA. *Health economists*: Fenn P, Gray M, McGuire AJ, Raikou M. *Quality-of-life questionnaire*: Battersby C, Bulpitt C, Yudkin JS. *Mathematical Modeller*: Stevens R. *Application Programmer*: Kennedy IA, Veness J. *Administration*: Alder P, Carter B, Cave M, Coster R, Croft D, Douglas P, Fitchie M, Harris F, Lampard H, Merle C, Nolan L, Stowell N, Tse A, Waring K, Wood C. *Data Entry*: Allen T, Aricescu AM, Byrne M, Harris E, Lindsay K, Sillence G. (Fig. 23.1)

Retinal Photography Grading Centre

Director: Kohner EM. *Manager*: Aldington S. *Grading Centre Staff*: Beattie E, Biggs T, Bodsworth L, Cockley S, Collum R, Dove S, Gradwell M, Harrison K, Leung L, Levien S, Lipinski H, MacIntyre C, Mortemore A, Nelson D, Skinner S, Staples S, Taylor F, Wilcox R.

ECG Coding Centre

Rose C, Keen N, Peachey B.

Figure 23.1 UKPDS Coordinating Centre.

Clinical Centres

Oxford, 00

Principal Investigators: Holman RR, Turner RC. *Centre staff*: Adler AI, Alexander A, Barrow BA, Bell NJ, Cook L, Eeley EA, Franklin SL, Frighi V, Hammersley MS, Levy JC, Matthews DR, Moss J, Nowell T, Palmer SL, Parker P, Spivey RS, Stearn MR, Steemson J, Tidy CR, Truscott E, Venuzzi A, Walker B, Walravens N, White S.

Aberdeen, 01

Principal Investigators: Murchison LE, Pearson DW. *Centre staff*: Brunt AHE, Callender P, Christie E, Church J, Farrow A, Lyall F, McHardy K, Patterson N, Petrie XMP, Rennie I, Stowers JM, Stowers M, Thomson E, Walmsley MEJ, Williams MJ.

Birmingham, 02

Principal Investigator: Wright AD. *Centre staff*: Bradbury M, Chakrabarti B, Eagle C, England P, Glover A, Graham J, Gyde S, Levi NA, Maiden S, Parkes C, Rayton S, Shearer ACI, Sherwell J, Smith J, Smyth-Osbourne A, Taylor G, Thompson RJW.

St George's Hospital, London, 03

Principal Investigators: Oakley NW, Panahloo A. *Centre staff*: Anderson M,

Hollier GP, Kean J, Martin S, Nisbett J, Pilkington T, Rice B, Rolland A, Simpson J, Soo SC, Whitehead MA.

Hammersmith Hospital, London, 04
Principal Investigator: Dornhorst A. *Centre staff*: Champman R, Doddridge MC, Dumskyj M, Elliott S, Forrester S, Foster M, Frost G, Kohner EM, Myers K, Nanka-Bruce M, Rose C, Roseblade M, Sharp P, Sleightholm M, Vanterpool G, Walji S.

City Hospital, Belfast, 05
Principal Investigators: Hayes R, Henry RW. *Centre staff*: Archbold GPR, Copeland M, Featherston MS, Foster M, Harper R, Martin S, McDermott M, Richardson I.

Stoke-on-Trent, 06
Principal Investigator: Scarpello JHB. *Centre staff*: Alexander L, Browne J, Hodgson E, Shiers DE, Stanley S, Strange RC, Teasdale M, Tucker RJW, Walton J, Worthington JRH.

Royal Victoria Hospital, Belfast, 07
Principal Investigator: Hadden DR. *Centre staff*: Atkinson AB, Bell PM, Culbert AM, Foster M, Hegan C, Holmes J, Kennedy L, McCance DR, Nesbitt S, Robinson I, Rutherford J, Tennet H, Webb N.

Carshalton, 08
Principal Investigator: Hyer S. *Centre staff*: Barron JL, Booth M, Clark D, Davis C, Haylock D, Hulland S, James LM, Nanson ME, Petrie H, Rice B, Spathis AS, Strugnell P, Tyrell JM, Wade R.

Whittington Hospital, London, 09
Principal Investigator: Yudkin JS. *Centre staff*: Alibhai K, Badenoch A, Clarke S, Cox C, Eckert M, Fernandez M, Gould BC, Howard E, Isenberg L, Lankester JA, MacFarlane S, Marriot E, McGregor M, Mehmed E, Price R, Ryle A, Singer J, Waite A, Walji S, Wallace G.

Norwich, 10
Principal Investigator: Greenwood RH. *Centre staff*: Brown C, Cook D, Denholm MJ, Duckworth E, Flatman M, Franklin S, Funnell M, Gorick S, Jackson L, Johnson F, Munroe C, Rainbow S, Temple RC, Whitfield K, Wilson J.

Stevenage, 11
Principal Investigator: Borthwick LJ. *Centre staff*: Bond M, Christie RA, McDougal S, Musk P, Raniga P, Seaman RJ, Wheatcroft DJ, Wheatcroft W, White J.

Ipswich, 12
Principal Investigator: Day JL. *Centre staff*: Almond J, Bayliss P, Doshi MJ, Graham A, Hexman S, Hicks K, Howard-Williams JR, Humphreys H, Ladbrook T, Murphy H, Pledger D, Wilson JG.

Dundee, 13
Principal Investigator: Newton RW. *Centre staff*: Burns J, Dick L, Ellingford A, Foster M, Hynd S, Jung RT, Kilby S, Kilgallon B, Roxburgh C, Waugh N.

Northampton, 14
Principal Investigator: Fox CJ. *Centre staff*: Beedie J, Coghill HM, Cowan W, Evans SJ, Fox A, French A, Hall K, Hein N, Hollway MC, Lawrence K, Nayani G, Quested K, Richard M, Staff C, Stoddart P, Willows M.

Torbay, 15
Principal Investigator: Paisey RB. *Centre staff*: Bower L, Brown NPR, Coysh T, Derby T, Frost J, Garrett F, Harvey P, Hogg J, Lemonides A, Mason S, Paisey R, Park P, Rocket P, Tucker AJ, Warren C, Wilcocks R, Williams K.

Peterborough, 16
Principal Investigator: Roland JM. *Centre staff*: Amps J, Ball V, Brown DJ, Church S, Donnelly D, Dunn G, Griffin P, King S, Maddison W, Mungall H, Palmer K, Smith S, Stanton-King K, Wilson A, Youens J.

Scarborough, 17
Principal Investigator: Brown PM. *Centre staff*: Armistead L, Davidson AJM, Garnett JFP, Humphriss D, Meldrum M, Nunn BR, Poon P, Rose R, Taylor J, Timms A, Townsend S.

Derby, 18
Principal Investigators: Donnelly R, Peacock IDA. *Centre staff*: Barrett J, Beeston W, Charlton MH, Connolly BPS, Culverwell NJC, Hill PG, King PG, Peacock J, Scott AR, Spendlove D, Wain J.

Manchester, 19
Principal Investigator: Boulton AJM. *Centre staff*: Abouaesha F, Abuaisha B, Booker J, Breislin K, Cole H, Curwell J, Davenport H, Grey J, Higgins S, Katoulis V, Knowles EA, Kumar S, McDonald H, Millichip M, Olukoga A, Parker R, Prest A, Raval P, Robertson AM, Sereviratne C, Shawcross G, Sunter J.

Salford, 20
Principal Investigators: Dornan TL, Gibson M. *Centre staff*: Clyne JR, Collantine J, Egan A, Floyd L, Maher J, McDowell D, Millichip M, O'Connell I, Tamkin E, Wallace C, Wilson SJ, Wong LM, Wright KL, Young RJ.

Leicester, 21
Principal Investigators: Burden AC, Gregory R. *Centre staff*: Burden M, Clarke J, Donley PJ, Grenfell J, Jackson S, Mansingh S, Meakin L, Morgan S, Roshan M, Sellen EM, Sherriff C, Vaghela N, Walyn L.

Exeter, 22
Principal Investigators: MacLeod K, Tooke JE. *Centre staff*: Green E, Higham A, Hoyle M, Hudson A, James AJ, Jones K, Leighton L, Martin B, Piper J, Pym C, Rammell M, Seamark C, Shore A, Stockman J, Yeo C.

Committees

Data Monitoring and Ethics Committee
Butterfield WJH, Doll RWRS, Eastman R, Ferris FR, Holman RR, Keen H, Kurinje N, Mahler RF, McPherson KFR, Meade TW, Peto R, Shaper AG, Siegel D, Turner RC, Watkins PJ.

Glucose Steering Committee
Alberti KGMM, Betteridge DJ, Cohen RD, Darbyshire J, Day N, Denton R, Forrester J, George C, Griffin J, Guppy T, Heller S, Home PD, Howell S, Jarrett JR, Johnston DG, Ledingham J, Marks V, Marmot M, McGuire A, Murphy M, el Nahas AM, Pentecost B, Robertson-Mackay F, Spiegelhalter D, Toy J, Ward JD.

Hypertension Steering Committee
Atkinson B, Holman RR, Ledingham J, Raine T, Turner RC.

Policy Advisory Committee
Bassett P, Cull CA, Fox CJ, Hadden DR, Holman RR, Matthews DR, Stratton IM, Turner RC, Wright AD, Yudkin JS.

Executive Committee
Adler AI, Bassett P, Carpenter JR, Cull CA, Holman RR, Lodge S, Manley S, Matthews DR, Mehta Z, Neil HAW, Stevens R, Stratton IM, Turner RC, Watkins P.

Data Committee
Cull CA, Frighi V, Holman RR, Manley S, Matthews DR, Neil HAW, Stratton IM, Turner RC.

Endpoint Grading Committee
Dornan TL, Fox CJ, Matthews DR, Wright AD.

Grant-giving bodies

Alan and Babbette Sainsbury Trust
Bayer
Becton Dickinson
Boehringer Mannheim
Bristol Myers Squibb
British Heart Foundation
Charles Wolfson Charitable Trust
Clothworkers' Foundation
Cortecs Diagnostics
Diabetes UK
Farmitalia Carlo Erba
GSK Glaxo Wellcome and Smith Kline Beecham
Health Promotion Research Trust
Hoechst Marion Roussel
Kodak
Lilly
Lipha
Merck Santé
Novartis
Novo Nordisk
Owen Mumford
Oxford University Medical Research Fund Committee
Pfizer
Pharmacia and Upjohn
Roche
UK Department of Health
UK Medical Research Council
US National Eye Institute
US National Institute of Diabetes, Digestive and Kidney Disease (National Institutes of Health)
Wellcome Trust
Zeneca

24 10 September 2008: late breaking 30-year results

The UKPDS 30-year results, reporting the 10-year Post-Trial Monitoring follow-up of the main trial survivor cohort, were presented at the EASD in Rome on 10 September 2008—exactly 10 years to the day after the primary results were presented at the 1998 EASD in Barcelona. The major glucose and blood pressure findings were published simultaneously as UKPDS80 and UKPDS81 in the *New England Journal of Medicine*. The abstracts for each of these are reproduced below.

The NEW ENGLAND JOURNAL *of* MEDICINE

ORIGINAL ARTICLE

10-Year Follow-up of Intensive Glucose Control in Type 2 Diabetes

Rury R. Holman, F.R.C.P., Sanjoy K. Paul, Ph.D., M. Angelyn Bethel, M.D.,
David R. Matthews, F.R.C.P., and H. Andrew W. Neil, F.R.C.P.

ABSTRACT

BACKGROUND

During the United Kingdom Prospective Diabetes Study (UKPDS), patients with type 2 diabetes mellitus who received intensive glucose therapy had a lower risk of microvascular complications than did those receiving conventional dietary therapy. We conducted post-trial monitoring to determine whether this improved glucose control persisted and whether such therapy had a long-term effect on macrovascular outcomes.

METHODS

Of 5102 patients with newly diagnosed type 2 diabetes, 4209 were randomly assigned to receive either conventional therapy (dietary restriction) or intensive therapy (either sulfonylurea or insulin or, in overweight patients, metformin) for glucose control. In post-trial monitoring, 3277 patients were asked to attend annual UKPDS clinics for 5 years, but no attempts were made to maintain their previously assigned therapies. Annual questionnaires were used to follow patients who were unable to attend the clinics, and all patients in years 6 to 10 were assessed through questionnaires. We examined seven prespecified aggregate clinical outcomes from the UKPDS on an intention-to-treat basis, according to previous randomization categories.

RESULTS

Between-group differences in glycated hemoglobin levels were lost after the first year. In the sulfonylurea–insulin group, relative reductions in risk persisted at 10 years for any diabetes-related end point (9%, P=0.04) and microvascular disease (24%, P=0.001), and risk reductions for myocardial infarction (15%, P=0.01) and death from any cause (13%, P=0.007) emerged over time, as more events occurred. In the metformin group, significant risk reductions persisted for any diabetes-related end point (21%, P=0.01), myocardial infarction (33%, P=0.005), and death from any cause (27%, P=0.002).

CONCLUSIONS

Despite an early loss of glycemic differences, a continued reduction in microvascular risk and emergent risk reductions for myocardial infarction and death from any cause were observed during 10 years of post-trial follow-up. A continued benefit after metformin therapy was evident among overweight patients. (UKPDS 80; Current Controlled Trials number, ISRCTN75451837.)

From the Diabetes Trials Unit (R.R.H., S.K.P., M.A.B.), the Division of Public Health and Primary Health Care (H.A.W.N.), and the National Institute of Health Research (NIHR) School for Primary Care Research (H.A.W.N.), Oxford Centre for Diabetes, Endocrinology, and Metabolism (R.R.H., S.K.P., M.A.B., D.R.M., H.A.W.N.); and the NIHR Oxford Biomedical Research Centre (R.R.H., D.R.M., H.A.W.N.) — both in Oxford, United Kingdom. Address reprint requests to Dr. Holman at the Diabetes Trials Unit, Oxford Centre for Diabetes, Endocrinology, and Metabolism, Churchill Hospital, Headington, Oxford OX3 7LJ, United Kingdom, or at rury.holman@dtu.ox.ac.uk.

This article (10.1056/NEJMoa0806470) was published at www.nejm.org on September 10, 2008.

N Engl J Med 2008;359.

The NEW ENGLAND JOURNAL of MEDICINE

ORIGINAL ARTICLE

Long-Term Follow-up after Tight Control of Blood Pressure in Type 2 Diabetes

Rury R. Holman, F.R.C.P., Sanjoy K. Paul, Ph.D., M. Angelyn Bethel, M.D., H. Andrew W. Neil, F.R.C.P., and David R. Matthews, F.R.C.P.

ABSTRACT

BACKGROUND

Post-trial monitoring of patients in the United Kingdom Prospective Diabetes Study (UKPDS) examined whether risk reductions for microvascular and macrovascular disease, achieved with the use of improved blood-pressure control during the trial, would be sustained.

METHODS

Among 5102 UKPDS patients with newly diagnosed type 2 diabetes mellitus, we randomly assigned, over a 4-year period beginning in 1987, 1148 patients with hypertension to tight or less-tight blood-pressure control regimens. The 884 patients who underwent post-trial monitoring were asked to attend annual UKPDS clinics for the first 5 years, but no attempt was made to maintain their previously assigned therapies. Annual questionnaires completed by patients and general practitioners were used to follow patients who were unable to attend the clinic in years 1 through 5, and questionnaires were used for all patients in years 6 to 10. Seven prespecified aggregate clinical end points were examined on an intention-to-treat basis, according to the previous randomization categories.

RESULTS

Differences in blood pressure between the two groups during the trial disappeared within 2 years after termination of the trial. Significant relative risk reductions found during the trial for any diabetes-related end point, diabetes-related death, microvascular disease, and stroke in the group receiving tight, as compared with less tight, blood-pressure control were not sustained during the post-trial follow-up. No risk reductions were seen during or after the trial for myocardial infarction or death from any cause, but a risk reduction for peripheral vascular disease associated with tight blood-pressure control became significant (P=0.02).

CONCLUSIONS

The benefits of previously improved blood-pressure control were not sustained when between-group differences in blood pressure were lost. Early improvement in blood-pressure control in patients with both type 2 diabetes and hypertension was associated with a reduced risk of complications, but it appears that good blood-pressure control must be continued if the benefits are to be maintained. (UKPDS 81; Current Controlled Trials number, ISRCTN75451837.)

From the Diabetes Trials Unit (R.R.H., S.K.P., M.A.B.) and the Division of Public Health and Primary Health Care (H.A.W.N.) and the National Institute of Health Research (NIHR) School for Primary Care Research (H.A.W.N.), Oxford Centre for Diabetes, Endocrinology, and Metabolism (R.R.H., S.K.P., M.A.B., H.A.W.N., D.R.M.); and the NIHR Oxford Biomedical Research Centre (R.R.H., H.A.W.N., D.R.M.) — both in Oxford, United Kingdom. Address reprint requests to Dr. Holman at the Diabetes Trials Unit, Oxford Centre for Diabetes, Endocrinology, and Metabolism, Churchill Hospital, Headington, Oxford OX3 7LJ, United Kingdom, or at rury.holman@dtu.ox.ac.uk.

This article (10.1056/NEJMoa0806359) was published at www.nejm.org on September 10, 2008.

N Engl J Med 2008;359.
Copyright © 2008 Massachusetts Medical Society.